The Ghosts of

Michael Young

Martyrs Square

AN EYEWITNESS
ACCOUNT OF
LEBANON'S
LIFE STRUGGLE

SIMON & SCHUSTER
NEW YORK   LONDON   TORONTO   SYDNEY

Simon & Schuster
1230 Avenue of the Americas
New York, NY 10020

First Simon & Schuster hardcover edition April 2010

SIMON & SCHUSTER and colophon are registered trademarks
of Simon & Schuster, Inc.

For information about special discounts for bulk purchases,
please contact Simon & Schuster Special Sales at
1-866-506-1949 or business@simonandschuster.com.

The Simon & Schuster Speakers Bureau can bring authors
to your live event. For more information or to book an event,
contact the Simon & Schuster Speakers Bureau at
1-866-248-3049 or visit our website at www.simonspeakers.com.

Designed by Davina Mock-Maniscalco
Maps by Paul J. Pugliese

Manufactured in the United States of America

1   3   5   7   9   10   8   6   4   2

Library of Congress Cataloging-in-Publication Data

Young, Michael.
The ghosts of Martyrs Square / Michael Young.
—1st Simon & Schuster hardcover ed.
        p.   cm.
Includes bibliographical references and index.
1. Lebanon–History–1990–   2. Lebanon–Politics and
government–1990–   3. Political culture–Lebanon.
4. Islam and politics–Lebanon.   5. Lebanon–Foreign
relations–Syria.   6. Syria–Foreign relations–Lebanon.
7. Hariri, Rafiq Baha', 1944–2005–Assassination.
8. Hizballah (Lebanon).   I. Title.
        DS87.54.Y68   2010
956.9204'4–dc22   2009053396
        ISBN 978-1-4165-9862-6
        ISBN 978-1-4391-0945-8 (ebook)

To my father

Contents

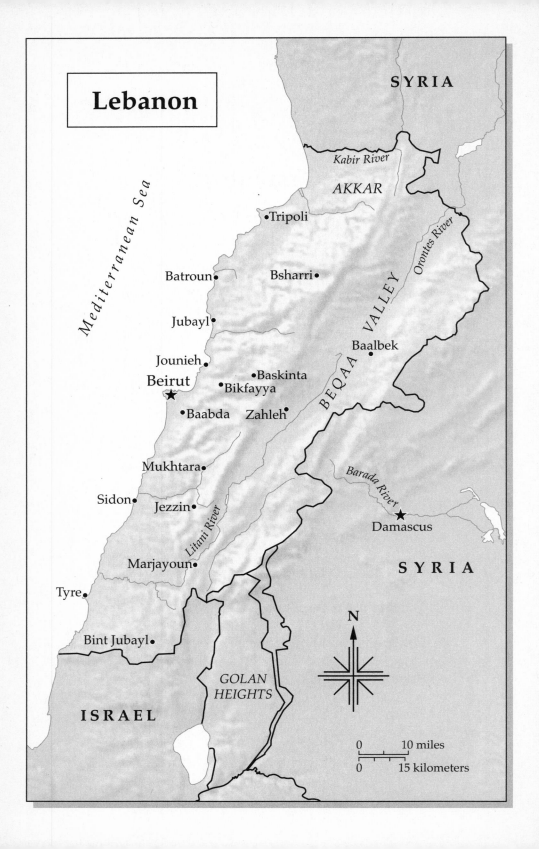

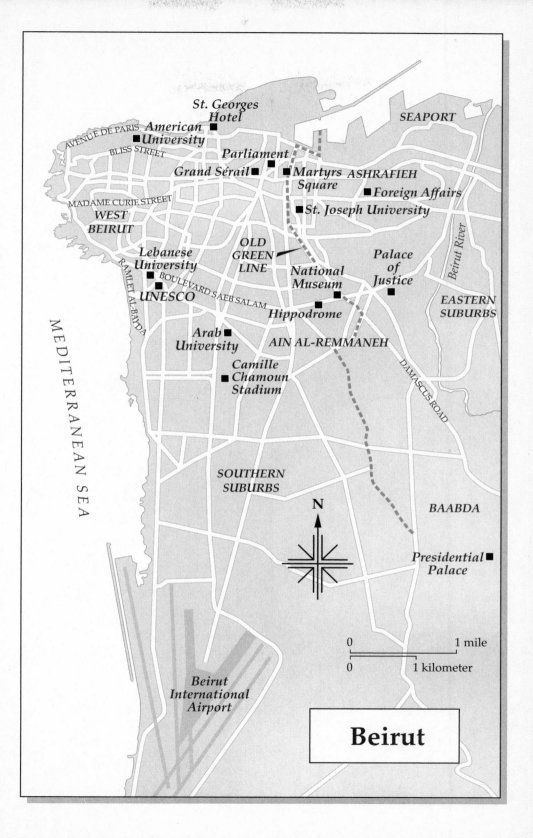

St. Georges
Hotel

SEAPORT

AVENUE DE PARIS
American
University

BLISS STREET

Parliament

Grand Sérail

Martyrs
Square

ASHRAFIEH

Foreign Affairs

MADAME CURIE STREET

St. Joseph University

WEST
BEIRUT

Lebanese
University

OLD
GREEN
LINE

National
Museum

Palace
of
Justice

Beirut River

RAMLET AL-BAYDA

BOULEVARD SAEB SALAM

UNESCO

Hippodrome

EASTERN
SUBURBS

Arab
University

AIN AL-REMMANEH

Camille
Chamoun
Stadium

DAMASCUS ROAD

MEDITERRANEAN SEA

SOUTHERN
SUBURBS

N

BAABDA

Presidential
Palace

0   1 mile

0   1 kilometer

Beirut
International
Airport

Beirut

Cast of Characters

Mosbah al-Ahdab—Parliamentarian from the northern city of Tripoli until he lost his seat in June 2009. An early member of the rump group of parliamentarians opposing the extension of President Émile Lahoud's mandate in 2004, and later a vocal figure in the March 14 coalition.

Michel Aoun—Former army commander and prime minister of a military government between 1988 and 1990. A leading opponent of Syria, he was forced into exile after his ouster by the Syrian army. Leader of the Free Patriotic Movement, he currently heads the Change and Reform bloc in parliament and is among the most prominent of Maronite politicians.

Talal Arslan—Parliamentarian and former minister allied with Syria and the Lebanese opposition. He heads the weaker faction in the Druze community, which opposes Walid Jumblatt.

Bashar al-Assad—President of Syria since June 2000.

Hafez al-Assad—President of Syria between 1970 and 2000, and father of Bashar al-Assad.

Daniel Bellemare—A Canadian former judge, currently prosecutor of the Special Tribunal for Lebanon based near The Hague, which is considering the assassination of the former prime minister, Rafiq al-Hariri, and other killings and crimes committed in Lebanon after 2005. Before becoming prosecutor, he was the third commissioner of the United Nations International Independent Investigation Commission investigating those crimes.

Nabih Berri—Speaker of Lebanon's parliament and head of the Amal Movement, which during Lebanon's civil war was the main Shiite militia.

Serge Brammertz—A Belgian judge, he was the second commissioner of the United Nations International Independent Investigation Commission investigating the Hariri assassination and subsequent killings and crimes. Currently, he is the prosecutor of the International Criminal Tribunal for the Former Yugoslavia.

Wissam Eid—A captain in the Lebanese Internal Security Forces, he was assassinated in a bomb attack in January 2008. At the time, he was working on analyzing telephone intercepts related to the Hariri assassination.

Jeffrey D. Feltman—U.S. ambassador to Lebanon between 2004 and 2008. Presently, the assistant secretary of state for Near Eastern affairs.

Elie al-Firzli—A former deputy speaker of the Lebanese parliament and a former minister, he is among Syria's stalwart allies in Lebanon.

Peter Fitzgerald—A former Irish deputy police commissioner, he was sent to Beirut by the United Nations soon after the Hariri assassination at the head of a fact-finding mission to prepare a preliminary report on the crime. On the basis of his findings, the U.N. decided to establish an independent international commission to determine who was responsible for the killing.

Suleiman Franjieh—Lebanese Maronite politician from the northern town of Zghorta and long a close ally of Syria. He is the namesake of his grandfather, who served as Lebanon's president between 1970 and 1976.

Samir Geagea—Leader of the Lebanese Forces party and a leading figure in the March 14 coalition. He formerly headed the Lebanese Forces militia during the latter stages of Lebanon's civil war, and fought a bitter war against Michel Aoun in 1990. He spent eleven years imprisoned at the Defense Ministry after being condemned in several postwar trials; he was released in 2005.

Amin Gemayel—Lebanon's president between 1982 and 1988, he heads the Christian Kataeb Party, founded by his father Pierre, and is a prominent figure in the March 14 coalition.

Bashir Gemayel—The younger son of Pierre Gemayel, the founder of the Kataeb Party, he forcibly united, then led, the Christian militias in the middle stages of Lebanon's civil war. In 1982 he was elected president in the wake of Israel's invasion of Lebanon, and was assassinated shortly thereafter, before formally taking office. He was succeeded by his brother Amin.

Pierre Gemayel—Founder of the Gemayel political dynasty and founder of the Kataeb Party, once Lebanon's leading Christian political organization, he played a leading role during Lebanon's post-Independence years, then during the civil war. He was the father of both Bashir and Amin Gemayel.

Pierre Amin Gemayel—Elder son of Amin Gemayel, he was an opponent of Syria and a member of the March 14 coalition before his assassination in November 2006, while he was serving as industry minister.

Antoine Ghanem—A parliamentarian from the Kataeb Party and a member of the March 14 coalition, he was assassinated in September 2007.

Rustom Ghazaleh—Head of Syria's Security and Reconnaissance Apparatus, effectively the country's military intelligence network in Lebanon, between 2002 and 2005. He succeeded Ghazi Kanaan in the post, after having served as his deputy responsible for Beirut.

Rafiq al-Hariri—Lebanese businessman who later was given Saudi nationality, he served several times as Lebanese prime minister after 1992. Hariri's governments until 1998 oversaw the postwar reconstruction of Lebanon. He was assassinated in February 2005, amid growing conflict between him and Syria following the Syrian-imposed extension of the term of President Émile Lahoud, a rival of Hariri, in September 2004.

Saad al-Hariri—Son and political heir of Rafiq al-Hariri, he became a leading figure in the March 14 coalition after the parliamentary elections of 2005. Formerly headed several of his father's companies in Saudi Arabia. At the time of this writing, Lebanon's prime minister.

Elie Hobeiqa—Formerly head of the Lebanese Forces militia, until he was ousted by Samir Geagea in 1986 after aligning himself with Syria. He began as the militia's security chief under Bashir Gemayel, and in September 1982, after Bashir's assassination, he ordered his men into the Palestinian refugee camps of Sabra and Shatila, where they massacred the inhabitants. Several times appointed a postwar minister, he was assassinated in 2002.

Salim al-Hoss—Lebanese politician who served several times as prime minister, most recently between 1998 and 2000.

Kamal Jumblatt—Leading Lebanese Druze politician since the 1950s, who played a significant role in the early stages of the Lebanese civil war. He opposed the Syrian entry into Lebanon in 1976 and was assassinated by the Syrians in 1977. The father of Walid Jumblatt.

Walid Jumblatt—Paramount leader of the Druze community, he heads the Progressive Socialist Party, which during the war was one of the leading Lebanese militias. Several times a minister in the war and postwar period, he was a close ally of Syria until 2004, when he had a falling out with Damascus over the forced extension of President Émile Lahoud's term in office. Thereafter and until the elections of 2005, he became the effective leader of the opposition to Syria and a leading figure in the March 14 coalition, until he announced in August 2009 that he would distance himself from his former comrades.

Ghazi Kanaan—Head of Syria's Security and Reconnaissance Apparatus, its military intelligence network in Lebanon, between 1982 and 2002. An Alawite, he was the effective ruler of Lebanon throughout the postwar years, until he was called back to Damascus. He was said to have committed suicide in 2005 amid signs that the Syrian regime was setting him up for a fall.

Omar Karami—Former Lebanese prime minister close to Syria, he headed the government in 2005 that resigned in the face of popular protests by the anti-Syrian opposition following the assassination of Rafiq al-Hariri.

Samir Kassir—Lebanese journalist and academic who was among the most vocal critics of the Syrian presence in Lebanon. He played an important mobilization role in the 2005 demonstrations that followed Rafiq al-Hariri's assassination. He was killed in a bomb attack on his car in June 2005.

Bishara al-Khoury—Lebanon's president in 1943 when the country gained independence from France. With Riad al-Solh, the Sunni prime minister, he agreed to the National Pact, the founding contract of Independent Lebanon.

Émile Lahoud—President of Lebanon between 1998 and 2007. A former commander of the Lebanese army, he was a close ally of Syria.

Detlev Mehlis—German judge appointed as the first commissioner of the United Nations International Independent Investigation Commission investigating the Hariri assassination. He left office in December 2005.

Walid al-Muallim—Syria's foreign minister and a former ambassador to the United States.

Hassan Nasrallah—Secretary-general of Hezbollah since 1992, when he succeeded Abbas Musawi, who was assassinated by Israel.

Naim Qassem—Deputy secretary-general of Hezbollah.

Moussa al-Sadr—Shiite cleric who was the first to mobilize the Lebanese Shiite community politically, starting in the 1960s. He founded the Amal Movement, Lebanon's first major Shiite political-military organization. He disappeared in Libya in August 1978, and is believed to have been killed by the regime of Moammar al-Qadhafi, though the motive remains a mystery.

Jamil al-Sayyed—Former head of Lebanon's General Security directorate and among Syria's strongest allies in Lebanon. A political enemy of Rafiq al-Hariri, he was forced to resign, along with three other security chiefs, in the aftermath of the Hariri assassination, and was later arrested, along with the security chiefs, as a suspect in the crime, on the recommendation of the United Nations International Independent Investigation Commission.

Nasrallah Boutros Sfeir—Patriarch of the Maronite Christian Church.

Fouad al-Siniora—Lebanese prime minister between 2005 and 2009. A close political ally of Rafiq al-Hariri, under whom he served several times as a minister responsible for Lebanon's financial affairs.

Riad al-Solh—Prime minister of Lebanon in 1943, when the country gained its independence. With Bishara al-Khoury, he came to an agreement over the founding contract of Independent Lebanon, the National Pact.

Michel Suleiman—Current president of Lebanon and commander of the Lebanese army between 1998 and 2008.

Gebran Tueni—Lebanese journalist and parliamentarian, he was for several years the publisher of Lebanon's leading daily, *Al-Nahar*. A prominent critic of Syria and one of the leaders of the March 14 movement, he was assassinated in December 2005.

Ghassan Tueni—Prominent Lebanese journalist, political figure, and diplomat, who was responsible for turning the *Al-Nahar* daily into Lebanon's leading newspaper. The father of Gebran Tueni, he took over his son's parliamentary seat following his assassination in 2005.

Lebanon Time Line

April 28, 1920—The Allied powers, meeting in San Remo, Italy, place Syria and Lebanon under a French Mandate. Both countries had been part of the Ottoman Empire, which the Allies defeated in World War I.

September 1, 1920—The French High Commissioner in the Levant, General Henri Gouraud, declares the establishment of Greater Lebanon, including Beirut and Mount Lebanon, the central Lebanese mountain chain, to which the French joined the Beqaa Valley, the north around and including the city of Tripoli, as well as southern regions around and including Sidon and Tyre.

May 23, 1926—Lebanon's constitution begins operating, following a statement to that effect by the French High Commissioner, Henri de Jouvenel, even though its formal publication into law does not come until 1930.

May 26, 1926—Lebanon's first president, Charles Debbas, a Greek Orthodox Christian, is elected by Lebanon's Representative Council and Senate.

October 12, 1927—The two houses of parliament approve a draft version of an amended constitution, pushed through by the French Mandatory authorities. The amended constitution, among other things, abolishes the Senate and affirms that the new parliament will have both elected and appointed representatives, the latter equivalent to half the number of elected ones. The aim is to stabilize the running of the state and give the president (and with him France) more power over the legislature. This ultimately proves unsuccessful.

May 14, 1930—The French High Commissioner, Henri Ponsot, publishes organic laws for the Mandatory territories, including Lebanon, as the basis for a policy to replace the Mandates with treaties to be concluded with elected governments in these territories. However, in November 1931, Ponsot is instructed not to apply the treaties policy to Lebanon, only to Syria, minus the autonomous Alawite region and Jabal Druze.

November 1933, March and October 1936—Amid prospects that Syria, then engaged in negotiations with France, would gain independence, Lebanese Muslim representatives hold three conferences, known as the Conferences of the Coast, to demand the reintegration of Muslim-majority areas into Syria from which they had been detached by France to form Greater Lebanon. The conferences reflect Muslim uneasiness with a Lebanon independent from Syria, even if a growing number of Muslim leaders seek to use such protests to enhance their role in a Lebanon not dominated by France and the Christians.

January 31, 1932—Lebanon holds a census, the last time this was done in the country, showing Christians holding a narrow 52 percent majority over Muslims.

January 2, 1934—Habib al-Saad, a Maronite, is appointed president for one year by the French High Commissioner, Damien de Martel. His term is later extended by one year.

January 20, 1936—Émile Eddé, a Maronite, wins the presidential election for a three-year term, against his Maronite rival, Bishara al-Khoury.

November 13, 1936—Two months after a similar treaty is signed between France and Syria, Lebanon and France sign a treaty stipulating that Lebanon will be granted independence within a three-year transitional period. However, because of the rising tension in Europe, successive French governments fail to ratify both treaties. During the Franco-Syrian negotiations, the Syrian delegation refuses to recognize an independent Lebanon, despite French pressure.

January 24, 1937—Damien de Martel restores constitutional life to Lebanon, and a new government is soon thereafter formed by a Sunni, Khaireddine al-Ahdab, setting an important precedent in Lebanese political life. Henceforth, Lebanon's elected presidents would be Maronites and its prime ministers Sunnis, an unwritten agreement later formalized in the National Pact of 1943.

October 5, 1937—As the tension between Eddé and Khoury rises, de Martel extends Eddé's term by three years. This is a poisoned chalice, as the conditions imposed on the presidency, like the conditions the High Commissioner forces on Eddé, including that he cannot seek reelection, undermine the president's ability to play an effective political role.

January 1939—Gabriel Puaux arrives in Beirut to replace de Martel. He later announces that France will not ratify the Franco-Lebanese Treaty.

September 21, 1939—Three weeks after the start of the war in Europe, Puaux suspends the Lebanese constitution, dissolves parliament and the government, and appoints Eddé as nominal head of state, with real power held by France.

June–July 1941—The Free French government proclaims the independence of Syria and Lebanon, and British and Free French forces invade the two countries, expelling Vichy forces. Georges Catroux is named Delegate-General.

November 26, 1941—Lebanese independence is officially proclaimed, one month after Syrian independence, a move immediately recognized by Great Britain, whose representative in Beirut is Major General Edward Spears, who would later be named British minister to Syria and Lebanon. However, the French look to delay implementation of the decision.

December 1, 1941—A Maronite judge, Alfred Naccache, is appointed president by Catroux.

August 28, 1943—Parliamentary elections are held in two stages, leading to the victory of the Constitutional Bloc led by Bishara al-Khoury, who is elected president on September 21 for a six-year term. Khoury asks his main Sunni Muslim rival, Riad al-Solh, to become prime minister. The government begins negotiations with the French Delegate-General, Jean Helleu, to amend the constitution and implement the provisions needed to realize independence.

October 8, 1943—Riad al-Solh presents his government to parliament and for the first time publicly outlines general principles that are later embodied in the National Pact, the agreement defining communal relations in post-Independence Lebanon, even if these principles evolved over time. The first is that posts in the state are to be allocated along demographic lines, perpetuating the custom from the Mandate years, so that the president is a Maronite Christian, the prime minister a Sunni Muslim, and the speaker of parliament a Shiite Muslim, and so on, while parliamentary seats are allocated in a 6:5 ratio in the Christians' favor, according to the 1932 consensus. The second is that Lebanon is part of the Arab world, having an "Arab face," but should neither join Arab unity schemes nor serve as an instrument for Western penetration of the Arab world.

November 8, 1943—In response to a French rejection of Lebanon's right to unilaterally amend the constitution, Lebanon's parliament does precisely that, formally endorsing measures granting the country effective independence. Three days later, Helleu orders the arrest of Khoury, Solh, and several ministers, who are imprisoned in the fortress of Rashayya in the western Beqaa Valley.

November 22, 1943—Amid popular pressure and British opposition, France is forced to release Khoury, Solh, and the ministers, marking the beginning of the end for French domination over Lebanon. The date is now recognized officially as Lebanese Independence Day.

May 25, 1947—Lebanon holds its first post-Independence legislative elections. Widespread fraud brings in a parliament friendly to Khoury, which one year later votes to amend the constitution to allow him to stand for a second term in office.

May 27, 1949—Bishara al-Khoury is elected for a second six-year term in office.

July 16, 1951—Prime Minister Riad al-Solh is assassinated in Amman, Jordan, by a member of the Parti Populaire Syrien, whose leader, Antoun Saadeh, had been executed by the Lebanese authorities two years earlier for organizing a failed coup attempt.

September 15, 1952—A general strike is called amid growing opposition to Khoury, whose administration never recovered from the illegitimate extension of his mandate in 1949, and from the subsequent death of Solh, his main Sunni ally. Two days later, Khoury resigns, naming the Maronite army commander, Fouad Shihab, as interim head of government until new elections can be held.

September 22, 1952—Camille Chamoun is elected president.

January 27, 1957—Prime Minister Sami al-Solh, speaking for Chamoun, expresses his support for Lebanon's adherence to the Eisenhower Doctrine, which aims to set the groundwork for collaboration between the United States and the Arab world against what is deemed to be the Soviet threat. This provokes a furor both inside Lebanon and in the Arab world, coming in the midst of deep polarization in the region between the West on the one hand, and the Arab nationalist regime of Egyptian President Gamal Abdel Nasser on the other, which had culminated in the Suez War of 1956. More specifically, this is a major test for Lebanon's National Pact, with many of Lebanon's Muslims siding with Abdel Nasser and many Christians sympathetic to the West.

March 16, 1957—Lebanon formally adheres to the Eisenhower Doctrine, to the displeasure of many Muslims, worsening Lebanese-Egyptian and domestic Lebanese relations. This is exacerbated by the fact that Chamoun's supporters begin a campaign to amend the constitution to allow him a second term.

June 1957—Parliamentary elections are held and bring in a majority favorable to Chamoun. The opposition accuses the president of manipulating the election results in order to ensure a friendly majority that will extend his term in office.

May 8, 1958—The assassination of a pro-opposition journalist provokes the start of an insurrection against Chamoun by his political rivals, which soon turns into a civil war. While this takes place mainly between Christians and Muslims, the president does have strong Christian opponents, particularly the Maronite patriarch, as well as Muslim allies. The army, led by General Fouad Shihab, remains neutral in the conflict, despite Chamoun's orders to the contrary.

July 14–15, 1958—Following a coup against the pro-Western monarchy in Iraq, the United States lands soldiers in Lebanon, answering Chamoun's request, fearing that his administration might fall as well. While this does not end the insurrection, the practical outcome is to end Chamoun's efforts to extend his term, and on July 31, Shihab is elected president, his term beginning when Chamoun's ends on September 23. This begins six years of relative stability under Fouad Shihab, during which the president repairs his relations with Abdel Nasser's Egypt but also comes to rely more heavily on military intelligence to contain his adversaries among the traditional political leaders.

August 18, 1964—Charles Helou is elected to succeed Shihab.

December 28, 1968—Following the Arab defeat in the June 1967 war, and as Palestinian armed groups based in southern Lebanon become more mobilized, Israeli commandos land at Beirut Airport and blow up the fleet of the national carrier, Middle East Airlines, as punishment.

April 23, 1969—Pro-Palestinian demonstrations in Sidon and Beirut lead to clashes with the Lebanese security forces, who open fire, killing some 20 people and injuring dozens of others. The incident illustrates the growing rift between those supporting the Palestinians and their growing militancy, and those, particularly in the Christian community, who oppose the Palestinians.

November 3, 1969—The Lebanese state and the Palestinian organizations sign the Cairo Agreement, regularizing the increasingly tense relations between the Lebanese army and armed Palestinian groups and permitting the latter to circulate along special corridors in the border area with Israel. The agreement is a compromise between the state and the Palestinians, but its net impact is to push Lebanon more deeply into the status of a "confrontation state" against Israel.

September 1970–July 1971—The Jordanian army begins attacking armed Palestinian groups in Amman, expelling them from Jordan in July 1971. The Palestinian leadership, in its majority, relocates to Beirut.

April 13, 1975—Following years of heightening hostility between Palestinian groups and their predominantly Muslim Lebanese allies on the one hand, and Christian paramilitary groups on the other, an incident in the Ain al-Remmaneh suburb of Beirut leads to a major outbreak of fighting. After gunmen shoot at a leading Christian politician, Pierre Gemayel, killing 4 of those with him, Christian gunmen fire on a bus full of Palestinians, killing 26 people. This is considered the formal start of Lebanon's fifteen-year civil war.

June 1976—Syrian forces launch an invasion of Lebanon in support of Christian militias, mainly to prevent a military triumph of Palestinians, which, the Syrians fear, might force them into a confrontation with Israel. This comes several months after the Syrians had already deployed pro-Syrian Palestinian units in Lebanon. The growing Syrian role in Lebanon receives American and Israeli acquiescence, so that Washington mediates a "red lines" agreement to regulate Syrian-Israeli relations in Lebanon.

March 11, 1978—Palestinian guerillas attack an Israeli bus in Galilee, provoking an Israeli invasion of southern Lebanon that lasts until June. The United Nations Security Council deploys an international force in southern Lebanon, known as the U.N. Interim Force in Lebanon (UNIFIL).

April 1981—Fighting between Christian militias and Syrian forces escalates into a confrontation between Syria and Israel when Israeli warplanes shoot down a Syrian helicopter. Syria responds by deploying antiaircraft missiles in Lebanon. The "missile war" ends thanks to Arab mediation between Syria and the Christians and the negotiation of a broader ceasefire by U.S. envoy Philip Habib.

June 6, 1982—Israel launches a major invasion of Lebanon, its aim to expel the armed Palestinian groups and bring to power a friendly president in Beirut, namely the leader of the Christian Lebanese Forces militia, Bashir Gemayel. Within a matter of days, the Israelis surround western Beirut, laying siege to the part of the capital where the Palestinian leadership is located.

August 23, 1982—As the Israeli siege of western Beirut nears its end, thanks to an international agreement to evacuate Palestinian guerillas, Lebanon's parliament elects Bashir Gemayel president to succeed Elias Sarkis. Three weeks later, Gemayel is assassinated in a bomb attack at a party headquarters.

September 15, 1982—Israeli soldiers enter western Beirut following Gemayel's assassination. A day later Lebanese Forces gunmen enter the Palestinian camps of Sabra and Shatila, killing what is estimated to be between several hundred and more than a thousand people, most of them civilians.

September 21, 1982—Bashir Gemayel's brother Amin is elected president. A multinational peacekeeping force that had helped evacuate Palestinian guerillas from Beirut, and that includes U.S. Marines, returns to Beirut to assist the Lebanese government. This brings on a period of relative calm, despite continued sectarian tension in the mountains between Christian and Druze militiamen.

July 1983—An Israeli redeployment from the Shouf Mountains toward the Awali River north of Sidon is followed by fighting between the Christian militias and Walid Jumblatt's Druze militia backed by Syria and Palestinian forces loyal to Damascus. This leads to a rout of the Christians and the expulsion of hundreds of thousands of Christians from the mountains.

June 1986—Several hundred Syrian soldiers, supported by the Syrian intelligence services led by Brigadier General Ghazi Kanaan, deploy in western Beirut to end the chaos there between mainly Muslim militias. This is the first time Syrian troops return to Beirut after withdrawing from the capital following the Israeli invasion of 1982.

September 23, 1988—Amin Gemayel's term ends without any successor being chosen. Gemayel appoints the army commander, Michel Aoun, as head of an interim military government. A rival government, headed by Salim al-Hoss and supported by Syria, is also in place, although because Hoss had submitted his resignation, Gemayel considers his government merely to have a caretaker role until Aoun takes over.

March 1989—Aoun, whose effective writ covers parts of the predominantly Christian areas of Lebanon, declares a "war of liberation" against Syria, which degenerates into destructive artillery barrages, leading to months of Arab mediation.

September 30–October 22, 1989—Lebanese parliamentarians meeting in Taif, Saudi Arabia, agree to constitutional amendments to redistribute political power among Christians and Muslims. This includes weakening the Maronite presidency and introducing a 50–50 ratio of Christians to Muslims in parliament. Michel Aoun rejects the agreement, arguing that it does not set a clear deadline for a Syrian withdrawal from Lebanon. Taif is effectively a compromise accord between Saudi Arabia and Syria, blessed by the United States.

November 5, 1989—René Mouawad is elected president, but remains in office for only seventeen days. On November 22, Independence Day, he is assassinated in a car-bomb attack in western Beirut. Two days later Elias Hrawi is elected to succeed him, even as Michel Aoun continues to challenge his authority.

January 31, 1990—Fighting breaks out within the Christian areas between army units loyal to Aoun and the Lebanese Forces militia led by Samir Geagea.

October 13, 1990—Syrian forces move militarily against Aoun's forces, entering the Christian areas of Beirut and its surrounding areas. The general takes refuge at the French embassy. This imposition of a Pax Syriana on Lebanon, one implicitly endorsed by the

United States and the Arab countries, brings an end to Lebanon's fifteen-year round of wars. Aoun soon departs for France.

October 31, 1992—Following Lebanon's first parliamentary elections since 1972, Prime Minister-designate Rafiq al-Hariri, a Lebanese businessman close to Saudi Arabia, announces the formation of a thirty-minister cabinet.

April 24, 1994—The leader of the Lebanese Forces, Samir Geagea, is arrested by the authorities for his alleged involvement in the assassination of a Christian leader in October 1990. A month later he is accused of responsibility in the bombing of a church in Zouq, north of Beirut. Supporters of Geagea say the arrest is politically motivated. Acquitted in the church case, he nevertheless later receives four life sentences in prison for other crimes.

April 1996—Israel, whose soldiers occupy the border area of southern Lebanon, launches massive air and artillery attacks against Lebanon, in response to cross-border rocket fire from Hezbollah. The sixteen-day war, which results in over 150 dead, leads to what is known as the April Understanding, an informal agreement between Hezbollah and Israel imposing limits on cross-border attacks. The understanding is a political victory for Hezbollah, because the party has been able to impose rules of engagement on Israel.

November 24, 1998—General Émile Lahoud, the army commander, is elected president, ending the term of Elias Hrawi, whose mandate was extended for three years by Syria. Replacing Lahoud as army commander is General Michel Suleiman. Rafiq al-Hariri is replaced as prime minister by Salim al-Hoss.

May 25, 2000—Israel completes its withdrawal from southern Lebanon, more than a month earlier than the stated deadline set by its prime minister, Ehud Barak. This brings to an end more than two decades of the Israeli military presence in southern Lebanon and represents a major victory for Hezbollah.

June 10, 2000—The Syrian president, Hafez al-Assad, who had ruled over Syria for thirty years, dies. He is succeeded by his son Bashar.

August–September 2000—Lebanon holds parliamentary elections under a hybrid law, drawn up largely by the head of Syria's intelligence service in Lebanon, Ghazi Kanaan. The results, which include a sweep by Rafiq al-Hariri of all the seats representing Beirut, are seen as a setback for President Lahoud, Hariri's bitter rival. In the election aftermath, Hariri returns as prime minister.

August 8, 2001—Maronite Patriarch Nasrallah Sfeir makes a three-day visit to the Shouf Mountains to meet with the Druze leader Walid Jumblatt. Both men formalize reconciliation between the Druze and Maronite communities after the expulsion of the Christians from the mountains in 1983.

September 2, 2004—Amid rising tension in Lebanon over the decision of Syria to extend the mandate of Émile Lahoud by obliging parliament to vote in favor of a constitutional amendment to that effect, the U.N. Security Council issues Resolution 1559 calling for a withdrawal of all foreign, meaning primarily Syrian, forces from Lebanon, the disarming of Lebanese and non-Lebanese militias, and noninterference in domestic Lebanese affairs.

September 3, 2004—Despite passage of Resolution 1559, parliament approves an amendment to the constitution allowing for an extension of Émile Lahoud's term in office. Rafiq al-Hariri, who opposes the extension, is nonetheless obliged by Syria to vote in favor of it, along with his parliamentary bloc, according to several accounts. Among those voting against an extension is the bloc led by the Druze leader Walid Jumblatt, who had been a close Syrian ally.

October 1, 2004—Marwan Hamadeh, a parliamentarian and former minister close to both Walid Jumblatt and Rafiq al-Hariri, narrowly survives a car-bomb attack near his home. The assassination attempt is viewed as the first sign that Syria will not tolerate growing opposition to its rule in Lebanon, amid indications that Hariri is moving closer to opposition figures critical of Syria in the run-up to parliamentary elections scheduled for summer 2005.

February 14, 2005—After weeks of growing tension between Syria and the emerging Lebanese opposition, Rafiq al-Hariri is assassinated in a massive truck-bomb attack in Beirut's hotel district. Twenty-one other people are killed, including the former economics minister, Basil Fuleihan, who survived the initial blast. This provokes what would be known as the Independence Intifada, or the Cedar Revolution.

The
Ghosts of
Martyrs Square

Introduction

IN LATE SUMMER 1983, the eighth year of Lebanon's civil war, Beirut's airport happened to be closed because of fighting. Many of us wanting to reach the city had to take an overnight ferry from Larnaca, Cyprus. As a matte sun rose over the Mediterranean and our ship drifted into Lebanese waters, I saw what it was about the country that I later hoped to describe. A group of Muslims began praying as other passengers looked on silently. Interrupting our introspection, a tall woman emerged on deck in an after-thought of a miniskirt, unsteady in her high-heeled shoes before she cut across the tranquil scene of those bent in prayer. The woman, an east European croupier from the ship's casino, was fol-lowed out by dozens of Lebanese still electrified by the night of gambling, their safari suits sodden with perspiration and scotch. The scene was neither unique nor especially powerful. But in its prosaic way it said much about the Lebanese, their resilience in a long journey that could often be punishing, their hedonism, even their intermittent spirituality, and those contrasts always seemed to me essential to understanding Lebanon's peculiar liberalism, a liberalism infused with the ideal of the many instead of the one.

This book is an effort to explain what this ideal can tell us about Lebanon's larger truths, particularly those pertaining to the country's social and political culture. For a long time I had wanted to write a book that would be one part reportage, one part essay on Lebanese society, and one part memoir. The events that followed the assassination of the former prime minister, Rafiq al-Hariri, on February 14, 2005, gave me an opportunity to do that, through a firsthand description of the defining developments in the country after 2005, when Syria ended its three-decade-old military presence here. They also allowed me to open windows on other aspects of Lebanon, its capital Beirut, its politicians, the war years and post-war memory, and the headaches brought on by hubristic leaders who, to our misfortune, have regarded themselves as better than the system.

I knew there was the possibility of a fourth ingredient: a post-mortem. Syria would not go easily, we knew in 2005, nor would its Lebanese allies, particularly Hezbollah, permit Lebanon to develop in ways that might require them to accept the authority of a sovereign Lebanese state, let alone carry the country outside Syria's and Iran's orbits. Indeed, what began in my mind several years ago as a story about the potentialities of Lebanese liberal inclinations became one about the five-year struggle to make that liberal moment meaningful.

On that fatidic February day, Hariri, along with almost two dozen others, was killed in a truck-bomb explosion outside the St. Georges, a once-legendary seaside hotel in Beirut destroyed during Lebanon's civil war. Its owner had been caught up in a bitter dispute over access to the sea with a property company effectively controlled by Hariri. The owner later said that when the bomb went off, he thought that he was the target. However, the man didn't rate over a ton of explosives. Hariri did and it was no small irony that he was served up at the St. Georges' doorstep. The only serious culprit in the crime was Syria, which had ruled over Lebanon in one way or another for twenty-nine years. Syrian power was virtually unlimited, its intelligence services and information networks ubiquitous. Yet Damascus protested that it was innocent, that it was all a ghastly plot to discredit Syria, another of those plots to discredit suspects in crimes with no other suspects. Syria's regime feared several things in Hariri: that the former prime minister would mount an electoral challenge against Damascus in the parliamentary elections that summer, almost a year after the United Nations Security Council, in its Resolution 1559, demanded the withdrawal of Syrian forces from Lebanon; but more generally that a Sunni Muslim like Hariri would, through the elections and his growing defiance, destabilize the established Syrian order in Lebanon and indirectly embolden Syria's own majority Sunnis, who, since 1970, have lived under an Alawite-dominated minority regime led by the Assad family.

The subsequent domestic and international furor was too much for the Syrian president, Bashar al-Assad, to deflect, and in a much-publicized visit to Saudi Arabia two weeks after Hariri's murder, he heard Crown Prince, later King, Abdullah, tell him that it was time for the Syrians to leave. In 1976, the Saudis had been instrumental in legitimizing Syria's entry into Lebanon during the civil war, so that this stopping of the clock had both political and symbolic meaning. According to Arabic press reports at the time, Assad tried to delay the pullout but was told that he had better order it soon or face Saudi enmity. The Saudis had few doubts about who had killed Hariri, however as patrons of immovability they were keen to avoid letting the Hariri assassination spin out of control and mar inter-Arab relations, particularly their own relationship with Syria. That required that Syria leave Lebanon quickly.

Hariri's murder provoked what would be known as the Cedar Revolution (a term coined by an American official, Paula Dobriansky, at a moment when popular movements in Ukraine and Georgia had, similarly, earned catchy brand names). For several weeks hundreds of thousands of Lebanese from all social categories, from most religious communities (with the exception of the Shiites, who in their majority, but by no means their totality, sided with the pro-Syrian Hezbollah and Amal movements), participated in peaceful rallies demanding that the Syrians go. The gatherings were held at Beirut's Martyrs Square, in the old downtown area that the latest martyr, Rafiq al-Hariri, had been instrumental in rebuilding after its destruction during the Lebanese conflict—a place doubly symbolic for being where Hariri was buried, if not triply so for being on the old wartime dividing line between predominantly Christian eastern Beirut and predominantly Muslim western Beirut, therefore embodying the surmounting of Lebanese divisions.

Initially, little heed was paid to Dobriansky's term among those assembling at Martyrs Square. The political allies of Hariri, who were demanding an end to Syrian hegemony, came up with the alternative name of Independence Intifada, which was regarded as more meaningful to an Arab audience, particularly a Sunni Muslim audience, because of the connotations it had with the Palestinian uprising against Israel. But gradually the Dobriansky label caught on, so that after a time many Lebanese themselves were referring to the "cedar revolution," not overly troubled that a revolution is more sweeping than an "intifada"—a word that in Arabic means a revolt but that can also mean something as modest as "shaking off" or "convulsion." And this coincided with a rising feeling among more than a few Lebanese, intense and vaguely expressed, and more powerful for being vaguely expressed, that what was taking place at Martyrs Square was the *possibility* of a revolution, an opportunity for a metamorphosis of their society into something more modern, where a citizen could be a citizen, not the factotum of a religious community; where political leaders could be held accountable to the law, not behave as overbearing patriarchs; and where (it was never quite expressed this way) everyone could fall into a fraternal embrace so often eluding the Lebanese, usually defined by their differences and parochial agendas.

If this was too idealistic for some tastes, including my own, idealism was also present in the way the outside world looked at the Cedar Revolution/Independence Intifada. So, too, was calculated cynicism. The reason was that both the Bush administration and its critics chose to interpret the shaking off of Syrian rule largely through the prism of what it said about American policy in the Middle East. Not for the first time, certainly not after the insular debate over the U.S. intervention in Iraq, an Arab society was afforded a bit part in its own story. Once Lebanon happened, it did not take long for American officials, and approving publicists in general, to insist that a "democratic wave" had overcome the region. This was destined to lend momentum to the faltering American endeavor in Iraq, and to George W. Bush's fluctuating "democratization" agenda. And precisely because the situation in Lebanon was eagerly picked up on by the United States, a disapproving backlash against the emancipation movement came from those who could not suffer the Bush administration. But Lebanon was never about Bush, and those who downplayed the impact of the Lebanese rejection of Syria for fear of overplaying Bush's merits, effectively silenced the voice of a majority of Lebanese who, Bush or no Bush, were simply fed up with Assad rule, and liked it that, for once, an American president agreed with them.

The "independence intifada" emerged from the convoluted realities of Lebanese society. That's why there was pragmatism in how the Lebanese played the situation outside. The American invasion of Iraq had not triggered rumblings of liberty in Lebanon in 2003, but Saddam's fall had allowed a prospect of change among Arabs more concerned with the message than with the American messenger. As far as the Lebanese were concerned, Iraq had usefully placed American forces on Syria's eastern border, a reminder to the Assad regime of its own vulnerabilities; and just as usefully it placed Lebanon higher in American attentions after Hariri's assassination. The Lebanese instinctively grasped the advantages to be gained. That's why, unlike most Arabs, they were prepared to employ American power against Syria. But most Lebanese hadn't planned their intifada. Indignation was their first impulse when Hariri was killed; from that indignation emerged an assumption that the absence of freedom and rule of law would only bring on more indignities, so that Syria's rule had to end because everything about it denied freedom, the rule of law, and indignation. It was a convergence of different interests that fed Lebanon's rebellion, and it told us an essential truth about the country's pluralism: in the pursuit of common goals the fractured Lebanese will create unexpected alliances.

• • •

THIS BOOK aims to unpack the Lebanon that emerged between 2005 and 2009, an essential moment in modern Lebanese history. During this time the country's very existence as a cohesive entity, more particularly the existence of its paradoxical liberalism and the reality of its emancipation from Syria, was overcome by doubt, after a beguiling moment following Hariri's killing that had pointed in a different direction. Some of this was predictable. It would be foolish to defend Lebanon as an ideal liberal example. Its system is in profound need of renovation. The country offers two roads: one of renewal through a new social contract; and one of failure to present itself as a sustainable model because of its unstable identities. Manifestations of Lebanese liberalism derive from a complex array of social and political relationships infused with illiberal drives and habits, enforced by numerous fathers who, like Saturn, devour their own children. But as I hope to show, these often illiberal relationships have also given rise to a system that, objectively, even reflexively, imposes equilibrium between Lebanon's political and social forces, allowing liberalism—albeit a paradoxical liberalism—to thrive in the spaces opened up.

Yet if only things could remain so simple. Throughout the post-2005 period, Lebanon's pluralism also became a curse. The society retained its diversity, but also saw its liberal tendencies on all sides wilt amid growing violence as its diversity turned to discord after the Syrian departure. This allowed Syria and Iran, with Hezbollah, to undermine systematically the consolidation of a fully sovereign and independent Lebanese state. Like many of my countrymen, I've spent much of my adult life observing, and hating, what the Syrian regime had done to Lebanon—its trashing of our constitutional institutions, its manipulation of our admittedly craven political class, its murder of civilians, politicians, and religious figures—and to watch the gains of 2005 being contested at every turn was not easy. Leading this effort was Hezbollah, toward which so many Arabs and "progressive" Westerners have displayed indulgence, but which I've seen to be mainly an autocratic, semisecret, military, political, and religious organization more powerful than the Lebanese state, that describes itself as, no less, the Party of God, is led by a leader who will probably remain in office for life, and that has made violent self-sacrifice and permanent armed struggle a centerpiece of its ideological mind-set, mainly on behalf of an autocratic clerical regime in Iran.

However, effective Hezbollah certainly has been, and in the aftermath of the Syrian pullout, the party adapted to a new situation where it not only protected Syrian and Iranian interests; it also shaped the environment in such a way as to protect its weapons and autonomy. The party's success has, arguably, been more threatening to Lebanon than the civil war between 1975 and 1990. For even at the height of the war, most Lebanese still retained faith in seeing a sobered, united country appearing out of the maelstrom.

That's why this book contains another ambition: to defend Lebanon, pluralistic Lebanon, warts and all, against the all-too-frequent accusation that because its system can be dysfunctional the country is not worth preserving as an independent entity. This has created a default attitude justifying subcontracting control of Lebanon to Syria, seen as the only state that can bring order to Lebanon's disorder, though Syria has always tried to make that clear by aggravating Lebanon's disorder. That doesn't lessen the responsibility of the Lebanese to agree to a reformed, consensual, functioning political system ensuring that outsiders won't have their way. Yet the conditions prevailing in the country don't allow for much optimism.

The most selfish reason for writing this book, however, is that Lebanon provokes powerful emotions in me, not all positive but that together offer the seductions of poignant imperfection. In 1970, at the age of seven, I was brought here by my mother, who had decided to rejoin her brother and his family after the premature death of my father. An American, he had dreamt of dropping everything and moving to Beirut. He dropped everything and we moved to Beirut. Those early years, which were supposed to bring consolation, were instead interrupted by a civil war that brought us a great deal more. The war, so ruinous in every other respect, was a valuable primer on the extent to which Lebanon is a country built on an absence of certitude, an embarrassment of myths. After all, no butchery can long be sustained where truth prevails. However, over the years I have also come to understand that those trying to cut through the myths, to present us with an uncompromising interpretation of Lebanon, have often only manufactured new ones of their own. The myths survive, metastasize, so that Lebanon's truth is frequently built on an immoderate accumulation of unsubstantiated perception.

That's why to better understand what happened after 2005, we might look at the foundations of Lebanon's political and social order and the discussion among publicists of something called the "Lebanese idea." On the one hand there have been those who see Lebanon as a "message," to quote the late Pope John Paul II, echoing earlier statements to that effect. Their reasoning is that Lebanon is something special, unique, and therefore that the Lebanese are special and unique. What has made Lebanon unique are many things: that it has eighteen recognized religious communities but that none can impose its will on the rest, requiring all to compromise; the country's openness to both East and West; its large Christian population when compared to that in other Arab countries; and the quality of its educational system and culture.

Defenders of this version have tended to regard Lebanese history as linear, stretching back millennia to the time of the Phoenicians and extending down to the present day, so that the formation of the modern state in 1920 and independence from France in 1943 were a culmination of historical processes leading toward a single point of national self-fulfillment. This linear interpretation is debatable; efforts to posit historical predestination often are. It has also been an outlook associated more with Christian publicists than Muslim ones. Yet it has earned a place of honor in the modern Lebanese identity—if only because the modern Lebanese identity is like a supermarket, where you can pick and choose what you want to be.

On the other side has been a less sanguine view of the country. From both the political left and from a segment of the Christian community uncertain of its fate in a changing Lebanon, there emerged in the 1960s and 1970s a profound critique of the Lebanese system, directed against its most upbeat ideologues. The left denounced a political order that it saw as inequitable socially and economically; retrograde for basing political and social life on the

religious community, or sect; and unsustainable for failing to impose an agreed-upon balance between Lebanon's Arab character
and what passed for its Western, or even Mediterranean, character.

From the Christian doubters, especially during the civil war,
came a narrower critique, that of a minority fearing its waning
power in a state where Muslims had become a majority. These
doubters emerged primarily from within the largest of the Christian sects, the Maronites. They maintained that because Christians
were losing ground demographically and politically, it was necessary to find a new arrangement guaranteeing Christian rights. That
proposed arrangement oscillated between plans during the war to
take back control of the state, which ended in predictable failure
since no single community can hope to control the state alone; to
promoting a federal structure for the country, which, though legitimate as an idea, has often come across as motivated by a yearning
for self-imposed isolation.

It is difficult for someone like me, a product of the war years,
not to smile when hearing Lebanon portentously described as a
"message." Too often I've seen Lebanese re-create a tranquil Lebanon of the mind as a palliative to the unsettled one encountered
daily. The critics are not wrong about the inequitable nature of the
system, the existence of little despotisms tarnishing the gentler image of the whole. Lebanon's sustainability as a unified state is an
unremitting worry, challenging the foundations of the optimists'
narrative. Even the country's historical-psychological prop—that
Lebanon is and always has been a "bridge between East and West"—
is dated. Of what value is such an attribute in a globalized world
where bridges have proliferated thanks to modern transportation
and technology?

Then there is sectarianism, the axial point of the Lebanese political and social system. Sectarianism has created an absurdity: a
bond between religious communities that derives far more from
their rivalries and mistrusts than from a sense of common national
destiny. Among the most influential ideologues of the Lebanese
idea was the journalist and banker Michel Chiha, who struggled
with the contradictions of a Lebanese reality he was instrumental
in helping define. He once wrote, "The dream would obviously be

to see the Lebanese, *all and suddenly in agreement*. But that's maybe only a dream. No one will perform the miracle of uniting them in one day." Chiha's way out of the dilemma was to argue that, with time, the Lebanese could develop a shared national sentiment, so that the primary goal in the interim was to create a system of equilibrium through national institutions representing everyone.

The point Michel Chiha made was and remains a compelling one. In a Lebanese system determined by laws of equilibrium, psychological or institutional, the mission shared by all, the common denominator accepted by all, consciously or unconsciously, has been self-protection by denying domination over the system to any one actor or coalition of actors—be they Lebanese or outside powers. Even Syria, which controlled Lebanon for nearly three decades, faced tenacious opposition throughout, always operated through a system it could direct but never truly change, and finally had to leave when it woefully misread the country's mood in 2004 and 2005.

What are the particularities of Lebanese sectarianism? Political office, civil service positions, and senior military and security appointments are apportioned according to the principle of religious balance. The unwritten National Pact of 1943, essentially the founding contract of Independent Lebanon, outlines that the president of the country is a Maronite Christian, the prime minister a Sunni Muslim, the speaker of parliament a Shiite Muslim, and so on down the hierarchical ladder. In parliament, Christian and Muslim seats are today distributed on the basis of a 50-50 ratio. Given that Christians roughly make up a third of the population, this provides them with representation beyond their numbers. Systems based on formulas of communal power-sharing in mixed or divided societies are known in the jargon of political science as "consociational" and are anathema to those defending one-man, one-vote. However, it can be shortsighted to apply majoritarianism as the sole benchmark of democratic legitimacy. Over the decades, the rationale has been that because Lebanon is a country of minorities, one-man, one-vote would only marginalize the smaller communities, would alter the equilibrium that Chiha wrote about, particularly with respect to the dwindling Christians, so that they might slowly abandon the system—through emigration, a heightened sense of paranoia, indifference. Lebanon would therefore lose an essential component of its pluralism, namely its scaffolding of religious coexistence. By and large, this is true, but it is all the truer in that resorting to one-man, one-vote would also risk destabilizing the far more sensitive relations today between Sunnis and Shiites, so that it would be misleading to limit the matter of representation to the Christian-Muslim dichotomy.

The late historian and journalist Samir Kassir observed that sectarianism, or what he referred to as "confessionalism" (Lebanon's religious communities are also known as "confessions"), was not a distillation of timeless communal prejudices, but something more contemporary. He wrote, "Far from being something archaic, confessionalism was a ransom paid to modernity," by which Kassir meant the modernity of the nineteenth century, when Lebanese society was transformed demographically and economically, and when Beirut grew into a cosmopolitan Mediterranean city. But individuality was also a ransom the modernizing Lebanese paid to confessionalism. For what was the value of the individual in a larger collectivity determined mainly by identities acquired at birth?

A leading detractor of the Lebanese sectarian system, the writer and former minister Georges Corm, has made a similar case. For him sectarianism has turned Lebanon into an "impossible state," a "state that cannot be found." Corm describes Lebanon as "a state in the conditional, with sovereignty limited by the forbearance of its constituent [religious] 'communities' and their foreign protectors." However, a detractor can also hide an optimist. In the early 1990s, Corm was mentor to a group calling itself the Movement of the Citizen. This spoke to his belief in the possibility of a Lebanese citizen who could transcend the religious community. Corm argues that the sectarian order is, in fact, of relatively recent vintage, dating back only to the seventeenth century. Like Kassir, he too has seen it as a ransom paid to modernity, and is right in attacking an essentialist approach to Lebanese communal identity. Sectarianism may be a characteristic of a particular Lebanese moment that will disappear into the mist of time. But where Corm falters is in not taking his argument for the transitory nature of the sectarian system to its logical conclusion. If sectarianism has endured, then it must have a certain measure of flexibility, seeking out an equilibrium that its flexibility reinstates. What is that equilibrium? The same equilibrium that Chiha outlines: a balance of power between the religious communities, which translates into a supple mechanism preventing the rise or consolidation of an authoritarian, exclusivist regime. While Corm believes that individuals represent less in such a system, their freedoms may sometimes be better preserved through its natural checks and balances.

That was the message in the Independence Intifada and its aftermath. Starting in 2004, before Hariri was killed, most of Lebanon's leading political figures began allying with each other against Damascus, including former wartime foes. There was no essentialism there. The Lebanese sects and their leaders responded pragmatically in defending their endangered prerogatives, which in turn created wider spaces later that allowed individuals to expand the range of their liberal ambitions when the Syrians withdrew. This was a different way the Lebanese had of reaffirming their individuality, rather than by presuming that a modern, nonsectarian Lebanese citizen could abruptly be invented. It was also much more realistic.

Is being weak the Lebanese state's worst fault? I believe not. In the hierarchy of evils, we should place much higher the limitations on freedom. What makes Lebanon relatively free in an unfree Middle East is that the country's sectarian system, its faults notwithstanding, has ensured that the society's parts are stronger than the state; and where the state is weak, individuals are usually freer to function. This goes against the modern view of statehood, where the nation-state is supposed to do away with primary loyalties and identities and mash them into an all-inclusive national whole. Modern democracies, in particular, have done this through institutions of representation and national integration. So to hold up Lebanon's divided order, its frail state, its sectarian atavisms, as worthy progenitors of its paradoxical liberalism, would seem absurd to a modernist. But that's precisely the case that will implicitly be made throughout this book, even if the shortcomings of the Lebanese system will be flagrant throughout.

Why adopt such a position? Because the affliction of the Middle East is the failure of its states. The Arab state has almost everywhere become a vessel for absolute rule, and many of the region's regimes have demonstrated the acute degradation of their political orders by establishing republican monarchies. Lebanon is not the only sectarian society in the Middle East; but it is the only one where the state is less powerful than the religious communities. Where the state has been more powerful, a secular ideology, usually some strain of Arab nationalism, was supposed to transcend sectarian or other identities. What happened, however, was that these ideologies became instruments of total control, so that at the top sat the autocrat, while at the bottom primary identities prevailed because the state offered no better than dictatorship. Syria and Saddam Hussein's Iraq are examples of this.

In Lebanon alone a formula was worked out to accept the reality of sectarianism and take advantage of the liberal openings it created. Despite two civil wars since independence and unrest recently, the system has been more capable of absorbing its contradictions than anyone thought possible. Lebanon may not quite be a message, but it is undoubtedly an outpost of invigorating variety in an Arab world that generally dislikes variety. The country's pluralism has allowed informal interstices to flourish in the society, interstices in which the Lebanese have developed their eccentric freedoms. Lebanon's women are allowed, by and large, to be just that: women; with personalities, exigencies, and determination, whichever community they come from, not shadows. Its youths, wherever they come from, take a functional view of the outside world, revealing an innate cosmopolitanism that makes them willingly pick up at any time to settle elsewhere. Lebanese clergymen lean toward the reassuringly shady rather than the dogmatically pure, often preferring the adulterated city of man to the austere City of God. The country's politicians are venal, but the better ones know that unless they value the needs and fears of their followers they could not survive. These examples are anecdotal, reply the pessimists, excuses to represent the impossible state as a possible one. That overstates things. Lebanon *is* an impossible state in its worst moments; it may well be an intangible one through its relentless permutations. However, these deficiencies only strengthen its paradoxical liberalism. For what kind of domineering order can easily take hold in a place of relentless permutation and exasperating impossibility?

After 2005, Lebanon suffered deeply from the open spaces its sectarian system created. The reason is that Hezbollah turned the Lebanese system on its head by using those spaces to defend its own parallel state, after having earlier used them to build up that state. The party could not impose its will on the rest of society, though it tried, but it was able to bring the political system to a standstill. It was able, as well, to take advantage of divisions in the society, which in turn allowed Syria and Iran to make considerable headway in reversing what the emancipation movement had achieved. The stalemate this created endures to this day, as Lebanese society is neither in a position to absorb Hezbollah nor to break with it, leaving a remarkably free system that also happens to be cripplingly unstable.

This might remind us of a conversation making the rounds after the American invasion of Iraq in 2003, and Iraq's subsequent descent into chaos. It centered on whether Arab countries were better off embracing freedom or stability. That the two should have been placed against each other implied that Arabs could not have both at the same time. It was a cultural thing, the agnostics whispered: what Arab societies needed was the time to develop democratic habits. The argument was both contradictory and circular: contradictory in that this assumption led to a counterintuitive notion that accepting, therefore legitimizing, what existed at the present, namely dictatorship, would eventually bring about more democracy; and circular because asserting that Middle Eastern societies were institutionally unprepared for democracy only encouraged regimes to make sure their societies remained institutionally unprepared for democracy. The argument also happened to be condescending and deterministic, condescending in its determinism.

However, Lebanese society has not required generations of democratic experience to appreciate that states are not there to blackmail citizens into surrendering their freedom to ward off instability. Lebanon is a country that has repeatedly failed to find the right balance between freedom and stability, but at no point has the society seriously considered that the two are necessarily incompatible. The years after 2005 only confirmed this basically sound view of what a society should seek to achieve. And that sound view came out of the social order of a country that too many people regard as no better than a failure. Yet to read Lebanon solely as a failure is terribly constricting. Fragmentation and a weak state can allow people to be who they are, even if they do not always allow them to be who they want to be. In today's Middle East just being who one is can be an extravagance. Lebanon is not the region's future, but it does offer valuable aspects of a better Middle Eastern future. The Lebanese were forced to find themselves after 2005, and are still doing so to this day, with mixed results. To their advantage is that their society is one in which, uncannily, liberal impulses have often come out on top, despite those who would prefer otherwise, who don't want to believe otherwise.

I

A Voluptuous Vibration

If men and women began to live their ephemeral dreams,
every phantom would become a person with whom to be-
gin a story of pursuits, pretenses, misunderstandings,
clashes, oppressions, and the carousel of fantasies would
stop.

Italo Calvino, *Invisible Cities*

THE PEOPLE GATHER at the top of Martyrs Square, near
where, some weeks earlier, he had addressed those demanding
that the Syrian army leave Lebanon. It is June 4, 2005, and the
procession—large but not nearly as large as the journalist Samir
Kassir deserves—is there to accompany him in the one starring role
(his brashness notwithstanding) that he would have surely preferred to delay.

Two days earlier—it was nearly 11 A.M.—Kassir had sat down in
his silver Alfa Romeo in an eastern Beirut neighborhood. One or
several people were watching him and detonated a bomb under his
car, killing Kassir instantly.

At that moment a great deal was ended: the biting pen of one
of Lebanon's most daring political commentators and a scholar of
the modern Middle East; but also the venomous antagonism between Kassir and a Lebanese intelligence official, who a few years
earlier had had the writer harassed after being criticized in two im-
pertinent articles. The bullying continued to the end. When he

was killed, Kassir was about to pick up a bodyguard—really more a burly driver accompanying him about town.

Not long after Kassir's assassination, the intelligence official was on the front page of the daily *Al-Hayat* peddling his version of events in a ten-part interview, as he defended a career brusquely terminated because of the Syrian pullout in April 2005. With his patrons gone, it was said that Major General Jamil al-Sayyed spent much time at the beach—an anteroom to irrelevance for a man moved by the tremors of authority and intrigue. But then things changed. Within weeks the beachcomber had become a jailbird, one of four Lebanese security and intelligence officials arrested as suspects in the February 14 assassination of Rafiq al-Hariri, Lebanon's onetime prime minister. Hariri's killing had prompted weeks of demonstrations against Syria at Martyrs Square, leading to the Syrian departure, Damascus being the prime suspect, indeed the only one, in the crime.

Kassir's funeral procession makes its way toward Nijmeh Square in Beirut's downtown area, the location of parliament and the Greek Orthodox St. Georges Church, where the requiem mass will be celebrated. A dozen or so members of the Democratic Left movement, to which Kassir belonged, hold up the casket at arms' length. Someone shouts, "Applaud the hero," and we applaud, because Kassir was nothing if not a superior performance. In the Lebanese tradition, when a young man dies, the funeral is often conducted as a wedding never had. There are horns and mourners feigning happiness, while a white casket, usually open, is pumped up and down by pallbearers in a wild salsa of death. Kassir's casket is being made to dance too, but this is no commemoration of aborted youth. Married twice, with two daughters, Kassir has instead been transformed into a medium of rage, his coffin waved angrily at the doors of parliament—though why parliament is not clear. There is something unbecoming about it all: the manipulation of a dead man; the immoderation that permeates Lebanese grief; a vague sense that the ceremony might dissolve into mayhem. But there is also a sense that this funeral means something, whether Beirut's streets are packed with onlookers or not.

As I walk toward the church, I see an old man hunched over,

framed by a breach in the crowd. It is the newspaper publisher Ghassan Tueni, who hired Kassir in the early 1990s to come work for *Al-Nahar*, Lebanon's leading Arabic-language daily. I greet Tueni, who responds with polite absence. The man who has serenaded into the grave most of the prominent Lebanese of the past half-century, who would do the same to his own son, Gebran, six months later, knows that this particular burial reverses the order of things. Kassir was a protégé, a taxing protégé for never shying away from a fight, but who was kept on the newspaper's front page even as he used his column to tear into the prohibitions bolstering Syria's order in Lebanon. Tueni was at ease with provocation, could rarely abide the smugness of power even as he searched power out, and likely heard in Kassir reverberations of his own effrontery. He stands defeated. I recall that the day before he mumbled a four-word fragment when asked what Kassir's death meant: ". . . the great Arab prison."

In an interview with Kassir in June 2004, I asked him whether he thought Lebanon had a message to offer, even though the values of the republic had been vandalized during the years of Syrian hegemony. "I don't know," he answered, "but I am sure the Lebanese deserve a better future. At least they deserve to find their own way, in accordance with a rich history that cannot be reduced merely to violence. Yes, we were a laboratory for violence, but we were also, before that, a laboratory for modernity, and in some ways we still are."

It is a paradox, one intimately understandable to the Lebanese, that the secular, worldly Kassir is to be buried in the ancient rites of the Greek Orthodox Church. The mass begins, but it is the marginalia that draws attention: the late arrival of Saad al-Hariri, the son of Rafiq al-Hariri, greeted by clapping, chased by the hissing of those annoyed with the interruption; the placement of Lebanon's grandees to determine which politician is sharing a pew with which ambassador; who is around the coffin and who is not. Then comes the ambulatory, slurred eulogy of Bishop George Khodr, also a weekly fixture of *Al-Nahar*'s front page, reaffirming the church's dominion over the service.

Ghassan Tueni's granddaughter reads a tribute that brings on another ovation. Kassir's former colleague from the Democratic Left, Elias Atallah, follows, but just as he's about to make a political statement, he is stopped by one of those anonymous dwellers of Lebanese sacristies. Atallah hesitates; he's been thrown off his stride. No one listens to what comes next. The scene moves to handshakes of sympathy for the family, a disquieting moment after the church has been emptied when the casket is opened for a last look, the procession to the Cemetery of St. Dmitri, only a short walk from Kassir's home, and his burial in an elevated family vault in the last aisle to the left behind the church, the closing of a story half-read on a humid Saturday at the start of a grimy Lebanese summer.

Theories circulated as to who was behind the blast. One was that Kassir made a good mark because he had close ties to the Syrian opposition and access to Arab satellite channels through his wife, Giselle Khoury, a prominent journalist at the Al-Arabiya station. He also had French citizenship, as well as Lebanese, so his death may have been a message to France to back off from its antagonism toward the Syrian regime—at least that was how French officials perceived it. According to one of Kassir's friends, his murder was a more general warning: Lebanon must no longer threaten stability in Damascus as it did during the 1950s and '60s, when Beirut hosted the region's exiles, becoming a nerve center for coups and malcontents of every stripe. To Kassir's wife he paid the price because he had designed a poster for the demonstrations organized after Hariri's killing, demanding the ouster of seven Lebanese officials, including Sayyed, all shown with dour demeanor, an *X* drawn through their faces.

Were the theories too convenient? Perhaps, but they were also quickly made irrelevant. The moment Kassir was killed, it was his outspokenness, and his outspokenness from the ramparts of his own city, that gave meaning to his death. The Lebanese had believed that the Syrian withdrawal offered them a new start. Kassir himself had recently been imbibing extra doses of optimism, a narcotic he never lacked in the first place, and presumed that the time of telephoned intimidation was almost over. Yet in his death was a warning that little had changed, that there were those who would fight Lebanon's liberal instincts, after months when those instincts were at the heart of efforts by the Lebanese to shake themselves free of Syria. Kassir had played a leading role in that shaking off. He had also been realistic about its limitations, so that his death affirmed that liberalism set free was also liberalism threatened, because it was itself threatening.

For all the abstract things Samir was to Lebanon, he was also, and quite incidentally, a friend of mine. I first met him at the old offices of *Al-Nahar* on Hamra Street in 1993, soon after his return from Paris. We mentioned squash and not long afterward began playing together in a run-down club near the remains of a Roman aqueduct in a Beirut suburb. Neither of us was any good, and when we weren't slashing at thin air, we could at least survey the bird's nest in the top corner of the court. The aqueduct would later hold meaning for me because Samir mentioned it in his last book, a history of Beirut. It supplied the Roman city with water and Samir's noticing it was an early step in his mentally reassembling the country he had spent years away from and would later embody better than most.

Samir's passage from those early days back in Beirut to his murder had many turns, yet also followed a straight line in that what he wrote, as George Orwell put it to describe his own motivations, came from a "desire to push the world in a certain direction, to alter other people's idea of the kind of society that they should strive after." In his more academic works, particularly his published doctoral thesis on the Lebanese civil war, Samir could sometimes read bone-dry—frigid analysis overwhelming his natural nimbleness, elaborate vocabulary gridlocking the prose. But in his newspaper and magazine articles the heaviness was gone as the urge to sting took over, to turn every article into a pamphlet. That style reflected a mind in ebullition. Samir did many things in the mid-1990s: he was put in charge of *Al-Nahar*'s publishing branch, before later editing *L'Orient-Express*, the political and cultural monthly magazine of Lebanon's French-language daily. He briefly hosted a television interview show; he wrote books; and he taught history at St. Joseph University, which allowed him to create relations with students who would later play such a fundamental role in the 2005 demonstrations and who would look toward him, as they would toward Gebran Tueni, for inspiration.

The ties between Samir and Gebran, distant cousins, were unusual. Gebran had taken over from his father Ghassan as the head of *Al-Nahar*, and he and Samir did not get on well. That was because in many regards they were alike: both of them conscious of the untapped power of the young, who had largely been ignored by traditional politicians who saw the world as a bargain between leaders; both also men of great egos, elegant narcissists, Samir more knowledgeable of Arab realities than Gebran, prouder of his cosmopolitan Arab identity, with his Palestinian father and Syrian mother, but less charismatic when speaking publicly, more self-conscious about avoiding Gebran's innate populism; and both viscerally angry with what the Syrian regime had done to Lebanon, its relegation of a country once an archetype of innovation in the Middle East to the status of a protectorate—even if Samir was far more incensed than Gebran with what Syria's rulers had done in the way of brutalizing their own people. I remember the look on Gebran's face as he stared down at Samir in his car shortly after the assassination—Samir broken in half, left as an exhibit for over an hour. It was a look of utter dread, perhaps at the realization that their destinies were more linked than either would have liked, for Gebran would not outlive the year, killed in a bomb explosion in December.

A few weeks before Samir's assassination, he sent out an email with an image of the front page of the *Washington Post*. The off-lead story was titled "A New Power Rises Across the Middle East." The photograph above it was of Samir standing at Martyrs Square next to a spray-painted slogan reading WE WANT THE TRUTH. The truth was, of course, the truth about who had killed Rafiq al-Hariri, and Samir had been chosen as a face of the changing Arab world. The cosmopolitan Arab man found amusing this sudden recognition by the Americans, but there was a limit. In one of his last writings he took issue with "a current of ideas inspired by American neo-conservatives [that] holds that one of the factors leading to the backwardness of the Arab world lies in the persistence of Arabism," by which Samir meant pan-Arabism and the Arab nationalist idea.

His was a brighter reading of Arabism, too bright, downplaying how Arab regimes had used the absoluteness of Arab nationalism to justify repressing their peoples.

However, this also showed that Samir, as he headed down toward Martyrs Square after Hariri's assassination, did so from one of numerous political and cultural vantage points gathering at the location. Panning out, you could see Arabists alongside Lebanese nationalists; dissident communists alongside Christian federalists; religious conservatives alongside hedonistic atheists; Francophones alongside Anglophones, conversing in approximate Arabic; the new faces of the Arab world alongside the old. It was about a moment when myriad strands met in a single spot. Samir and his more prescient comrades understood this—and even better that their efforts were playing out against a backdrop of calculations by politicians on all sides, which they tried to counter through their actions on the ground. Ultimately, their fears were confirmed when calculation won out. If Samir's death invited a medley of interpretations, we can add one more. Always practical, he was nonetheless corrupted by romanticism. As he stood among those who made possible the popular revolt against Syria, he also wrote its obituary in several of his final articles. In retrospect, that obituary prefaced his own.

I MISTOOK the explosion that killed Rafiq al-Hariri for a sonic boom, as it rattled the wooden curtain box above my balcony window. It was almost 1 P.M. on Monday, February 14, 2005, and I was working in our apartment in eastern Beirut, 3 kilometers (about 2 miles) from the blast. The first sense I got that something had happened was my wife telling me, as she walked into the house, that what she had heard was no sonic boom. By midafternoon we knew that Hariri had been assassinated, that the image many of us had seen on our television screens of the charred remains of a victim being lifted onto a stretcher was of the charred remains of Rafiq al-Hariri. In the car sitting next to him was Basil Fuleihan, formerly an economy minister and a friend from my university days.

Basil survived but was so badly burned that when he passed away on April 18, the miracle of his being kept alive seemed a curse. A friend who saw the explosion described cars, heavy armor-plated cars, tossed up dozens of meters into the air, as the shockwave made him feel like the flesh was being torn from his body.

Hariri's killing struck me as astonishing. His enemies had gone too arrogantly far, without gauging the consequences. Unlike a surprising number of other people who had *not* known the former prime minister (I had met him only twice), I did not take the assassination personally. But I do recall telling a friend that it was the end for Syria in Lebanon, and feeling that now we had to deal with the enormous vacuum left behind by Hariri, because, like or dislike him, he had filled center court in the country for almost fourteen years. I had never been close to the Hariri entourage, and had criticized the prime minister's social and economic program in the mid-1990s. But Hariri was no thug; he enjoyed defending his ideas against argumentative journalists, and wouldn't crack your knees for disagreeing with him. He had a tendency to see the state as a version of himself writ large, and collected people without allowing himself to be played by them. The son of a modest family from the southern port city of Sidon, throughout his social rise he had had the determination and astuteness of the upstart who hasn't yet acquired a vanity fed by the city. Hariri's feat was to conquer Beirut, to reinvent himself as a personification of the capital by way of a successful contracting career in Saudi Arabia during the 1980s. But with Syria always looking over his shoulder, Hariri usually won his hands with three aces, never four. Nothing demonstrated this better than the fact that he was now dead, having tried but failed to pick that fourth ace.

That evening I went to the Hariri residence in the Qoreitem neighborhood to see what the atmosphere was like. As I stood in a crowd outside the door waiting to enter, I heard a young man shout, "If we want to know the truth, it is Syria that killed Hariri." This was an audacious statement to make then, but not because Syria was innocent, for it was plain that Syria alone had the motive, the means, and the intention of killing Hariri; but because the young man was almost certainly a Sunni Muslim, from a community that had long resisted condemning the Syrians in Lebanon. Inside the building were hundreds of people, as leaders of the opposition to the government of Prime Minister Omar Karami gathered to issue a statement. When it came, the statement held Syria and the pro-Syrian government responsible for the crime, demanded an independent international investigation, called for the government's resignation, and demanded that Syria withdraw its forces from Lebanon. The last point restated the central demand of United Nations Security Council Resolution 1559 approved the previous September, which had also called on armed groups in Lebanon to surrender their weapons—a provision directed primarily against Hezbollah. The participants insisted that the Syrian withdrawal take place before parliamentary elections in May and June, and declared a three-day general strike. These ideas would be given a label on Friday the eighteenth, when the opposition declared the launching of the Independence Intifada.

I sat next to a European ambassador who told me he had seen Hariri the previous week and inquired whether he was being careful about his security. Hariri had been confident, the ambassador remembered, persuaded that he was protected by his international connections, particularly French President Jacques Chirac. That didn't quite square with what Hariri's ally, the Druze leader Walid Jumblatt, said after the killing. Jumblatt had more openly defied Syria than Hariri in recent months and mentioned that he and the former prime minister would discuss which of them would be killed. "He was," Jumblatt later laconically told me. But if that was Hariri's thinking, then it indicated no certainty that he was safe, unless he was convinced that Jumblatt would be the unlucky one.

The relationship between Hariri and the Syrian regime had always been complicated. For much of his time as prime minister, Hariri had propped up the postwar Syrian order, if not always by conviction. Syrian rule after 1990 rested on a foundation of Arab and international consensus, and Hariri was the Saudis' stake in Lebanon. However, the bad blood had grown in the months between passage of Resolution 1559 and the assassination. The previous August, Hariri, who headed a parliamentary bloc, had been summoned to Damascus for a meeting with Syrian President Bashar al-Assad. He was told to approve a constitutional amendment extending the term of President Émile Lahoud, Hariri's enemy. According to Jumblatt, Assad told the former prime minister: "Lahoud is me, if you and Chirac want me out of Lebanon, I will break Lebanon." The Syrians held Hariri responsible for Resolution 1559. This overstated things but was true in that Hariri had influence with Chirac, whose government had jointly sponsored the resolution with Washington. Hariri had even quietly congratulated some Security Council members voting in favor.

In reaction to the extension of Lahoud's mandate, a small group of politicians and parties formed what became the "Bristol Gathering," for the hotel where they met. This coalition coalesced around a core of longstanding Christian foes of Syria, as well as, for the first time, previous Syrian allies, most prominently Jumblatt, leader to Lebanon's 200,000-strong Druze community. Hariri officially remained neutral, but in the weeks before his assassination he and his bloc members more openly displayed their sympathy for the Bristol opposition, earning them threats from government ministers and even from the prime minister. Hariri had his eye on the summer legislative elections, hoping he would be able to reconfirm his popularity and widen his margin of maneuver with the Syrians. Yet he and his allies expected, at best, to win a substantial minority in parliament. However, Syria's perception of its domination of Lebanon was inflexible. The Assad regime's fear of what Hariri, backed by the international community, might do to this domination; its paranoia with regard to Lebanese Sunni mobilization, fortified by Christian and Druze antipathy, which risked giving the wrong ideas to Syria's own majority Sunni population ruled by a minority Alawite regime—all this made the former prime minister a premier target. It should have been obvious why Hariri risked more than Jumblatt. He was playing a high-stakes game so that his successes endangered Syria's twenty-nine-year-old rule over Lebanon as well as Assad's authority at home. Yet the Syrians were wrong in assuming that his removal would impose tranquility. All it did was bring about the outcome the Syrians had sought to avert: the unity of a majority of Sunnis, Druze, and Christians against Syria.

The Hariri funeral, held on February 16, was billed a popular funeral rather than an official one, to avoid the presence of Émile Lahoud and those who had tried to destroy Hariri. Most Sunnis were not yet ripe to turn against Syria, but they were nearly there. Surrounded by Christian political groups or independents who had spent the postwar years contesting Syrian rule in Lebanon, whose activists had been mistreated with little discernible sympathy from the rest of Lebanese society; surrounded by later arrivals in the opposition to Syria, Walid Jumblatt's Druze and the more recently established Democratic Left, with its Christian and Muslim members; surrounded by these groups, the Sunnis began to organize and mobilize, even if those who had been with Hariri were still finding their bearings. The absence of any obvious successor to the former prime minister had an impact on how the Sunnis framed their response to the crime. Should the priority be to seek the truth about the killers? Should it be to drive Syria out of Lebanon? Among Hariri's sister, Bahiyya, a parliamentarian, and his wife, Nazeq, as well as his two eldest sons, Bahaa and Saad, all of whom held a piece of Rafiq al-Hariri's legacy and financial inheritance, no answers were forthcoming. This allowed the more assertive allies of the Hariris to pilot them into a conflict with Syria the family had not immediately settled on but did not oppose.

As the Hariri funeral procession headed through the streets of western Beirut toward Martyrs Square, those with Syria on their mind began unfurling their banners. An apolitical events organizer, Asma Andraos, who would soon set up a civil society tent in Martyrs Square with her friends, held up, with those friends, signs saying IT'S OBVIOUS. NO? What was obvious to her and her friends was that Syria had killed Hariri. The followers of Michel Aoun, a former commander of the Lebanese army who had launched a failed "liberation war" against Syria in 1989 before being exiled, also held up anti-Syrian slogans. Walid Jumblatt later told an interviewer (with feigned sorrow) just how low Syria had fallen in Lebanon by repeating a rhyming chant he had picked up around him, whose last line referred to Syria's President Bashar al-Assad as a "pimp," even if Jumblatt stopped short of using the word. The Democratic Left also had its banners, which the marchers had concealed so they would not be confiscated by intelligence agents. Ziad Majed, a Shiite from south Lebanon who was vice president of the Democratic Left, remembered what happened:

> We chose our slogans prior to the funeral because we feared people would be silent. . . . I remember when we started our slogans, people around us were shocked, scared, and many tried to change their place in the procession so as not to be associated with us. Then suddenly more and more people began joining in the songs and the slogans against Bashar, Lahoud, against the Baath and for independence. . . . I cannot forget the scene when we passed near [the predominantly Sunni quarter of] Aisha Bakkar, through Munla, and to Karakol Druze, how people started screaming from the balconies when we were chanting against the *mukhabarat* [the intelligence services] and the Syrian regime and then women started throwing rice and sugar at us. We were probably a group of 150 to 200 when we gathered at Verdun. By Karakol Druze there were thousands with us.

For the lawyer Nabil Aboucharaf, a Christian with memories of being slapped around by the security services as head of the Amicale de Droit, the student representative body at St. Joseph University's law faculty, who had once lost 5 kilos (11 pounds) in twenty-four hours after being abducted and mistreated by military intelligence agents, this was a moment he had been waiting for. "Hariri's assassination showed that there was no cover for anybody. A Sunni leader had been killed and the reaction was rage, but also a sense that this alone could move the Muslims."

Even before Hariri's funeral, the vibrations had begun within Lebanese society to ensure that the page of the assassination would not be hastily turned. What occurred in the subsequent weeks showed how the liberal impulses in Lebanese society, when roused, could pack a tremendous wallop. There was the start of a campaign of demonstrations against Syria and its local partners; the establishment of a tent city at Martyrs Square by independents and youths affiliated with political parties to build on the momentum of public outrage; and there was an awareness by some participants that this popular movement needed to be branded, since branding meant defining the demonstrations and imposing on them a unity of purpose and goals.

However, the uprising against Syria was not just a case of a population imposing its liberal will on illiberal adversaries. The move against Damascus began in late 2004 as a revolt by a rump of Lebanese politicians against Lahoud's extension. The president was unpopular because he had tried to be the sole conduit to Damascus and had often used the army to keep his adversaries in line. The revolt was justified, even admirable, but it was also limited in scope. Hariri's assassination changed that, for in the month after February 14 it was the public that led the way, that turned the Bristol revolt into a national objection against Syria. The politicians later reasserted their grip on developments before the summer elections, disappointing those who saw in the uprising the basis of a new Lebanon that could rise above the small despotisms of their leaders. That would account for the disagreements in evaluating what the Independence Intifada was about, which to this day mar recollections of that period.

The demonstrations against Syria were also about a place. It was not inevitable that the Lebanese would transform Martyrs Square into the scene of their activities, and yet it was, because there never was anywhere else, physically or symbolically. From its origins dating back to Mameluke times as a public area outside the old city's walls, the *maidan*, to its later incarnations under the Ottomans and the French, to the period following Lebanon's independence, the space that became Martyrs Square had been constantly changing, invisible in its multiple personas. As the sociologist Samir Khalaf reminds us, "the idea of the *maidan* emerged as a result of human intervention directed not toward the addition of identity, events, or character but rather towards keeping land free and indeterminate and therefore negotiable." Negotiable spaces are liberal spaces, because freedom is left for their interpretation. That explains why Martyrs Square was so perfect a place for combining the metaphors that the very dissimilar people present at the site brought there after February 14.

There were the more obvious reasons. But were they indeed so obvious? The Hariri family buried Rafiq al-Hariri near Martyrs Square, in a plot of land bought immediately after the assassination, next to the unfinished Mohammed al-Amin Mosque that the former prime minister had erected on the western side of the square. In burying Hariri there, in an area he had played a pivotal role in rebuilding, at the crossroads of predominantly Christian and Muslim quarters of Beirut, on a rare open space in the capital, the family helped set in motion a fortuitous process they had not planned for. The mosque was controversial for having been built out of proportion with surrounding buildings, especially a church; for also being in the classic Ottoman style, which was unfamiliar in Beirut. Initially condemned as an expression of Hariri's inflated ego, it became after his assassination, next to his mausoleum, a place of convergence, even a practical instrument to trick the pro-Syrian security services. When activists needed to set up a perimeter around their tent city to protect themselves from hostile youths, the pretext used with police was that the building material being trucked in was needed for the mosque.

But the square was also a place of separateness. If Hariri's tomb drew people from all over, that didn't mean that those who came to pay their respects necessarily came to partake of Martyrs Square's other activities. Some did. There were those who drifted from the mausoleum to the tent city to see what was going on. But there were also many who did not, who considered Hariri's death disconnected from the political demands being formulated only 100 meters (330 feet) away. This tells us something about the events that immediately followed February 14: that the unity of purpose between the divergent forces that later sought to transform Hariri's killing into leverage to get the Syrians out of Lebanon was never a foregone conclusion.

There were three simultaneous magnets attracting people to Martyrs Square: Hariri's makeshift mausoleum, the tent city, and the space between and around them open to the tens, then the hundreds, of thousands of unaffiliated demonstrators neither completely of the tent city nor completely of the mausoleum, who for weeks came down to protest, listen, watch, mingle, and enjoy the collapse of all political interdictions. It took organization and a plan to bring and keep these diverse elements together; but it took, above all, an understanding of the symbolic possibilities of Martyrs Square. In retrospect, the most remarkable achievement of the organizers and protestors was to grasp how important it was to allow the square to be whatever one wanted it to be, to materialize from the depths of Lebanon's untidy pluralism.

Martyrs Square was given its name in honor of Lebanese nationalists hanged by the Turkish governor, Jamal Pasha, in 1915 and 1916. However, as late as the 1970s, when I was growing up, the square was usually referred to as the Burj, the Arabic word for tower, named for a tower once dominating the space. But it was also known (only in French for some reason) as the Place des Canons, the Square of the Cannons (because the Russians in 1772, at war with the Ottoman Empire, had bombed Beirut's medieval walls from there). During the civil war, Martyrs Square was a front line in the fighting, with Christian militias on its eastern side and predominantly Muslim militias on its western one, earning its names many times over, a place of martyrs and cannons, as gunmen spent a decade and a half obliterating its buildings and landmarks. By war's end, parts of the old city had been abandoned for so long that they were grown over with vegetation many stories high, a feral Amazonia in the heart of the capital. My only vivid memory of that period, it must have been in 1995 before the rebuilding of the area started, was of strolling with a friend to see what was left, only to discover amid the devastation a ramshackle coffeehouse with the name Café of Peace.

Nor should we underestimate the elegiac stimulations of Martyrs Square, so essential in transforming a place into an idea. Take these lines from an article on the cinemas of the Burj by Farés Sassine, the director of the Dar al-Nahar publishing house, recalling what was showing decades ago. "Was she heading toward Weygand Street or was she preparing, or preparing once again, to walk around the square? Was she walking, or was her pace that of a dance? Everything was beyond measure in the Swede with the velvety name painted in oil on the immense sign above the Rivoli Cinema in the year of our Lord 1960: her blond mane, the shoulders broad and bare, the armpits full and the arms asway, the generous breasts, the black dress with a train, a slit down the middle revealing the birth of a thigh, the feet without shoes to allow more sensation, more liberty . . ."

Through vapors of memory and desire, aficionados will recognize Anita Ekberg in Fellini's *La Dolce Vita*, and that thigh, Sassine would later explain with relish, was the origin of our world, from the thigh of that splendid celluloid fertility goddess prancing atop the Rivoli, whose demolition in 1995 would mark the beginning of the reconstruction of Martyrs Square and downtown Beirut. It would have been difficult to warn Sassine that reverie had gotten the better of him, for somewhere in there was the reality of rebirth.

But if those of Sassine's generation could reach for their memories of Martyrs Square, could convert them into ephemeral dreams, what of the younger generations? What of those in 2005 who had no memories of the prewar area, who were familiar only with the square as a largely vacant space offering an open vista toward the sea, but otherwise neither especially attractive nor evocative? Though the question was not posed in that way, the answer was on the mind of political and civil society activists who met on the day after Hariri's burial. Their ambition was to turn Martyrs Square into a place where politics and imagination could feed off each other. Ziad Majed later summarized the practical considerations in setting up a permanent tent city at the square. "The idea was to build up momentum after the funeral, and to benefit from the different elements that [Martyrs Square] contains and offers: the tomb of Hariri, the [Mohammed al-Amin] mosque and the [St. Georges Maronite] church nearby; the symbolism of the place and the statue [commemorating the 1915–1916 martyrs]; the good access to media and the neighborhood's access to *Al-Nahar*."

There was something for everyone. The presence of Hariri's tomb meant the security forces could not readily deny people the right to assemble. The religious sites spoke to the unity of the once-divided participants. The proximity of the Al-Nahar Building, where Gebran Tueni and Samir Kassir worked, allowed the organizers and youths from the tent city to meet in a space closed off to the security forces and coordinate their activities. The nearby Virgin Megastore, located in the old Opera Cinema, a fine example of early 1930s Art Deco architecture, served more prosaic purposes—as restroom and refuge from bad weather. As for the statue of the martyrs, erected in 1960, the work of the Italian sculptor Marino Mazzacurati, its recent history was of interest. It had been damaged during the war, punctured by wayward bullets, before being restored once the war ended, though holes had been left in as a memento. The enmity between Lahoud and Hariri had delayed the statue's return to its location, but not for long enough to prevent it from becoming a backdrop to the demonstrations. For without the statue as aesthetic anchor and measuring rod, the anti-Syrian protestors would have been lost in the vastness of Martyrs Square.

Rafiq al-Hariri's funeral was the first sign of division within Lebanese society, as the Shiite community, led by Hezbollah, was largely absent from the public manifestations of grief, as were others loyal to Syria. Hezbollah's leadership paid its condolences to the Hariri family, but the party knew something menacing was in the air, that Hariri's murder, if the consequences were not contained, could alter the balance of power in Lebanon to Syria's disadvantage, and therefore to that of Hezbollah, which had benefited from the Syrian presence to build up a virtually autonomous army and ministate within Lebanese society. The party was also aware that many suspected Hezbollah, with its extensive intelligence capabilities, at least of having been aware of the planning for Hariri's assassination, if it did not play a more active role in it, at Syria's request. Hezbollah's sense of vulnerability would shape its behavior in the following weeks in ways that unintentionally galvanized Syria's foes.

The establishment of the tent city gave body to the powerful but diffuse moment that had been the funeral. Though it would be easy to overestimate the impact of the tents on later developments, they served an essential early role by defining a space where things could happen, so the intifada against Syria could survive. They also gave political meaning to Hariri's mausoleum, which gave emotional meaning to the tent city. But most importantly, the tents made it compulsory for a large number of people to set up networks of collaboration, to feed, lodge, and stimulate the youths inside, so they would not abandon the site. For without this, the army and the security services would have been able to segregate Hariri's burial place from everything around, smothering the uprising in its egg.

Everything seemed to fall into place. Asma Andraos and her colleagues, almost by accident, started a petition at Martyrs Square after finding a white sheet on which they wrote DÉMISSION!— "resignation" in French, meaning the resignation of the government. The petition grew as people added their signatures, until it became some 200 meters (over 600 feet) long. The idea of headlining the petition with a demand for resignation was the brainchild not of a politician, but of a lawyer, Chibli Mallat, who suggested it over the telephone to his brother-in-law, Selim Mouzannar, a jeweler hanging out with Andraos. Before long, Gebran Tueni had added an *s* to the word, making it plural. These haphazard gestures were sharpening the intifada's goals, which were those outlined by the opposition at Qoreitem on the night of Hariri's assassination, but later refined to include the resignation of the four intelligence and security officials—the directors-general of the Internal Security Forces and General Security (the latter the man who had threatened Samir Kassir), as well as the heads of the Presidential Guard and of military intelligence. That was the meaning of Tueni's added *s*, even if he was not alone in turning his attention to the security chiefs, nor even the first.

When Andraos and her comrades set up their tent, they spontaneously took on certain duties. Surrounded by youths from political organizations that had fought each other during the civil war, it made sense for the neutral civil society group to act as a moderator, to hand out food and deal with other collective tasks. This was sometimes done in ingenious ways. Initially, food was distributed to the tents, until those in the civil society tent decided to serve the food in their own so that representatives of the political parties, still unsure of what to say to each other, could meet in line and chat while awaiting their servings.

There was also significant assistance from people with ties to opposition leaders and from apolitical figures. Nora Jumblatt, the wife of Walid Jumblatt, played a key role in the protests, organizing walks between the location of Hariri's assassination and Martyrs Square. She provided a sound system for the tent city, as well as a stage and portable toilets; while the owner of the Virgin Megastore, whose losses from the commotion next door were substantial, supplied electricity and a link to the Internet. The Hariri-led Future Movement footed a large bill for the cost of the demonstrations, as well as for printing posters and other material. A prominent banker opened an account at his bank to collect donations to finance the protests. Even the kitchen employees of a nearby restaurant came in on their day off to prepare, without payment, sandwiches for those in the tent city.

While the intifada picked up momentum, the obstacles remained immense. The army and the internal security forces were controlled by men close to Damascus. The army commander, Michel Suleiman, today Lebanon's president, was more of an enigma. No adversary of Syria, he was nevertheless not about to split the armed forces and ruin his own reputation by ordering his men to fire on the crowds at Martyrs Square. Instead, he preserved the status quo, never allowing the anti-Syrian protests to overturn the established order.

On the first Monday after Hariri's murder the opposition called for a march between the St. Georges Hotel, where Hariri had been killed, and Martyrs Square. It was a test to see how many people would show up, but also how many would show up at 12:55 P.M., the moment Hariri was assassinated, in the middle of a working day. With two friends I made my way on foot from the

Beirut port to the gathering place, as the army had closed all access roads to traffic. We were surprised to see that there were more people than expected. Someone handed us a red and white scarf, the colors of the Lebanese flag. Soon after 1 P.M. we began walking up the hill toward the Fouad Chehab overpass, the main thoroughfare between eastern and western Beirut, a place that had once been Lebanon's "sniper's alley," long before Sarajevo had its own, but which on that day was serene in the Mediterranean winter sunlight. I looked behind, to see that we were being followed by several rows of riot policemen. Near us was a group chanting (and this was becoming a habit) that Bashar al-Assad was a "pimp," because the word "pimp" in Arabic rhymes with the word "Beirut," and the demonstrators were telling Assad that they did not want the pimp in Beirut. On the incline leading down from the overpass toward the old city center and Martyrs Square, we were enclosed by two lines of soldiers. They didn't look belligerent, but no one could be sure. The marchers broke into "No army in Lebanon except the Lebanese army," one of those appropriate, neutralizing chants that showed there were some among us who had done this before.

While the numbers of demonstrators that first Monday were inflated, there was more life in the Independence Intifada than anyone had suspected. In fact, some of us left with two impressions from that day: that there was some method to what was going on, suggesting that people were thinking through the protests, its colors, aims, and catchphrases; and a second, more intriguing, impression, namely that a majority of those in the march were Christians, with a smaller number of Druze and Sunnis, as well as Shiites opposed to Hezbollah. And this Christian majority seemed to include a fairly high percentage of people from the educated middle class.

Such a thing was not difficult to understand, since only that category of Lebanese could afford to take time off in the week. But it also pointed to a larger truth about the sociology of the first month of the intifada: While most of those present at Hariri's funeral were Sunni Muslims, in the month between the funeral and the great demonstration of March 14, when the Sunnis again came out in massive numbers, the spontaneous thrusts of the intifada were kept largely alive by Christians, not least a Christian bourgeoisie residing in the neighborhoods east and southeast of Martyrs Square. That is not to downplay the merits of the other participants or sectarian groups, which each in its own way made the whole possible, but to emphasize the growing complexity of the intifada and its implications for Lebanon's paradoxical liberalism. What was happening was a delineation of the political, cultural, and sectarian roles in and around Martyrs Square. There was the religiously and politically mixed tent city, which "held" Martyrs Square for the opposition; there were the mostly Christian demonstrators who protested every Monday for a month after the assassination (in addition to daily activities that fewer people attended); and there were the Sunnis, whose attention continued to be drawn mainly to Rafiq al-Hariri's mausoleum, even as their timorousness vis-à-vis the Syrians began to dissipate.

This wasn't a tale of dissonance, however; it was an example of how Lebanese society tends to work best through an alignment of parallel interests between its constituent groups, interests usually defined, in the most unmodern of ways, by primary identities—religion, regionalism, social category, education, or various combinations of each. That's why more than a few people, Lebanese and foreigners alike, sneered when they saw middle-class Christian protestors descending on Martyrs Square from their comfortable neighborhoods, dismissing what was happening as a "Gucci Revolution." There was something supposedly inauthentic here; true protestors were burly, poor, coarse; they had dirt on their nails as opposed to nail polish. But that mockery told us more about the prejudices of the critics than about the demonstrators themselves, who took to the streets flaunting their paradoxes.

That much of that flaunting came in bright colors, red and white especially, was due to a relatively small group of people who worked on branding the independence intifada, who sometimes paid for this out of their own pockets, but also who worked long hours to design, print, box, and transport the hundreds of thousands of posters, flags, scarves, banners, and placards that gave the demonstrations their visual energy. By the time the Lebanese began their protests against Syria, a number of so-called "color revolutions" had taken place elsewhere, in Georgia, Ukraine, even in Iraq. These events had a limited bearing on what was taking place in Lebanon, but they had a powerful impact in showing how displeasure could be portrayed visually and how the media, particularly the foreign media, could be used to the advantage of those voicing the displeasure. This combining of imagery and political slogans, so they would become a cornerstone of a political stratagem, was new in Lebanon. Those who thought of it displayed a canny understanding that dictatorships, like the one in Damascus, are effective only when imposing the grayness of silence, and that it is almost impossible to silence a population reacting to the same symbols, wearing the same colors, holding up the same signs, and shouting the same slogans, as part of an emotional leviathan that intelligence services can do little to counter.

By coincidence, much of the branding for the Independence Intifada had been prepared before Hariri's assassination, the intention being to launch the campaign during the summer 2005 parliamentary elections. Samir Kassir played an important role in terms of conceptualization, collaborating with an experienced advertising hand, Eli Khoury, the head of Quantum Communications in Beirut. Together, they had also worked on slogans that Quantum was preparing for the Iraqi elections. In late 2004, with members of the Bristol Gathering, they began planning for what would become the "Independence '05" brand, to be unveiled at demonstrations during the election period. Resolution 1559 had given them hope that the time was ripe to demand a Syrian withdrawal. As Khoury, with whom I was working, later told me, "the idea of setting a deadline of '05 was to tell the subconscious, 'This one is for real.'" For such a campaign to be meaningful, however, Hariri had to endorse it and participate in it. There were signs that the former prime minister had made his choice as 2004 ended, particularly after a failed assassination attempt against a member of the Bristol Gathering. But it was Hariri's assassination that prematurely kicked off the branding campaign, just as it prompted civil society activists, like Khoury's counterparts in other ad agencies, to pool their resources and consider what might appeal to the diverse groups protesting against Syria.

The colors of the Independence Intifada were red and white; however, agreement over this obvious color pattern was not immediate. Khoury had wanted the Independence '05 regalia to be all red, particularly the scarves. According to Khoury, Kassir had argued in favor of red and white, though personally, as his wife recalled, he was not taken by the Lebanese flag motif, which he considered too overtly nationalistic. However, in the first days Nora Jumblatt had already printed red and white scarves, and there were others—the overt nationalists such as Gebran Tueni—who liked red and white, so the colors were adopted. However, there was a different color pattern in the Hariri camp, implying a different set of priorities—for if red and white were the colors of independence from Syria, the sky-blue chosen by the Hariris' Future Movement accentuated the search for the "truth" of who had killed Rafiq al-Hariri—the word emblazoned on the scarves and buttons worn by most Sunnis. The Hariris were still adrift, and their differentiating themselves from the other protestors was a matter of no small exasperation to those wearing the red and white, who wanted the truth certainly, but who above all wanted Syria out. Even years after the intifada, this would still be a sore point for some participants in the Martyrs Square events, held up as an example of the lack of solidarity from the Hariris, proof that the former prime minister's family had taken too much time to break with Syria.

The judgment is severe. There was no doubt that the Hariri camp, without a recognized leader at the time, was unsure of its options immediately after Rafiq al-Hariri's killing, just as there was no question that its allies saw the assassination as the galvanizing event that could force a Syrian pullout. In that context it was understandable that the Hariris would hesitate before being railroaded into an intifada they had not really thought through, and about which, we should add, their Saudi patrons might think differently; just as it was understandable that those focused on Syria would grow impatient with seeing the Hariris dither, when it was obvious who had murdered the former prime minister. This misunderstanding would feed into the political divisions that followed the termination of the intifada against Syria, magnified by the parliamentary elections of summer 2005. Yet somehow the sky-blue and the red and white would find their equilibrium before then, as the public generally proved less attuned to the nuances of colors than the advertisers and politicians. The Sunnis, no less than the Christians and Druze, were already well advanced in their enmity toward the Assad regime by the time the crowning event of the uprising against Syria took place: the demonstration of March 14, in which hundreds of thousands, perhaps nearer a million, Lebanese gathered at Martyrs Square. The Hariris, caught up in their own affairs, were behind the curve of their community on Syria. The Sunnis may have worn sky-blue, but by March 14 most of them were thinking in red and white.

IN LATE February, I was assigned to do a portrait of the Svengali of the intifada against Syria. I had asked the *New York Times Magazine* before Hariri's assassination whether they would be interested in an article on Walid Jumblatt, who had turned against his Syrian allies several months earlier. The answer was no, the magazine had more pressing stories. However, once Hariri was killed, Lebanon became a pressing story and Jumblatt an American one. I set an appointment to meet with the person whose decisions had, in one way or another, affected the lives of most Lebanese since 1977, the year his father, Kamal, was assassinated—not surprisingly by the Syrians.

My feelings about Jumblatt were mixed. Not yet thirty when he became leader of the Druze, he had the reputation then of being a lightweight, a playboy. Yet Jumblatt proved as imposing as his father, less feted as an intellectual, but in some ways shrewder politically for having understood the lessons of his father's murder, a murder that imposed humility with respect to Syria, but also with respect to the convolutions of Lebanon itself, that Kamal Jumblatt for a moment had thought he could prevail over. Walid Jumblatt's men had been at the vanguard of militia abuse during the war, and were responsible for a brutal round of sectarian cleansing in 1983 against the Christians, leading to the expulsion of virtually the entire community from the Shouf and Aley districts. My wife and her family were among the many who could not return to their home for a decade. On my first visit there after the war, I drove through expanses razed to the ground, in one instance a village whose highest feature was the road sign at its entrance. But it was also true that in the logic of the war, Jumblatt and the Druze had protected their turf against Christian militias that had entered the Shouf and Aley in 1982 behind the Israeli army, the Druze having behaved no better or worse than others in those bestial years. And in the peculiar logic of the postwar period—but which made perfect sense given Lebanon's counterpoint—it was Jumblatt who returned the Christians to the mountains as minister for the displaced.

Now Jumblatt had allied himself with his Christian enemies from the war years, and I wanted to see what he was all about. What I saw was Lebanon's great pessimist, its Cassandra, who had made it alive through the wreckage of the war by virtue of his litheness and hard-nosedness, an ability to manipulate inconsistency, his eyelids forever sagging under the weight of his impossible choices. Those who described Jumblatt tended to be drawn to his stylishness and irreverence, his jeans and Western habits that played so aesthetically off the primeval relationship he entertained with his own community. Jumblatt was a tribal patriarch to his followers, and despite the "progressive" visuals, he was among the most conservative of leaders; he gave a great deal to the Druze but demanded near complete obedience in exchange, a daunting memory enforcing that contract on a daily basis. He was also someone whose sense of derision concealed how disciplined he was when imparting information, how focused he was in shaping the message he wanted to get out, so that in our first meeting he did not offer much more in private than in public. Jumblatt was under a sentence of death, but without sentimentality he sought to use that to strengthen his hand, to build up an impression that America, or if not America at least the readers of the *New York Times*, should want to be on Walid Jumblatt's side against Bashar al-Assad. America was little mentioned in our exchange, but it was at the forefront of Jumblatt's thinking, because he knew that America

and American public opinion were among the few effective coun-
terweights to Syria. He recounted the details of Hariri's murder,
presaged his own by asserting "not a single Jumblatt died in his
bed, my father would say," a phrase he would often repeat without
any intention of confirming it himself. And he divulged what
might lie ahead by adding, despite condemning the Assad regime:
"We must cut a deal with Syria; those who went after Hariri won't
leave Lebanon so easily."

At one point Jumblatt remarked that Ahmad Chalabi might
become defense minister of Iraq. He worried that Chalabi's appointment would enhance Iraqi federalism, which could have adverse effects throughout the region, particularly in Lebanon, where
it might harm communal relations. Here was Jumblatt scouring
the horizon for calamitous icebergs that might sink him and his
own, the natural reflex of the minoritarian. As I would later learn,
that first encounter, which would be followed by many more as
we became friendlier, told me little about that enigmatic political
acrobat perched on his high rock alone, whose every premonitory
move was dissected by those trying to get a sense of Lebanon's
political winds. He had become the dominant leader of an emancipation movement he would infuse with life, then ride, then
deflate—testament all to an exceptional political mind, yet the
mind of someone whose single-minded motive remained, as the
Lebanese filled Martyrs Square in larger numbers, as their intifada
took on new layers of symbolic meaning, each more idealistic than
the last, as Walid Jumblatt was transformed—in fact transformed
himself—into the atypical incarnation of that idealism; whose
single-minded motive remained protecting his Druze community and his leadership over that community. This betrayed a poverty of low expectations but also reticence toward what Jumblatt
expected he could achieve, toward what a Druze and the Druze
could achieve; but also what could be achieved by Lebanon's
system, whose exasperating rules, strangely enough, Jumblatt respected more than most, more than his father anyway; and reticence about what the Independence Intifada could achieve amid
the loose talk of revolution circulating around Martyrs Square, no

less audacious than a barefoot Anita Ekberg in her yearning for more sensation, more liberty.

There was something anomalous in Walid Jumblatt's sudden turnaround with regard to the United States, just as there was something anomalous in Samir Kassir's writing slogans for Iraqi parliamentary elections organized under American occupation. Both were self-declared men of the left, although in Jumblatt's case that concept could be elastic. However, their political markers, like those of most Lebanese who participated in the intifada against Syria, had little to do with America—even as they read American books and magazines, watched American movies, and otherwise drank from the fountain of American knowledge. Yet in 2005 most Lebanese found themselves aligned against the temper in much of the Middle East. Where the region reviled America for what it had done in Iraq, or so everyone told us, the Bush administration's willingness to help push the Syrians out of Lebanon created a very different reaction among many Lebanese. America was the ally against Syria they had spent decades waiting for, after Washington had upheld Syrian hegemony for much of that time. Of course, there were a substantial number of Lebanese who did not like America, who could not be ignored for doing so, but it would be fair to say that a majority in the weeks after Hariri's assassination had a more pragmatic reading of their situation. The United States, but also the France of Jacques Chirac, Hariri's chum, were leading an international effort to force Syria to withdraw and bolster Lebanese sovereignty, and not many in Beirut were picky about whom they were in bed with. So as the Arab world, and not just the Arab world, railed against America, against Bush, the Lebanese, like the Iraqis, used America to help create a new order—whether America was appreciated or not, thanked or not. That's why a leftist like Kassir wrote Iraqi election slogans with his friend Eli Khoury; it's why he welcomed the ouster of Saddam Hussein (then lamented America's wasted opportunities afterward); and it's why the feudal leftist Jumblatt, far less of an optimist on such matters, nonetheless had the dexterity to tell the Americans what they wanted to hear, if only to keep Lebanon alive in their attentions, when he explained to the *Washington Post* columnist David Ignatius, "I was cynical about Iraq. But when I saw the Iraqi people voting three weeks ago, 8 million of them, it was the start of a new Arab world."

It was not the start of a new Arab world, as Jumblatt knew for having spent decades navigating the old one, and for having warned that Hariri's assassins would not abandon Lebanon so lightly. However, it was a moment when the notion didn't seem quite so ridiculous. One reason was that the international community, through the Security Council, established legal scaffolding to uphold Lebanon's post-Syria stability. The United Nations ordered a preliminary investigation of the Hariri assassination, a demand of the opposition, sending to Beirut an Irish deputy police commissioner, Peter Fitzgerald, to report on what had happened. He concluded

> that the Lebanese security services and the Syrian Military Intelligence bear the primary responsibility for the lack of security, protection, law and order in Lebanon. The Lebanese security services have demonstrated serious and systematic negligence in carrying out the duties usually performed by a professional national security apparatus. . . . The Syrian Military Intelligence shares this responsibility to the extent of its involvement in running the security services in Lebanon.

Fitzgerald did not directly accuse Syria of killing Hariri, but he didn't need to when affirming that security in Lebanon was in Syrian hands, and that it took "considerable finance, military precision in its execution, [and] substantial logistical support" to carry out the assassination. In other words, it took a conspiracy that the omnipresent Syrian and Lebanese security services could hardly have avoided noticing. And if there were lingering doubts, Fitzgerald accused Lebanese officials of tampering with the evidence at the crime scene, in a ham-fisted cover-up effort. On the basis of the report, the Security Council passed Resolution 1595 establishing a U.N. investigation to look into the assassination, naming the German judge Detlev Mehlis as its first commissioner. This was a novelty in the Middle East, where political crimes had always gone unpunished. Within weeks the Lebanese security chiefs were obliged to resign, another novelty in a region where security officials are untouchable.

It was a very different Bush administration acting in Lebanon than the one that had planned and executed the invasion of Iraq. The United States adopted a template of intervention in Lebanon that it had avoided in Iraq. The administration worked through the U.N., in consultation with other nations, in the shadow of an international consensus, in support of international law and justice. There were those who could never be satisfied with anything George W. Bush did, who would criticize Washington's behavior in Lebanon as a case of unnecessarily alienating Syria, of giving much too much credence to the Martyrs Square demonstrators while ignoring the Shiites. But by and large, this was the outlook of a minority then. Only when the Bush administration's difficulties in the Middle East began multiplying did the dissenters gain ground. The worsening situation in Iraq in 2006 combined with the Syrian backlash in Lebanon and the summer war that year between Hezbollah and Israel led to a new perception overseas that the intifada against Syria had been an interlude that the administration had exploited to defend its failed Middle Eastern democratization project—Bush's so-called "Freedom Agenda."

In 2006, Francis Fukuyama published *America at the Crossroads*, his essay denouncing the behavior of American neoconservatives in the administration. While the much-discussed book covered issues beyond the Middle East, Iraq was Fukuyama's Exhibit A against the neocons. *America at the Crossroads* received notice because Fukuyama had been an intimate of the neocon household, had even signed on to a letter drafted only days after the 9/11 attacks by the right-wing Project for the New American Century (PNAC) advocating the removal of Saddam Hussein by force, because that had to be part of "any strategy aiming at the eradication of terrorism and its sponsors." Strangely enough, Fukuyama wrote, he was "never persuaded of the rationale for the Iraq war"—strange because he failed to mention his participation in that particular PNAC letter, which expressed a rationale for the Iraq war.

But it was Fukuyama's skepticism toward democratization in the Middle East that demonstrated how American political realists had reentered the Washington debate over the region, mainly to tell the administration that Arab societies did not have institutions to "move from an amorphous longing for freedom to a well-functioning, consolidated democratic political system with a modern economy." Maybe, but Lebanon was as good an example confirming Fukuyama's judgment as exposing its central flaw, namely that societies caught up in the fragrances of emancipation don't pause to consider where they stand in terms of their institutional evolution. But Fukuyama was only echoing what other prominent American realists were saying, and the fact that they tended to be conservative and had once been Cold War warriors lent their statements authority. Which is why it hit closer to home for George W. Bush when a former national security advisor, Brent Scowcroft, told the *New York Observer* in 2004: "[T]he notion that within every human being beats this primeval instinct for democracy has not ever been demonstrated to me." Scowcroft had served under President George H. W. Bush, and they had together looked away when Saddam Hussein crushed the Shiite and Kurdish uprisings against his regime following the Gulf War of 1991. Both felt more comfortable with predictable connections to the region's despots than with woolly concepts such as "freedom" and "democracy." And in this they echoed a half-century of U.S. policy toward the Arab world.

The discussion in America went largely unheard by those who had been at Martyrs Square. But they were at its very heart, because what the disbelievers were questioning was the value of universal principles in foreign policy: Were liberty and democracy, or simply liberal pluralism, ideas the United States was obligated to defend and spread worldwide, and if so how? There was no agreement in Washington, let alone in the international community, over the way to answer the question with regard to Lebanon. The Bush administration had shown interest in the Lebanese experiment of 2005, which began only a month after George W. Bush had vowed, in his second inaugural address, that "[a]ll who live in tyranny and hopelessness can know: the United States will not ignore your oppression, or excuse your oppressors. When you stand for your liberty, we will stand with you." But Bush became less passionate about going after Arab autocrats, since the ones in Egypt, Saudi Arabia, and Jordan were useful in helping contain Iran, once it emerged as a regional nuisance after President Mahmoud Ahmadinejad's election in August 2005.

It was not that Bush was insincere. Lebanon lent momentary conviction to his inaugural pledge, which perhaps explained why he remained so tenacious about its liberal promise when the Lebanese themselves had started doubting it. But Lebanon and its intifada had also taken Bush by surprise. Until the Lebanese uprising against Syria, the president, like Brent Scowcroft, had not seen very many symptoms of an Arab world yearning for liberty. There were the Iraqi elections, of course, but they had really taken place *against* the United States, an affirmation of the Iraqis' desire to release themselves from Bush's wellspring of democracy. Lebanon was less ambiguous in showing, to those who wanted to believe, the potential for democratic idealism in the Arab world, one that did not need to be directed against the United States. If Washington's old enemies, the leftists like Jumblatt, were prophesying a new Arab world, then it might be true.

But Lebanon was never about the United States, just as the manner in which the Independence Intifada was represented internationally was not about Lebanon. The power of modern emancipation movements is their ability to generate narratives the media can pick up on, render arresting, and make understandable to home audiences. In that process truth is lost, but both sides get what they want. Those pursuing emancipation get publicity and access to the airwaves, and media get a good story. The instinct of the Lebanese was not to resort to violence after Hariri was murdered; it was to take up the terrible weapon of opinion by lending romance to their endeavors, so outsiders would take sides. This not only revealed a liberal outlook, it revealed a grasp of how modern politics work.

It was not all about image, however. Personalities could make a difference, and few were more influential in Beirut at the time than the U.S. ambassador, Jeffrey Feltman. He had arrived in the summer of 2004, and his second meeting with Rafiq al-Hariri occurred on that August day when the former prime minister was called to Damascus and instructed to vote in favor of Émile Lahoud's extension. The encounter perplexed Feltman, a relatively young Ohioan in his first ambassadorial posting, after serving in Hungary, Iraq, and Israel. Feltman was still finding his feet in the tortuous ways of Lebanese politics, and he and a visiting State Department official, Elizabeth Dibble, were not sure how to read Hariri. Washington was impatient to know what the Syrians had told him, because the administration was preparing the groundwork for Resolution 1559. It must have been a perplexing meeting for Hariri as well, facing two envoys he didn't know well, so soon after he had been threatened in Damascus for sympathizing with an international effort to get the Syrians out of Lebanon. For someone who suspected that his own home was bugged, he must have also worried that this conversation with representatives of a country leading that effort might soon find its way to the desk of a Syrian intelligence officer.

Feltman came to know Hariri better, but, more important, he came to know the Syrians better and what they were capable of doing. This made him sensitive to the risks the Lebanese took after the assassination. As Feltman later put it, "I believe strongly that it was the combination of international and local pressure that made the Syrian withdrawal inevitable. Had the international community been looking the other way when Rafiq Hariri was murdered, Syria's proxies in Lebanon would have crushed even mass demonstrations. . . . But had the international community been working on its own, without an active partner in the Lebanese people, I'm not sure we would have been able to get that first step of a Syrian withdrawal. . . . I'm proud that the international community played an important supporting role, but I don't forget that it was the Lebanese who led the process."

What Feltman outlined was a more sensible model for democratization in the Arab world than one achieved through a unilateral resort to outside force or, conversely, sole reliance on domestic pressures in Arab societies. But there was no polemical intent on his part; only a keen sense of the limitations of absolute ideas from a foreign policy practitioner on the ground. What Feltman was hinting at, and what the Lebanese at Martyrs Square made more explicit, as did the Iraqis at the ballot box, was that to have a fighting chance of succeeding, efforts at emancipation in the Middle East sometimes had to combine a domestic popular impetus with outside coercion. There were surely exceptions to this rule, places where both components were lacking or where their combination would flounder. However, in Lebanon everything somehow came together at the right time and in the right place, and by so doing showed how myopic were those who echoed that "democracy can only come from within" in the Middle East—a platitude repeated by Arab autocrats, who realized how easily they could inhibit what came from within. Lebanon showed that emancipation sometimes required something from within and something from without, and that the something from without did not necessarily have to be detrimental; and that nothing was quite as effective as a population looking beyond the medium of change, whether America, France, the United Nations, or anyone else, to define what it wanted for itself. That, too, was a liberal impulse, and it is why the Independence Intifada was important—a seamless meeting of multiple interests, for which the Lebanese deserve their due.

AFTER THAT first demonstration on the Monday following Hariri's assassination, three days came to define the Independence Intifada. On February 27, a Sunday, the Lebanese army and security services were ordered to block off Martyrs Square to those who intended to mark the second week after the assassination the next day. This prompted hundreds of people to enter the square through a haphazard cordon of soldiers and spend the night to prevent the security forces from clearing the area. With a friend, I went in, then came back out of the square. We could see that the army was not enforcing the order with particular conviction.

By the next morning a new situation had developed, one with

all the makings of a Levantine deal. In the neighborhoods around Martyrs Square, the army directed the tens of thousands of arriving demonstrators through designated streets. At the entrance to the square, volunteers maintaining order stopped us and told us to wait for a moment while a group ahead passed through a line of soldiers. Then it was our turn. A volunteer yelled "Say God!" which in Arabic is another way of saying "God Help Us," a superfluous appeal considering what was going down. As we hit the wall of soldiers, we pushed, and if we didn't push, the soldiers murmured to us to push, because the quicker we pushed, the quicker the absurdity would end for them. And as we pushed, they gave way, making it seem like a struggle, one that fooled nobody but that allowed the army command to say it had implemented its orders short of firing into the crowd.

It seemed like a joke, but it avoided more dangerous repercussions had the situation been handled differently, because the army was caught between clashing interests: that of keeping in check the growing protests and preventing the Syrian order in Lebanon from collapsing, or collapsing too quickly; and averting a bloodbath that would discredit the military, even split the armed forces. That night the Independence Intifada scored its first victory when Prime Minister Omar Karami resigned. The activist Nabil Aboucharaf later described how he finally felt that change was coming: "This was a concrete result, something we could work on. Christians and Muslims had brought down a Muslim prime minister. The taboos had fallen."

The taboos were beginning to fall, certainly, but the Syrians and their sympathizers had not called it a day. On March 5, Bashar al-Assad made a speech before the Syrian parliament—the kind of parliament that applauds a dictator's semicolon and stands up at a full stop. Three things were worth remembering in what was, otherwise, a distillation of Assad's contempt for the Lebanese and their politicians who had turned against Syria: The president announced that Syrian forces would withdraw toward the Lebanese-Syrian border, without specifying whether they would cross over into Syria; Assad mocked the Beirut demonstrations by saying that if cameras "zoomed out" they would see how small they really were; and he made a promise to his people, a forewarning of what Syrian intentions would be in the event of a pullout: "A Syrian withdrawal from Lebanon will not mean a disappearance of Syria's role in Lebanon. This role is imposed by several factors, including geography, politics, and others."

Three days later, on March 8, Hezbollah organized the largest demonstration since Hariri's funeral. It took place at Riad al-Solh Square, only a few hundred meters west of Martyrs Square, but far enough to prevent a confrontation between those in each area. This was a party rally, one in which Hezbollah used its substantial means of mobilization to guarantee that a large crowd would be present. Yet those at Riad al-Solh were no less convinced by what they were doing than those at Martyrs Square. Hezbollah's leader, Hassan Nasrallah, had three objectives in his speech to them: to break the momentum of the Independence Intifada by showing that the other side, the side ignored by the foreign media, could gather more people; to publicly "thank" Syria for what it had done in Lebanon; and to take a step that, with Assad's speech and the reappointment on March 10 of Omar Karami to form a new government, would spearhead a counterattack by Syria and its allies.

In his speech, Nasrallah called for the formation of a national unity government after parliamentary consultations to name a prime minister. This was not innocent. Because Syria's allies had a legislative majority, they could name the prime minister and retain a cabinet majority while also drawing the opposition into the sterile byways of government bargaining, neutralizing what was taking place in the streets. The ploy failed when the opposition rejected it. Karami was reappointed to form a new government, but when he failed to do so, the task was assigned to a more neutral politician acceptable to all. This coincided with the March 14 demonstration that changed all the rules, but which in retrospect changed very little.

Syria's intentions were not clear. In his speech Nasrallah told French President Jacques Chirac that the Lebanese people "are saying to you that they want to safeguard our historic and special ties with Syria." Foreign envoys in Beirut were uncertain about what

Assad had meant in *his* speech. The Syrian president had heard from the Saudis that his army had to go home, but all he told his parliament was that they would redeploy to the border. As Jeffrey Feltman later explained: "[T]he international experience of dealing with Bashar gave us no confidence to trust his words. We suspected he would employ excuses, trickery and delays." And as Feltman knew better than most, in the months after passage of Resolution 1559, Washington was willing to advance in stages on a Syrian withdrawal—to avoid allowing the perfect to be the enemy of the good, in the ambassador's words—by initially working toward a partial pullout to Lebanon's Beqaa Valley. Assad was aware of this American flexibility, but he may have misinterpreted it as meaning that the United States was not serious about a full Syrian withdrawal. In January 2005 an influential Syrian journalist told me that this was indeed the thinking in the Syrian leadership, which believed the administration was only raising the heat in Lebanon to gain Syrian cooperation over Iraq. If that was Assad's evaluation, and it was one that perhaps explained a great deal about why Hariri was killed when he was, then nothing by the time the March 8 rally occurred confirmed that the Syrian leader had reconciled himself with abandoning Lebanon.

Then came March 14, the vortex of the Independence Intifada, which drew more people into Martyrs Square, or anywhere, than a Lebanese event ever had; an exceptional moment, but also one that raised unrealistic expectations and reflected much more Lebanon's pluralistic cacophony than its unity. It's difficult not to become lyrical when recalling the day itself, its images and sounds and irrepressible energy. The breakers upon breakers of human beings splashing into Martyrs Square from all directions; the tens of thousands of people backed up on Charles Helou Avenue, arriving through Beirut's eastern suburbs, themselves backed up by tens of thousands more who never even made it near the city because the traffic was too dense; the rude, flippant posters and billboards directed against Syria and its local peons—the one in particular reminding Bashar al-Assad to "zoom out" and see how many people *really* hated his army's presence in their midst; the pointless struggle by intelligence agents to force down banners mocking Émile Lahoud; the consciousness of people absolutely everywhere, filling out Martyrs Square, all its side streets, the Fouad Chehab overpass, Riad al-Solh Square, where Hezbollah had organized its thank-you to Syria a week before, and all without a single security incident, a single shop broken into, almost no trash left behind, just an overpowering bash with everyone in a trance.

Yet so intense was March 14 that many Lebanese regarded it as something it was not. In its unity of purpose they saw the stimulus for deep change, something new—revolution instead of intifada. In truth, March 14 was a manifestation not so much of Lebanon's liberalism, but of how its sectarian thermostat could kick in to defend a pluralistic order that, in turn, safeguarded its liberal instincts; for in the end very little about the day was new, and that was its significance. It was a reaction against March 8, and in particular against the Shiite gauntlet thrown down on March 8. That was what allowed the Hariri camp to massively mobilize the Sunnis, from Beirut to the easternmost depths of the country, to the far north. For those who had watched March 8 with a disabused knot in their stomach, March 14 was payback, sectarian assertion a powerful motive behind that payback.

Yet March 14 was also, like the Independence Intifada itself, a perfect merging of interests. The participants all agreed that Syria had to go, but otherwise their priorities varied. The Christian group known as the Lebanese Forces wanted their leader, Samir Geagea, to be released from prison, where he had been languishing for eleven years; the followers of another mostly Christian group, the Free Patriotic Movement, wanted *their* leader, Michel Aoun, to return from exile in Paris; the Sunnis were there to show fidelity to Rafiq al-Hariri; the nonsectarians were there to save the intifada from the sectarian political leaders, who were already assessing how to convert it into political gains. A large majority, however, had less lucid thoughts and was there because no one could escape March 14, a day, like Martyrs Square itself, that was whatever you wanted it to be.

March 14 was also the day when the youths were forgotten.

The previous afternoon, at a meeting in Mukhtara, the mountain home of Walid Jumblatt, opposition leaders had met to decide who would make speeches the following day. One idea had been to keep the speakers to a minimum. The lawyer Samir Abdelmalek, who helped organize the activities of the tent city, thought there should be only three speakers: someone chosen by the Hariri camp; someone representing the tent city; and a third person to be agreed upon. Instead, there was a mad rush to the rostrum, with between twenty and thirty speaking and nobody from the tent city invited. Of the speeches only two were memorable. That of Bahiyya al-Hariri, who made conciliatory gestures toward Syria, confusing many in attendance, but echoing what Jumblatt had told me, namely that the opposition had to "cut a deal with Syria" if it was to have any hope of stabilizing Lebanon. It was also a speech destined to calm Sunni-Shiite tensions. The second was that of Gebran Tueni: an oath to Lebanese unity that he had the crowd repeat, but which many remembered better after Tueni was assassinated, just as that unity was breaking down.

There began the denouement of the Independence Intifada, and the carousel of fantasies stopped. Within days the politicians had begun to prepare for their separate electoral interests. Walid Jumblatt opened channels to Hassan Nasrallah and to the speaker of parliament, Nabih Berri, both prominent allies of Syria. Jumblatt would later say he was trying to bring them both into the post-Syria system. This wasn't completely untrue, because Jumblatt, a perfect triangulator, could gain by positioning himself between the anti-Syrian opposition and Syria's allies; but, more important, Jumblatt needed Hezbollah's support to win the Shiite vote in a constituency that would determine his own political relevancy in the post-Syria era.

In April, the Syrians finally withdrew their forces, though they remained very much present in manipulating Lebanese affairs. Legislative elections in May and June, during which Samir Kassir was assassinated, brought in a majority of parliamentarians hostile to Damascus. The opposition label changed sides, and Lebanon would begin the difficult process of finding an equilibrium between the people of Martyrs Square and those of Riad al-Solh Square. However, by then the disagreement over which law would govern the elections had split the anti-Syrian opposition. The inability to agree on a new law led to the de facto adoption of an earlier law, that of 2000, which alienated a majority of Christians. The reason was that the four political-sectarian groups that most benefited from it were the Sunnis, who by election time had seen Saad al-Hariri anointed by Saudi Arabia as Rafiq al-Hariri's political heir; Jumblatt and his Druze followers; and the two Shiite parties, Hezbollah and Amal—all at the expense of the Christians who had sustained the Independence Intifada in its embryonic moments. The Christians felt cheated and voted massively for Michel Aoun, freshly returned from France, giving him a large parliamentary bloc, its members now opposed to their allies of the weeks before.

Ill feeling having swept away the good vibes of the Independence Intifada, a narrative took form among many of those who had gone down to Martyrs Square that the politicians had betrayed their ideals, displaying an aversion to change and an even deeper dedication to their own survival. But their reimposition of old hierarchies on weeks of popular abandon was not a story of dreams suffocated. Most of those affiliated with political organizations at Martyrs Square ended up following their leaders, often for complex, contradictory, unsatisfactory reasons of their own. As Ziad Majed later recalled about those in the tent city: "They did not form a strong movement to pressure their leaders. Maybe they did not have time to do so, or they were not capable of doing so. But I believe there was and is a certain degree of romance about the camp. This is understandable. But the political impact of the camp was more symbolic than effective, and it is clear that the 'leaders' are popular, have legitimacy and that many of their acts are justified even by the youth."

The appraisal was tough, inasmuch as the tent city had managed to keep alive Martyrs Square as a space of protest. But it was on the money in admitting to the essential legitimacy of the sectarian leaders. The idealists descending on Martyrs Square had misdiagnosed the nature of their protests, seeing them as a lever for change when they ended up being mainly a mechanism for balance. In the behavior of the youths was a deeper, maybe involuntary, understanding of Lebanon's reality. They concluded, to their enduring regret, that theirs was a country of pluralistic immovability. Liberalism would not emerge from overhauling the political or religious leadership, which was secure for reflecting the country's sectarian interactions; it would emerge from those spaces created by the inability of any one leader, party, or coalition of parties, to impose a single will on all.

That was the real meaning of the events of 2004 and 2005. It was an intifada that, at important junctures, was propelled forward by a popular aspiration for revolutionary change, but an aspiration never fully formed or truly achievable, never really convincing, because the Lebanese had no idea what revolution was supposed to bring; because there was no consensus over what should replace the system's pluralistic immovability. There were quite a few who saw in this shortage of ambition, in the supposed inertness of the Lebanese, a sign of the sickness of their system, its lack of democracy. In fact, things were more complicated, and subtle: It was a case of the system defining its boundaries, reminding the Lebanese of its rhythms and mechanisms of continuity, uncompromising rhythms no doubt, but boundaries and rhythms that had characterized the system for decades, that were its bane but also its safeguard against too-sudden political and social shifts that, in the name of revolution, of absolute change, might bring about only chaos and violence.

When their power was at stake, the politicians were monuments to egoism. But in their own way they and their followers were only upholding the Lebanese way. Here was an invisible hand at work, whereby the political self-interest of each could add up to the general interest of the whole, or at least the pluralism of the whole could protect the paradoxical liberalism in each. This wasn't a country of revolutions, one young Aoun follower admitted to me, right after admitting that he wanted a revolution because he hated how politics in Lebanon were played. His contradiction was no different than the contradictions of countless others. The Independence Intifada started as a revolt of a group of Lebanese politicians against Syria, but Hariri's assassination turned it into an unprompted popular movement that allowed the politicians' revolt ultimately to succeed and for an enthralling moment looked like more than what it really was. However, Syria was gone because this time it had overestimated its ability to terrorize the Lebanese, and that was nothing to spit at.

2

A Forest of Fathers

In our childhood we experienced, rather than really knew, a power we can today define as completely criminal, but a power we can also, and paradoxically, say was in good health, always in the sense of crime, of course, in relationship to the schizophrenic power of today. . . . Needless to say, I prefer schizophrenia to good health. . . .
Leonardo Sciascia, *The Knight and Death*

THE FRENCH-LEBANESE AUTHOR Amin Maalouf ends his 1993 novel *The Rock of Tanios* with a disappearance. That may not be a coincidence. A winner of France's prestigious Prix Goncourt, the book is interesting not least because of its multiple evasions—above all Maalouf's skill in evading himself.

The novel takes place in the Lebanese mountain, circa 1831–1840, when an Egyptian army under Ibrahim Pasha occupied the area, supported by the emir of the mountain, Bashir II. It was a time when Ibrahim, son of the viceroy of Egypt, threatened to capture Istanbul and alter the balance of power in the Levant. In the village of Kfaryabda, Tanios is born to Lamia, perhaps fathered (we're never sure) by the local feudal lord, the Sheikh, whom Lamia's husband serves. Tanios's life, henceforth, will be a recurring struggle to coexist with this legacy, the legacy of an elusive social status, of having disgraced one father by possibly being a bastard of the other; a struggle also through the turmoil of mid-nineteenth century Mount Lebanon, amid men who will influence him, educate him, kill for him, die for him, and manipulate him. At the end of the tale, as the Egyptians withdraw and the Sheikh returns from an exile imposed by the Emir, and as Kfaryabda prepares for the possibility of a round of sectarian revenge killings with a neighboring Druze community because of Tanios's failure to act decisively to prevent this, Tanios walks out of the village and sits on a rock, where, legend has it, he vanishes. The narrator adds this comment: "Many were the men who left the village in the invisible steps of Tanios. . . . That's the way of my mountain. Attachment to the land and an aspiration for departure. A place of refuge and a place of passage. Land of milk and honey and blood. Neither paradise nor hell. Purgatory."

Evasion as purgatory, too. The evasion, first, of Tanios himself, in the presence of a place and a society he cannot adjust to, let alone govern. But that evasion is only a manifestation of the evasions of the author, for it is striking how Maalouf sinks Tanios into the contradictions everywhere without guiding him out, because he is himself unsure how. Then there is the fact that Maalouf writes about the Lebanon of the 1830s to avoid writing about the 1970s, when Lebanon's civil war began, forcing him and many from his generation to vanish, to disappear into exile, their homeland a place of passage. And in the most discreet evasion of all, Maalouf, the historical novelist, never tells us that his story has little to do with nineteenth-century Lebanon at all and everything to do with something more personally felt: the affliction of perpetual disappearance imposed on the Lebanese by their leaders, the fathers all around—political, familial, social, or religious—purveyors of despotism who allow little latitude for imagination and renewal, and who impose exile on the indomitable and an erasing of the self on those who remain.

For those like me who came back to Lebanon after the end of the civil war but who didn't disappear into a cloud of self-conscious futility, Maalouf's verdict sounds harsh—the harshness of the émigré whose attachment to his land has morphed into a complicated aversion. Certainly, the despotism of Lebanese leadership has always been a valid theme, so saturated with leaders is the society, so omnipresent the silhouettes of hierarchy. But where there are many

leaders, there is also pandemonium, so that the burgeoning dictator loses his footing. And if some saw the triumph of the leaders,
and of their despotisms, as the singular lesson that came out of the
2005 Independence Intifada, then there was something lacking,
even undeserved, in that sour view.

That's because while Lebanon's political leadership thwarted
change after the March 14 demonstration in the name of equilibrium, it was the pursuit of equilibrium that made possible the
fantasy of change before. Had a handful of parliamentarians not
decided to vote against an extension of President Émile Lahoud's
term in September 2004; had that refusal not led to the formation
of the Bristol opposition; and had Rafiq al-Hariri not decided, in
his roundabout way, to exploit that opposition to make gains in
the 2005 elections, particularly in the shadow of Resolution 1559,
he would not have been killed. And had Hariri not been killed,
the popular uprising against Syria would not have taken place, at
least in the way it did. The reason why once pro-Syrian politicians
turned against Syria, or at least tried to rebalance their relationship
with it, was that Damascus had transgressed the unwritten stipula-
tions of their contract: It had too maladroitly, too overtly, flaunted
that its priorities alone mattered in Lebanon, whatever the preferences of its allies, and Lahoud's extension put those leaders on
guard that the president and those upgraded at the same time as
he, particularly Jamil al-Sayyed, the head of the General Security
directorate, would continue to be Syria's favored sticks in Lebanon, at their expense. Sayyed was one of the generals arrested after
the Hariri assassination, but also before then a principal Lebanese
enforcer on behalf of the military intelligence network the Syrians
used to rule Lebanon.

Émile Lahoud did not generate enough fear to compensate for
the pervasive loathing he elicited from Lebanon's political class. It
wasn't always like that. When the president was selected by Syria
in 1998, he rode a brief populist wave into the presidential palace.
He was a man different from other politicians, people would whis-
per, someone who *drove his own car*. Even normally lucid observers
of Lebanese politics suggested he would clean up Lebanon's act,
end corruption, and show that the state was boss against the poli-

ticians. It was an illusion. Very quickly, we discovered that the man was indeed different, so different that newspapers were instructed not to publish cartoons of him, because it was unbecoming. But Lahoud was also like everybody else in wanting to sit his son in parliament, a desire duly fulfilled in the 2000 elections, and he was drawn as much to the returns of power as others.

My own brushes with the Lahoud system were negligible— writing in English gave me more latitude than Arabic-language journalists. However, the calls did sometimes come to the *Daily Star* newspaper after my commentaries. I remember Sayyed contacting my publisher and friend Jamil Mroueh in early 2004, following an article in which I had mentioned that Lahoud might try to extend his mandate. "So now you're letting foreigners theorize about Lebanese politics?" Sayyed had asked Mroueh, who answered that I was Lebanese. It was a rare lapse for a man who kept a close eye on the media and who happened to sign everyone's passport. Then again, our overestimating Sayyed was another sign of his talent for shaping perceptions of his near infallibility as a Syrian sentry.

Lahoud and Sayyed shared as a main duty the political containment of Hariri. The tensions this released were immense. In 2000, Lahoud was humiliated in parliamentary elections from which Hariri emerged the greatest winner, but that made the president more determined than ever to break him. The uneven distribution of power perpetuated by Lahoud's remaining in office in 2004, Syria's overreliance on a man with little legitimacy and on other lesser officials whose role was to do what Syria told them to do, under the watchful eyes of the Syrian and Lebanese security agencies, went against the balancing grain of Lebanese politics. Even close Syrian allies warned Bashar al-Assad that keeping the president in office might backfire. "Lahoud has failed," one such politician told Assad, before hearing from the Syrian president that Lahoud was the choice, like it or not. To disregard the advice of those with the most to lose from Syrian setbacks was an example of hubris on Assad's part.

In an indispensable essay written in 1976 titled "Ideologies of the Mountain and the City," the British-Lebanese historian Albert

Hourani offered a nuanced reading of Lebanon's sectarian relations. While accepting that sectarianism was at the heart of the country's political and social system, he maintained that the religious communities "are not, beyond a certain limit, solid bodies having a single interest or attitude, and the division into religious communities is not the only division which can be made of the population of Lebanon, and in some ways may not be the most significant."

Hourani pointed out that Lebanese politics were the product of an agreement between sectarian leaders and their ideologies, each the consequence of specific social, geographical, and political conditions. "To the extent to which they entered the Lebanese political alliance, they did so with their own modes of action and their own traditions," Hourani wrote. Modern Lebanon emerged from a combination of the ideologies of the mountain and of the city, of rural, more insular, more populist traditions on the one hand, associated primarily with the Maronite Christian community; and on the other, of urban concerns associated mainly with the mercantile elites of the coastal cities, Sunni Muslim principally, but not solely, who viewed Lebanon as a place that needed to be open to the outside, "a plural society in which communities, still different on the level of inherited religious loyalties and intimate family ties, co-existed within a common framework."

Though these ideologies fed into each other and changed over time, as did the identity of those advocating them, the consequences of what Hourani described very much survive to this day. It was Bashar al-Assad's inability in 2004 to grasp the continuities of that arrangement between Lebanese leaders themselves, but also his inability to anticipate the repercussions of his undermining the parallel Syrian-Lebanese arrangement when Damascus ordered the assassination of Hariri, that led to Syria's setbacks in 2005, after most Christians, Sunnis, and Druze had unified their efforts against it. Yet the Syrians had previously been able manipulators of the Lebanese system, having their way with the country for far longer than most others, even if they never built anything durable there. And they did so because they understood precisely what Hourani explained, namely that if Lebanon was a compact between sectarian leaders and their sundry ideologies, then Syria could dominate Lebanon by creating a new compact respecting the rules of the old but also allowing Damascus to introduce innovations of its own into these to dominate the whole. So what emerged—in its most stable expression after 1992 when Hariri became prime minister, and before 1998, when Lahoud became president—was a system that was pluralistic when it came to relations between Lebanese politicians, above and around which existed a tight and elaborate structure of Syrian control, underpinned by implicit violence that exploited this pluralism to divide the politicians, but that also allowed them to pursue their interests within defined limits.

What were the ways of Syrian power, and what did the Lebanese overthrow in 2005? A good start to an answer is acknowledgment of the power of forgiveness—official forgiveness. In August 1991 the first postwar Lebanese government issued a general amnesty covering the war years, pardoning, among others, individuals who had fomented civil and confessional conflict and engaged in politically motivated murder, a designation describing most wartime killings. In a grotesque touch, pardons were denied to perpetrators of bank fraud, smugglers of antiquities, and sellers of property to foreigners without a license. There was a quirky but explicable logic here: The amnesty covered the war, over which the state had no control; but forgiving civil crimes meant undermining the essence of what the state stood for, at a time when the state was back.

Many Lebanese considered the amnesty a cynical whitewash of those who had tormented us for so many years. Who could deny it was, and that Lebanon never went through a process of reviewing the war years as a prelude to some form of national reconciliation.* But absent a whitewash, how would Lebanon have realistically emerged from its war, since virtually all major leaders had committed crimes or transgressions, of which the Lebanese, depending on their political loyalties, had probably at one time or

---

* A subject that will be discussed in Chapter 4.

another approved? So we all waded in a pool of guilt better toler-
ated for being ignored or forgotten.

The amnesty had several purposes as far as Syria was concerned.
It set the foundations for a Syrian-dominated postwar order in
which everyone's slate was legally wiped clean. But the essence of
it was that the Syrians were doing the wiping. Those whom they
declared innocent could also, given the right judicial incentives,
be declared guilty if Damascus needed to do so. That's what happened to Samir Geagea, the head of the former Christian militia,
the Lebanese Forces, who was sentenced to multiple life terms in
a string of trials after his arrest in 1994. Geagea was no altar boy.
He had come out the strongest from the viper's nest that was the
militia's Executive Committee, but the Syrians did not like it that
he had never embraced their hegemony over Lebanon, indeed had
been one of their bitterest enemies during the war years and might
rally refractory Christians to his side against Syria's postwar impo-
sitions. So, Geagea was falsely accused of being behind the bombing of a church in February 1994, which, politically, facilitated the
opening of several trials for wartime crimes. This permitted Syria,
through the Lebanese legal system, to put Geagea away for a long
time. Amnesty International condemned his trials as "unfair," but
his fate was a useful reminder to other wartime leaders of what
Syria could do against them if they ever got out of line.

The Syrians had other means of asserting their power. One was
the manufacturing of politicians entirely reliant on them, which
Damascus then inserted into, and used to encroach upon, the
more established political class—itself having gone through numerous permutations during the war years. There is a cliché that Lebanese politicians exemplify a "feudal" or "tribal" type of leadership
that is all-embracing and unchanging. The reality is that Lebanon's
leadership is much more versatile and complex than that sleight of
hand suggests, and substantially re-created itself in the three decades after the war began, and particularly once it ended. There has
been continuity in the behavior of the political oligarchy, but
Syria, in order to impose itself, shrewdly engineered systematic political overhauls in the post-1990 period to keep Lebanese leaders
off-balance.

Several types of politicians emerged from the civil war years, in a sectarian landscape even more bewildering than the one Hourani had written about in 1976. There was, once again, Walid Jumblatt, the descendant of an old feudal family and self-described "tribal chieftain" over the Druze, who also headed an "ideological" party, the Progressive Socialist Party, which happened to be his armed militia during the war years. Jumblatt was one of the few with an effortless talent for reinventing himself through the multiple identities he adopted—that of mountain aristocrat, leftist political leader with ties to the Socialist International, and warlord. He was an anomaly of relative continuity in a sea of change. His adaptability was made possible by the absolute loyalty Jumblatt commanded among the Druze during the war and after, and by his skill in marginalizing his communal rivals, even as he avoided eliminating them since that would have only divided the Druze and eaten into his own power base.

The story was a different one in the Maronite community, the largest and most influential of the Christian sects, which by war's end had gone through perhaps the most far-reaching convulsions of all. A constitutional document ending the war, the so-called Taif Accord of 1989, had taken power away from the president, by common agreement a Maronite, and with it the community's leading political privilege, while the Maronites' old enemy, Syria, now lorded over Lebanon. Many of the notable Christian political families survived the war, but their overall power declined in Syria's shadow, even if several avoided this outcome by taking up a role as mediator in the Syrian-dominated system. The Maronites' downfall followed a savage conflict between the community's two principle leaders in 1990, Samir Geagea and Michel Aoun—between the Lebanese Forces militia led by the first and Lebanese army units loyal to the second. The ascent of Aoun and Geagea illustrated the extent to which power among the Maronites during wartime had gravitated toward men of the geographical and social periphery. Geagea hailed from a modest family in a northern mountain town, while Aoun was born in Beirut's southern suburbs, also to a family of few means. Where Geagea had used the violent meritocracy of the war to reach the top, Aoun had climbed a more traditional route of social promotion through the officer corps, though it was the Lebanese conflict that allowed him to pretend to a national role. For Syria the marginalization of both became a priority after the war, for though they were foes, both men were also fierce adversaries of Syria, leading to Geagea's imprisonment and Aoun's exile.

In the Sunni and Shiite communities, very different types of leaders intruded on what was in place before the war and during its early stages. There, new leaderships coexisted with the traditional notable families, but also came to dominate them politically, even if they could not eliminate their presence completely. The Sunnis had Rafiq al-Hariri, a billionaire, also someone born to the periphery, who had made his fortune in Saudi Arabia. In 1992 he was chosen prime minister as the offspring of the Taif Accord, which was really little more than a Syrian-Saudi deal blessed by the United States. Where Hariri's money ended and that of the Saudis began remained a mystery, as he often served as a front man for the kingdom's investments and patronage and aid networks in Lebanon. Hariri overwhelmed the recognized Sunni families, to the extent that he pushed several out of their parliamentary seats, his way of showing that a new dynasty had taken over. But this supremacy flouted political tradition, and it was the Syrians, promoters of pluralism through their incitement of division (until they forgot that lesson in 2004), who were the most alarmed by Hariri's sweep of all the Beirut seats in the 2000 elections. That event, probably more than any other, made the Syrian regime fear the outcome of the 2005 elections for their own continuity in Lebanon. As the late Lebanese journalist Joseph Samaha perceptively put it two years before Hariri's killing: "Hariri won a victory in Beirut, but it was too big a victory."

In the Shiite community, too, by the end of the civil war the traditional families had lost what remained of their political stature. The process had actually begun before the Lebanese conflict, in the 1960s, when a cleric who had returned from Iran, Sayyed Musa al-Sadr, began to use one part of the traditional Shiite leadership structure against the other to create his own alternative leadership, while buttressing this with middle-class Shiite support and that of an urban underclass gleaned from the shantytowns of Beirut's suburbs, particularly its northeastern suburbs (where a future Shiite leader, Hassan Nasrallah, would grow up). During the war years, Musa al-Sadr established the Amal militia, but when he disappeared in Libya in 1978, his fate unknown to this day, it was left to his political heirs to build on what he had created. Israel's invasion of Lebanon in 1982 pushed the Shiites to new levels of affirmation. The invasion freed the community from under the thumb of the Palestinian paramilitary organizations then dominating southern Lebanon. However, when the Israelis overstayed their welcome, this gave rise to what would become a largely Shiite-led resistance movement. Early on, the Shiite revival domestically was led by Amal, armed and backed by Syria. However, Iran, whose Islamic revolution had spawned a new sense of regional militancy, also began forming its own armed groups under the name of Hezbollah, later reorganizing them into a more centralized party. By the end of the 1980s, Hezbollah had defeated Amal in Beirut's southern suburbs, the seat of Shiite power in the capital. When the war ended, Syria continued to favor Amal, whose leader was appointed speaker of Lebanon's parliament in 1992. However, it was the more effective Hezbollah that gradually won over a majority of Shiites, even as the party continued to ally itself with Amal and the traditional families when necessary.

Faced with this array of new social and political forces in the major religious communities, the Syrians played a balancing game. They co-opted the older leaders, promoted new ones entirely dependent on Damascus, including former militiamen with no independent political base of their own, and hit out against the incorrigibles. To Hezbollah they granted considerable leeway to arm, allowing the party to fight Israel's occupation of southern Lebanon, which Syria used as leverage in its negotiations with Israel during the 1990s. Also, and more perniciously, the Syrians used Hezbollah as a counterweight to Rafiq al-Hariri, pitting the party's vision of Lebanon as a state focused on "resistance" to Israel and the West against Hariri's predilection for turning Lebanon into a Western-oriented services and commercial entrepôt. As the years went by, Syria reinforced its grip on Hariri, whom they never trusted for being a Saudi venture, even as they welcomed him as the only man who could rebuild Lebanon, stabilize its economy, and build up financial confidence in the country's potential—lending legitimacy to what was, after all, a Syrian protectorate. Hariri, in turn, exploited his indispensability to expand his influence in the system, so that for a time it was still possible to candidly inquire who was the master and who was the slave, who was taking advantage of whom—the Syrians or Hariri? Hariri's reconstruction efforts and the postwar apportionment of the economic pie also spawned networks of corruption that generated vast sums of money and patronage capabilities largely benefiting Lebanese and Syrian politicians and senior military and intelligence officers.

Hariri's sway notwithstanding, there never was any doubt who was leading and who was following. It was Syria, and at the top of the pyramid of Syrian rule was the president—until his death in 2000, Hafez al-Assad, thereafter his son Bashar—the final decision-maker on all matters Lebanese. It was under Hafez that the Syrian system was set up and worked most efficiently. In day-to-day affairs, the president ceded considerable power to the head of his intelligence branch in Lebanon, the Security and Reconnaissance Apparatus, officially a branch of Syrian military intelligence. However, one had to distinguish between three phases of Syrian rule. In the period between 1990 and 1998, Hafez al-Assad installed a more amorphous structure of relations between Damascus and Beirut. His head of intelligence in Lebanon was General Ghazi Kanaan, an Alawite from the president's own Kalbiyya tribal confederation, who aside from being in charge in Lebanon was also head of the foreign intelligence section of Syrian military intelligence. While Kanaan had the advantage of being on the ground, until 1998 he was not alone in managing Lebanese affairs. The Syrian vice president, Abdel Halim Khaddam, as well as the chief of staff, Hikmat Shihabi, both of them Sunnis, as well as other Syrian officials with variable influence, also played important decision-making roles in the country, and often had privileged relations with specific Lebanese politicians. This multifarious structure was also reflected inside Lebanon, where the president, prime minister, and speaker of parliament, their mandates ill defined in the postwar constitution, competed for power, while they and most other politicians, in the absence of a single Syrian reference point, would bring their major disputes to Damascus for arbitration. Atop this hierarchy of checks and balances sat a serene Hafez al-Assad, playing his subordinates off against one another through the parallel lines of authority he had laid down, keeping the Lebanese divided and allowing everyone, Syrian and Lebanese, to benefit from the spoils the arrangement offered in order to better safeguard its continuity.

Kanaan's philosophy when it came to Syria's role in Lebanon was expressed thus: "You Lebanese, you are shrewd, creative and successful merchants. . . . Create light industries. Engage in trade and commerce. Indulge in light media, which does not affect security. Shine all over the world by your inventiveness, and leave politics to us. Each has his domain in Lebanon: yours is trade; ours, politics and security." One didn't expect better from someone like Kanaan, but no one could quite be sure what the British author William Dalrymple's excuse was when he described Syria approvingly as "a police state that tends to leave its citizens alone as long as they keep out of politics." Yet his phrase perfectly expressed Kanaan's logic in Lebanon.

In the early postwar years, on his visits to Damascus, Kanaan would see Khaddam and Shihabi, while he also reported to his hierarchical superior Ali Douba, then head of military intelligence. In 1998 that reportedly changed. The reason was that Hafez al-Assad did two things: he brought in Émile Lahoud as Lebanese president and he much reduced the power of Khaddam as well as Shihabi, who retired. There seemed to be a streamlining of Lebanon policy in Damascus, but also in Beirut, where Lahoud, backed by the Lebanese army and intelligence services, was, in theory, to be the main funnel of decisions coming down from Syria. But the effort to militarize Lebanese politics, which took place in parallel to preparations for Bashar al-Assad's rise in Syria to succeed the dying Hafez, failed. In fact, it allowed Kanaan to consolidate his authority in Lebanon, as Lahoud proved even less willing than his predecessor to challenge Syria. Adnan Shaaban, a former Lebanese intelligence officer who knew Kanaan well and who, improbably enough, became friends with him after being abducted and mistreated on Kanaan's orders, put it this way: "After 1998, Kanaan would go to Damascus and report personally to Hafez al-Assad. He would not see anyone else in Damascus anymore. There was Ghazi Kanaan in Lebanon and Hafez al-Assad in Syria."

By all accounts, Kanaan was an unusually intelligent individual, ruthless and agile for having risen through the pitiless school of Syrian military politics. Yet he, too, like Rafiq al-Hariri, may have done too well. Little during his glory days in Lebanon presaged what would happen on October 12, 2005, when Kanaan, by then Syria's interior minister, shot himself (or was shot) in his office in Damascus, amid signs that the Assad regime was setting him up for a fall. The evening before, a Lebanese television station had accused him of corruption, almost certainly on orders from Damascus, and that morning he had called the mellifluous radio interviewer Wardeh Zamel to deny the charge. Zamel had immediately put him on the air even though she was not on the schedule that day. A quarter of an hour later he was dead. Did the Assads fear that this man, who had grown wealthy during his Lebanese interregnum, despite the denials, who also had decisiveness and Alawite legitimacy, might foment a coup against them? It's difficult to say, although such a rumor spread, likely encouraged by Damascus itself. Whatever the truth, it was difficult not to conclude that it was Kanaan's Lebanese successes that led to his death.

Kanaan's day in Lebanon would begin at 7 A.M. Based in the Beqaa Valley, on the highway between Beirut and Damascus, he would start by exercising in the town of Shtaura, around a house he had confiscated from the family of a prominent Lebanese newspaper publisher, before heading for Anjar, near the Syrian border, where he had his headquarters. At noon he would receive telephone intercepts sent by his deputy responsible for Beirut, Rustom Ghazaleh, one of almost two dozen officers overseeing intelligence matters in different parts of Lebanon. The lines of most people of any prominence in politics, the media, or elsewhere, were as a rule assumed to be tapped. Kanaan was effectively a head of state and few details fell below his radar. He would order Ghazaleh to call people if he required something—or if he simply wanted them to make the long drive up to his office. In another af-firmation of power, those without an appointment could be kept waiting for hours, so that it became a tactic of Kanaan to have peo-ple encourage visitors to drop by unannounced, only for them to be left cooling their heels once they arrived. The more experienced ones would do so at a restaurant on the Beirut-Damascus highway owned by a friend of Kanaan's, their delight at the early informal-ity of it all having by then long dissipated. Kanaan kept an eye on what the politicians were up to, followed what was going on in state administrations, kept track of lucrative projects, cut his fol-lowers into illicit money-making arrangements in public institu-tions, and spent his day otherwise meeting people and pushing pieces around on his Lebanese chessboard. No one refused a sum-mons to Anjar—politicians, ministers, civil servants, even presi-dents, albeit secretly. Kanaan made governments; promoted or demoted politicians, senior civil servants, and security cadres; de-cided who could be invited onto political talk shows; and elevated or shuffled around Lebanese army officers, even deciding where they would receive their staff training.

Soon after his election, Émile Lahoud received a sobering les-son in Kanaan's power. Just before vacating the presidency, Lahoud's predecessor, Elias Hrawi, had asked for three favors in a meeting with Hafez al-Assad. On all three the Syrian president was said to have left the final decision to Kanaan. Two were rebuffed, but the third, the appointment of a Hrawi crony as ambassador to Tunisia, Kanaan accepted. Yet when the person in question went to meet Lahoud to see the matter through, the new president said no, that he only wanted ambassadors from the diplomatic corps. The man complained to Hrawi who complained to Kanaan, who was overheard by Adnan Shaaban saying: "Lahoud said that? That's big for his neck. Tomorrow [your man] will sleep as an ambassa-dor." And indeed Hrawi's man did sleep as an ambassador, but only after Kanaan called Ghazaleh and told him to instruct Lebanon's new prime minister, Salim al-Hoss, to make the ap-pointment, or to call him back if there was a problem. Here were all the ingredients of the Syrian way: the putting of two presidents in their place; the humiliation of a prime minister; and Kanaan's allowing Shaaban to overhear the conversation, knowing it would make the rounds and confirm that Kanaan could put Émile Lahoud in his place and humiliate Salim al-Hoss.

The backdrop to the Syrian order in Lebanon was violence, or more precisely its latency. Just as Kanaan would order Ghazaleh to call people on his behalf, so the Syrians would usually use the Lebanese army and security services, as well as the Lebanese judiciary, civilian and military, to abuse on their behalf. This had the advantage of making the Lebanese mistrust their security institutions while keeping Syria in the background, preserving a mystique of Syrian coercion more fearful for seldom being used. The rise of Jamil al-Sayyed was very much a consequence of this calculation and was very much a Kanaan project. Even early on, humbleness was not a Sayyed trait. A mutual friend called him in the mid-1980s to congratulate him on being promoted to the rank of lieutenant colonel, or *muqaddam* in Arabic. But *muqaddam* was also the title of regional mountain chiefs in Lebanese history, and my friend offered up a pun, telling Sayyed that under the Mamelukes it was the *muqaddams* who ruled Lebanon. It was a subtle way of reminding Sayyed that outsiders had promoted him, and wrapping this in a compliment, but the officer showed he could match that in repartee: "Yes," he answered, "but when the Mamelukes left, the *muqaddams* still ruled Lebanon."

In point of fact, Sayyed did not long outlast the Syrian withdrawal. And his power never came unconditionally. As in Syria, where the Assad regime set up various security and intelligence agencies to watch and offset each other, so, too, did it set up such a system in Lebanon. Sayyed's General Security directorate, under the nominal authority of the Interior Ministry, was given more power than before, but also collaborated and competed with the military intelligence service, the Internal Security Forces, the State Security service, and, after Lahoud's selection, the Presidential Guard, whose de facto prerogatives were enhanced. A consequence of this was that Lahoud found himself "accompanied" by Sayyed on his foreign visits, where the General Security chief sat in on the president's meetings with heads of state, one watchdog watching another.

Throughout the period of Syrian domination, Lebanese from all religious groups disappeared into Syrian prisons, victims of equal-opportunity callousness. While this may not have been as widespread after 1992 as it was during the war years, given the Syrian preference for letting the Lebanese deal with their household troubles, such behavior never stopped. And for too long the tale of the Lebanese in Syrian prisons was one of cruelty and silence. The window was momentarily opened on April 29, 2005, after the Syrian departure, when a popular Lebanese television talk show host interviewed several former prisoners. They all described arbitrary brutality, of finding themselves in a Syrian intelligence prison, particularly the one near Kanaan's headquarters at Anjar, where they were beaten or tortured, before disappearing into Syria itself, where a more sustained cycle of abasement and extortion began. One prisoner recounted how he had spent five years in solitary confinement. Another recollected how his family had paid $30,000 to a senior Baath Party official to secure his release. Particularly feared was the military prison at Palmyra, described to me by a onetime Syrian prisoner, Yassin al-Haj Saleh, as "a place that literally eats men . . . where every day primitive and vengeful torture is carried out at the hands of heartless people." This was the repulsive face behind the mask of normality the Syrians and Lebanese erected after the war, one built on the degradation by Syria of a Lebanese political oligarchy that often invited such degradation, and of the Lebanese in general. There was something especially nauseating in this image: that of grandees visiting with Kanaan, of waiting in his anteroom and laughing at his jokes, while down the road their countrymen were being softened up for their long journey into the twilight zone of Syria's prisons, many never to return.

A third phase in the method of Syrian control over Lebanon began in 2002, when Rustom Ghazaleh took over from Kanaan. By then Bashar al-Assad had succeeded his dead father, and his appointment of Ghazaleh showed he was beginning to bring in officers entirely loyal to him. Ghazaleh happened to be a Sunni. This meant he posed less of a threat to Assad inside Syria, where Alawites ruled, but it was also Assad's way of telling Lebanon's Sunnis, particularly Hariri, that he could sic his own Sunnis on them.

Ghazaleh was a very different organism than Kanaan, whom he had served under and reportedly addressed only with the greatest deference. He was less impressive, in the sense of crime, and among his drawbacks was that Lebanese leaders knew him from the time when he was taking orders, not giving them, therefore someone to be feared more than respected. There was a yearning for intellectual recognition in the man. He had received a Ph.D. in history at the Lebanese University, though there was a tongue-in-cheek debate in Beirut over how he found the time to write a dissertation. Ghazaleh defended it before a committee of professors, and afterward one of them would take great pride in the fact that he had asked the Syrian officer difficult questions. His academic bent notwithstanding, Ghazaleh was not usually someone who would make his points by drafting a treatise. For example, it was very likely he who ordered a rocket attack against Hariri's Future Television station in June 2003, a week after the prime minister declared, while in Brazil, that Arabs and Israelis should enter into a dialogue to resolve their problems, adding "we believe in trusting" the United States. Who was Hariri to "trust" anyone, Ghazaleh must have muttered. Yet that action only created an understated sense that he had reached too quickly for his gun, that things were not as frigidly graceful as they were under Ghazi Kanaan.

It was Ghazaleh's misfortune to take over at a volatile moment in the Middle East, in the aftermath of the 9/11 attacks and just before the American invasion of Iraq. Those events, while they did not affect Lebanon directly, could not fail to jolt a Syrian regime that in 2003 found itself with an American army on its border. Even earlier than that, in May 2000, just days before the death of Hafez al-Assad, Israel had changed the ground rules in Lebanon by withdrawing its soldiers from the south of the country. That pullout provoked appeals in Beirut for redefining Syrian-Lebanese relations, since if Israel was no longer in the south, why should Syria be everywhere else? The appeals hadn't changed minds in Damascus, but combined with the American presence in Iraq and the

American and French sponsorship of Resolution 1559 in 2004 demanding a Syrian departure from Lebanon, they made the inexperienced Bashar al-Assad take fateful decisions that backfired.
Lahoud's extension was the most significant of these, and by the
time the Bristol Gathering began convening, the fear imposed by
the Syrians was beginning to fray.

That explained, for instance, why one parliamentarian, Mosbah al-Ahdab, could decide to attend the first Bristol meeting,
even though as a Sunni from Tripoli he was doubly vulnerable to
Syrian retribution. He was vulnerable for being a Sunni, therefore
more likely to face payback from a Syrian Alawite regime on perpetual alert against Sunni discontent; and for being from Tripoli, a
city the Syrians viewed as their back yard, close to Sunni Islamist
power centers on their side of the border, whose conservatism
made it more amenable to intimidation than cosmopolitan Beirut.
Ahdab, whom someone once referred to as "the Ken doll" of Lebanese politics, also had the intelligence and dexterity to go with his
pop idol looks, and had won reelection in 2000 because voters in
Tripoli had appreciated his refusal to support a pro-Syrian slate in
the municipal elections of 1998. Before heading to the first Bristol
meeting, he was contacted by the Syrian intelligence officer responsible for Tripoli, Abdel-Latif Fahd, who told him in so many
words that it would not be a good idea to attend. When Ahdab
said he was going anyway, Fahd asked him to see Ghazaleh in Anjar. Ahdab obliged, but again stuck to his guns. From Anjar he
went to the Bristol, and as he entered the hall, Fahd called him
again, with a more pointed threat: "If you go in, consider this the
last communication between us. You live in Tripoli and you know
what that means." Ahdab went in nevertheless, and during the session another Ghazaleh call came, which Ahdab didn't take. He delivered his speech, and on Ahdab's way out, by this time the stress
having brought on a migraine, Fahd called yet again to say, "Are
you finished; I was talking to [Ghazaleh] and he said, 'Why did
you anger Mosbah al-Ahdab, he is a nationalist.'" Then yet one
more call arrived, this time from a Tripoli doctor with a message
from Ghazaleh: "The *mua'llim* (master) says you are a man. He
likes you very much and when he can he will see you." To which a

relieved Ahdab, not wanting to push his luck, responded, "I will make it a priority when he wants." However, it seemed an awful lot of phone calls for so meager a result, and all to end up with a statement of esteem from Ghazaleh, sincere or not. Perhaps something really was changing in Lebanon.

A VERY different book than *The Rock of Tanios* was published in 1999, but it managed to address a similar topic: the cannibalism in Lebanese leadership. The book in question was titled *From Israel to Damascus: The Painful Road of Blood, Betrayal, and Deception*, by one Robert Maroun Hatem, alias Cobra, the name of a brand of submachine gun. Cobra had been a bodyguard of Elie Hobeiqa, a former Christian militia leader who was a comrade of Samir Geagea until Geagea staged a coup that sent Hobeiqa into the arms of his onetime enemies, the Syrians. Those were still the war years, but what made Hobeiqa's embrace by the Syrians so remarkable—and so illuminating about the depravity of Syrian co-optation in Lebanon—was that he had ordered his men to butcher several hundred, perhaps even over 1,000, people at the Sabra and Shatila Palestinian refugee camps in Beirut in September 1982, when Israel occupied the Lebanese capital. For the Baathists, noisy defenders of Arab renewal and the Palestinian cause, inconsistency in the pursuit of self-interest was no vice. Once the war ended, Hobeiqa entered parliament and was appointed a minister in several cabinets. He was a superlative example of the kind of politician who, though he had lingering support among his former militiamen in Christian areas, was otherwise entirely owned by Syria—reliant on its goodwill for his political and physical survival, since many had not forgotten his road of blood.

Cobra's book was an illiterate masterpiece. But to call the effort a book may be too kind; it was page after page of invective, written, or more likely recorded, in wretched English, directed against Hobeiqa (and likely paid for by one of his enemies), apparently because Cobra and Hobeiqa had had a falling out over money. The book, in the unremitting ugliness it described, captured perfectly what the war years were about, and what the men of the war were about. It made the rounds in Beirut in photocopied versions, particularly the chapter on Hobeiqa's sexual exploits with prominent society ladies. Cobra was out to settle a score, but the broad lines of what he remembered were how others had also remembered Hobeiqa. And as Cobra portrayed it, during the war years Hobeiqa's life was that of a predator, another of those cunning predators which the war had promoted. His attentions were said to be mainly devoted to making money, eliminating rivals, accumulating power, fornicating, and stealing cars. Not much changed after the war, the bodyguard reported, even if there was less killing going on and the stealing was now part of the "authorized" plunder of the reconstruction years.

It was not Cobra's objective to do so, so sordid a figure was he, so preposterous a moral paragon; but in describing Hobeiqa he was also denouncing the foundations of the Syrian postwar order. He may have overstated things, but one thing Cobra managed to get right was that Hobeiqa had been recycled into someone vaguely palatable by Syria, to the extent that he was photographed for the covers of glossy celebrity magazines. He had come a long way from his days as a minor gunman in the Christian working-class neighborhood of Gemmayzeh. But what Cobra did not get right, because his book came out too early, was that the veneer mattered little. Hobeiqa, more than others, perhaps unfairly for those like him were all over, would always be looked upon as someone who had just crawled out of the killing pit, who couldn't rinse off his heavy past. In 2000 he failed to win a parliamentary seat, a sign that Syria had lifted its protection of him. And so in January 2002, while driving to work, he and his bodyguards were killed in a car-bomb explosion, the reason for the assassination never elucidated.

Hobeiqa's ending showed there was more to recognized leadership in Lebanon than the outward affectations of social arrival. When the Syrian safeguards fell, Hobeiqa became a marked man, amid great indifference. But that was only another way of saying that the Syrians were mostly unable to insert a group of followers into the political class with an independent standing of their own—something, in contrast, that the Ottomans and the French were

able to do with more success. This was normal: How could the
Syrians build up a legitimate class of political followers when their
point was that those whom they fabricated were nothing without
Syria? Implicit in this arrangement was that the Syrians also needed
to keep on board politicians having more credibility, to lend legitimacy to the enterprise as a whole, while using their peons as ther-
mostats to preserve their rule. Yet when Jumblatt and then Hariri
turned against Damascus in 2004 and found willing collaborators among the long-marginalized Christians, the Syrians should
have sensed that their edifice was beginning to shake. Jumblatt
had a committed following, as did Hariri, while the Christians, divided over everything else, were united against Syria. However, instead of defusing this, the Syrians accelerated the deterioration by
hitting out against Rafiq al-Hariri. In doing so, the Assad regime
came to overrely on a government top-heavy with Syrian political
creations having ersatz authority. When Hariri was murdered, the
wobbly edifice came crashing down, and Syria found only Hezbollah with the legitimacy and wherewithal to resist the Independence
Intifada. But that was hardly enough. Bashar al-Assad and Hezbollah provoked the majority in March 2005, when Assad taunted
that the cameras should "zoom out" and expose the tiny crowds
crying for Syria to go home, and Hezbollah brought out the faithful to show that Shiite numbers could silence everyone else's
numbers. Both steps aimed to delegitimize the other side, but the
battle over legitimacy was not one Syria could win, certainly not
when it was now so dependent on sycophants; nor that Hezbollah
could win, because the pluralism of Lebanese sectarianism did not
allow it.

When looking back on the events of 2004 and 2005, a recurring question is what allowed the Lebanese oligarchs opposing
Syria to win out? Two systems had clashed, that of the Syrians and
that of Lebanon's more recognized politicians, and the Lebanese
had come out on top, at least momentarily, even though it was
Syria that held the guns. One explanation is that the fathers all
around us, whichever side of the Syrian divide they were on, had
an implied compact that would always be sturdier than what Syria
offered, because it was based on a collective agreement to retain

power. This was possible because the oligarchs were tied with one another, and with their electorates, in an intricate web of relationships that the Syrian arrangement, once it had fallen back on raw intimidation, could not match.

That which enhances power and legitimacy in Lebanon is not so very different than what enhances power and legitimacy elsewhere. In their biography of the influential Chicago mayor Richard J. Daley, who for two decades ran the city's Democratic political machine, Adam Cohen and Elizabeth Taylor describe him as someone whose "primary test of a political cause was whether it would increase or decrease his power." That statement applies, with few adjustments, to most Lebanese politicians, for whom ideas and causes are mere adjuncts to influence. Daley's way was patronage, as it is in Lebanon. Where self-declared modernizers will groan at such a system, in the absence of necessary reform the Lebanese have generally embraced the patronage system, bestowing different degrees of acceptance on their leaders. The result is a vicious circle: the leaders perpetuate a system that perpetuates their leadership. But the system also imposes on leaders duties and responsibilities that, if they don't build a modern state, nonetheless inject into politics self-regulating mechanisms that sanction those who fail to play the game effectively.

As any Lebanese navigating the world of the leaders will tell you, patronage alone doesn't generate legitimacy, which requires a number of other characteristics, both variable and intangible, to take anchor: family origin and political history, wiliness, proof of accomplishment over time, networks of relationships, the ability to do harm but also to show compassion, a memory for names, and such lesser things as physical bearing and command of Arabic. In various measures all these traits are picked up and weighed by the severely politicized Lebanese, canny in the ways of authority, allowing them to assess who merits respect and who merits less or none—even as they will take advantage of a politician's favors regardless of which category in which they place him or her.

Take the former deputy speaker of parliament, Elie al-Firzli. A Greek Orthodox from the West Beqaa, Firzli came to power sponsored by Ghazi Kanaan as a benign version of Elie Hobeiqa and

Jamil al-Sayyed. I first met Firzli in 2008, to get a better sense of how the pro-Syrians were faring with their sponsors gone. A man over the top by temperament, his angled face bearing the scars of a bomb explosion he survived during the war, Firzli takes pleasure in the physics of his oratory, even if the gestures are usually there to lend color to the colorless edicts transmitted from Damascus. Firzli had been out of parliament, and office, for three years, a victim of the 2005 elections that brought in the anti-Syrian majority. In front of him Firzli had a pile of small white pieces of paper with notes and telephone numbers written on them. I inquired what they were. He said that each one was a request for a favor, with contact details. It was not the most sophisticated of methods, but Firzli had over a dozen in hand. Several days per week he would also receive people in his village of Jib Jannine, leaving little time to do anything else but call people up for services on behalf of an electorate that in its majority had not voted for him. But Firzli was liked among Christians, and when I asked what kind of pull he still had, he answered: "No one has ever refused my requests. Many Christians help me out because they see me as a Christian in a Muslim majority area." That may have been true in part, but people also responded to Firzli because they reasoned it was best to stay on good terms with Syria's defenders.

Firzli is interesting, and in a way almost touching, because for him patronage, bolstered by the relation with Syria, is the only way he has of combating obscurity. His task is an ungrateful one. At the end of the day he has to run harder after his political clients than they after him, because neither the family name nor the Firzli money will ever be enough to turn his electoral victories into dead certainties. The West Beqaa will always be able to dig up another Elie al-Firzli, even if his stamina and histrionics make him a difficult act to follow. And though he had lost his seat, Firzli still took the calls and walked around with his little white papers. "The day after the elections is for me like the day before," he explained, sounding ever so slightly like Tantalus condemned to drinking from a lake forever drying up.

At the top end of the spectrum are the more established politicians, those who stand at the nexus point between the government bureaucracy, local government, the private sector, and communal institutions. They are the ones who can more readily place their people in ministries, local administrations, and private companies or banks; who can also arrange for administrative favors, asphalt roads, and see to it that their followers have better access to water and electricity. Until his assassination Rafiq al-Hariri personified the ability to combine politics and business in a way unmatched by others. In a country where the political class had traditionally expanded its interests into the private sector and forged alliances with the commercial and financial bourgeoisie, this combination was nothing new. What was new was that Hariri had come to politics from the fringes of the society by way of business—a less common phenomenon—but, more significantly, had done so in such a way that he came to dominate the space the Syrians left open for him, which was substantial during his first years in power. Hariri's wealth and latitude to dispense Saudi funding allowed him to create his own political constellation and finance social, educational, and charity associations that provided him with valuable patronage ability and enhanced his popularity. His Hariri Foundation had given loans to help educate tens of thousands of students over the years, allowing Hariri to gather around him professionals whom he could employ in his companies and in the state institutions he controlled or set up to circumvent certain ministries. Hariri also gave the Sunnis a strong leader at a moment when they most needed one, at the end of a civil war that left the community with no compelling leaders. That combination is what brought tens of thousands of Sunnis down into the streets for Hariri's funeral, and who then on March 14 were willing for the first time to accept the consequences of a bitter divorce from Syria.

Saad al-Hariri landed in what his father had set up, but the fit was not as snug. Soft-spoken and thirty-something when he took over from Rafiq al-Hariri, Saad often seemed an uncomfortable politician for dealing with counterparts usually a generation older in age, and several more in duplicity. Upon inheriting the Future Movement, he had to adjust to a system he had not created and a situation his father had never faced. In 2005, Saad knew few people in the Hariri archipelago and came to depend on those who had surrounded his father, with whom he had no close ties. He would later explain that it was his father's people who helped him through the formative years, most of them having chosen to stay on "because I get along, I don't threaten people . . . because there was a lot of understanding between my mentality and theirs in running the show." No doubt there was, but staying with Saad al-Hariri also meant staying at the center of power. Complicating the transition was the fact that Saad was not someone with a history of involving himself in the details of retail politics, while the political assassinations after 2005 further limited his movements and capacity to familiarize himself with his constituency. "We've made some mistakes, but some were fixed and some will be fixed," he admitted in an interview. Money circulated, but was usually doled out with abandon, so the impact could be uneven. For example, as late as 2008, pro-Hariri Sunnis in Tripoli, emerging from a round of fighting with Alawites, complained that the Future Movement was absent in filling the political and aid vacuum in their destitute areas. This was overstated, but it reflected a larger reality, namely that Syria had not allowed Rafiq al-Hariri to organize in most areas of Lebanon, and that those his son appointed as his representatives after 2005 could be mediocre and corrupt. As Saad himself pointed out, "we have to experience new people in those regions, and that's where we make mistakes." While the Future Movement enjoyed communal loyalty, and Saad personal popularity, these came with expectations of how he and it should perform. Money was not enough; Hariri also had to show to his followers that he was in control of his ungainly movement; that he could play the political game with skill and be on top of things, wise to the ways of what the public necessarily assumed, fairly or unfairly, was a scheming entourage.

For the Druze leader Walid Jumblatt, Saturday mornings are open house in his mountain palace at Mukhtara. I once asked him whether I could sit in and watch, and he obliged. There is little formality on such days—when I was there, a woman manhandled Jumblatt out onto a balcony in front of visitors to ask for a favor—but there is also a well-oiled system. Depending on what people need, they are taken in hand by one of Jumblatt's dozen or so assistants responsible for a particular file: social affairs, health, public or private sector employment, and much else. In his distribution of favors and services, Jumblatt balances out the interests of those he effectively rules over.

At one point Jumblatt signaled for me to follow him into another room, where his assistants gathered. There I spent an hour listening to reports from most of these men on the condition of roads, electricity outages, dispensaries to be opened, water distribution, projects Jumblatt had set up or that others had offered to finance. Many of the issues involved looking for ways to get ministries to act favorably on Jumblatt's behalf. Sometimes they would, sometimes they wouldn't. It was a question of who was most capable of grabbing a piece of the pie. At the end of the session, Jumblatt sat with an older aide who read a list of names of people, between thirty and fifty in total, who needed financial assistance, presumably out of Jumblatt's own funds. "So and so needs to send his son to school, he's a decent chap, one million pounds." Jumblatt would sleepily nod his head, but everything would register. As Jumblatt accompanied me out, I suggested there were an awful lot of details to remember. He answered, "I've been doing this a long time. But this is real politics."

It *was* real politics, or a version of it, and what Jumblatt does on Saturday, other oligarchs, high and low, do on preferred days of their own, within their means. And this applies just as much to those who opposed or were skeptical of the Independence Intifada—who stood against Hariri and Jumblatt and all the other politicians who went down to Martyrs Square, but who also belong to the same loose brotherhood that they do. Some come from Lebanon's more rural areas, dispensing favors to communities mainly in need of agricultural amenities, or simply cheap health and educational services. Others operate in more economically developed areas, where the labyrinthine rules and regulations imposed by the state affect all forms of business enterprises. This means the successful politician there is the one who can mediate on their behalf with the bureaucracy and the judiciary. Yet other politicians combine aspects of urban and rural leadership.

Then there is Hezbollah, the Lebanese party that many wrongly view as being above the fray when it comes to patronage, that allegedly lets conviction and ideology do the talking, and yet that is an unmatched personification of patronage. It is startling to see how outsiders to Lebanon, particularly Westerners, tend to misconstrue Hezbollah, seeing it as a genuine alternative to traditional Lebanese politics by virtue of its ability to set up institutions. Hezbollah indeed oversees an array of social service organizations, hospitals, clinics, schools, and agricultural facilities. There is the Martyrs Foundation, to help families of dead combatants, and the Jihad al-Bina, to oversee development and construction projects and to help dig wells and set up electricity networks. Hezbollah does not pursue personal leadership, its defenders maintain; its assistance is there only to compensate for the dearth of Lebanese state services provided to the Shiite community. The argument is disingenuous. The party pursues its narrow institutional power with no less tenacity than the politicians do their personal power, and the politicians try to fill the vacuum left by the state when it comes to providing services no less than Hezbollah does. That such behavior on the part of the traditional politicians and Hezbollah marginalizes the state is undeniable; but it is also true that many Lebanese look at that reality as a glass half-full: better to have a politician or party on one's side when the problems come, and they are many, than to face one's travails unassisted.

That's why 2005 was such a disappointment for those expecting an end to this paternalism, and why the optimists were myopic in failing to see that the Syrian departure, far from bringing in a new order, only allowed the old order to consolidate itself—albeit with fewer Syrians around. And that is why Lebanon will remain a forest of fathers, so limiting in its own way, yet so much more tolerable than a place with a single father who cuts down the rest of the forest.

When Rafiq al-Hariri was killed, two breakdowns ensued: a breakdown in the system that Hafiz al-Assad and Ghazi Kanaan had first set up in collaboration with the Lebanese oligarchs; and a breakdown in the cohesiveness of the Lebanese political class itself, as several of the more prominent politicians decided that by sticking with Syria they would only prolong a system circumventing their authority. Yet to reduce everything about 2004 and 2005 to a cold evaluation of how power was preserved or accumulated would be excessive. The dangers involved would have made anyone pause. Almost two dozen people were killed in a string of bomb attacks and assassinations after the Syrians left Lebanon. Between 2005 and 2008, Syria's most prominent enemies, particularly ministers and parliamentarians, were prisoners of their homes or hotels for long stretches of time, rarely venturing out for fear of being murdered, their lives and livelihoods in suspended animation. In July 2008, after a new president was elected and a new government formed, I asked the outgoing justice minister, Charles Rizq, whether I could congratulate him on leaving office, since he had been a leading target of assassination. The question was half-serious since I knew that Rizq, a political animal par excellence, had harbored ambitions of becoming president himself. Nevertheless, he said that congratulations were definitely in order. He was planning to travel and return to private business. Rizq seemed sincere, and yet the guards were still outside his building, his street still arrayed with metal obstacles and closed off to parking for fear of a bomb.

Bashar al-Assad and those around him in the Syrian regime took Lebanon for granted. Unlike his own father, who had patiently engineered an extension of Elias Hrawi's mandate in 1995 over a period of many months, Bashar failed to prepare the terrain for Émile Lahoud's extension. In an interview with a Kuwaiti newspaper a few weeks before deciding he would keep the Lebanese president in office, Bashar said it would be up to the Lebanese to decide. In August, however, he showed he cared nothing about what the Lebanese decided, forcing Hariri and parliament to amend the constitution and make it seem like *they* wanted Lahoud to stay. This only compounded the shame, displaying recklessness on Bashar's part—an inability to take the measure of a country his father had handed down to him. Lebanon can be unforgiving to those who think that fear alone can long maintain order. It is a country where formal rules mean little, where adherence to the law and its implementation is often erratic; but it is also a place addicted to form, particularly the forms of hierarchy, so that most politicians could spend years being demeaned by Syrian intelligence officers but at the same time accept this because the Syrians worked through a façade of counterfeit consideration and deference. It was all very hypocritical and guarded, but it made the Lebanese feel better, feel like they had salvaged some self-respect in bargaining for their proscribed autonomy, all until Bashar tore that façade away and replaced it with a condensed lump of humiliation, and before long everything came tumbling down.

There was a definite machinery of emancipation that had confounded the Syrians. It was a machinery made up of very dissimilar parts, even contradictory ones. There was the swelling discontent the oligarchs felt toward Syria, multiplied by Assad's errors, against a background of declining international patience for Syria's presence in Lebanon. And there was the public's impetus to pick up on that after Hariri's killing and stamp a more liberal imprint on the events of 2005. It was a dramatic interplay, and it was the leaders who initially made possible that public reaction by turning against the Syrians and forming a core that a majority of Lebanese would later follow and surpass, but always somehow regard as legitimate.

But without the public, without that brief moment when the Lebanese responded to Rafiq al-Hariri's assassination by declaring it an outrage to their liberal sensibilities and taking to the streets, the fathers would have gone nowhere. The Bristol Gathering would have shriveled on the vine; Rustom Ghazaleh would have continued running Lebanon by telephone and rocket fire; and eventually some new balm would have been applied to appease the oligarchs, until a new tectonic shift in the region provoked new outbursts. In the electoral aftermath of the March 14 demonstration, the day when the clock finally ran out for Syria in Lebanon, the fathers on all sides, those against Syria and those with it, scrambled to fill the vacuum left by the Syrian departure through strange election alliances with their former adversaries. It was musical chairs, not democratic but polyphonic, to avoid being left standing once the music stopped. Much of the public went along with this. But that only showed how, in the weeks and months after Hariri's assassination, the mostly illiberal leaders on all sides canceled each other out, as so often happens in Lebanon; and where there is a canceling out of leaders, liberal manners are more likely to flourish. For what could be more liberal than the collapse of the house that Bashar al-Assad and Ghazi Kanaan and Rustom Ghazaleh had built and maintained in Lebanon—in its own way a house of the dead?

3
Total War

We shall, in fact, work to turn the whole of Lebanon into a country of resistance, and the state into a state of resistance. . . . There is a dialectical link, here, between the resistance and the internal situation in Lebanon, because for the resistance to survive there should be a community that adopts it and adopts the resistance fighter. This means that, in order to remain steadfast, that fighter needs to secure all the support he needs politically, security-wise, culturally, and economically—and be provided with the means of livelihood.

Hassan Nasrallah, Interview with
Al-Watan al-Arabi, September 11, 1992

THE SUMMER WAR of 2006 between Hezbollah and Israel was the first perilous confrontation between the two Lebanons that emerged from the Independence Intifada the year before. Until then, the anti-Syrian majority in parliament on the one side and Hezbollah on the other had managed to coexist in a unity government, albeit united only in name. Afterward, the possibility of violence, never far away during the preceding months, would come to engulf relations between the Lebanese, casting a pall over any hopefulness of early renewal in a country going through the first paces of emancipation.

The war was also something else, a reminder that conflict in Lebanon is often part of a longer train of events. For what happened in 2006, at least as far as I could see, could only be fully understood in the context of an earlier war, that of the summer of 1982, when Israel invaded Lebanon to expel the Palestinian Liberation Organization. It was 1982 that had led to the creation of Hezbollah, shaping where we stood twenty-four years later; it was also a war that had fundamentally altered political relations in Lebanon for the worse, subsequently dividing the society for a long time; and it was a war of transcendent ambition, at the center of which stood a man, Bashir Gemayel, who thought he could use the Israeli invasion to reorder to his liking a Lebanese sectarian system for which he had little tolerance. Yet Gemayel only foreshadowed another figure, both similar and dissimilar: Hassan Nasrallah, Hezbollah's secretary-general, a son of the 1982 invasion, whose war in 2006 would, similarly, result from his impatience with the rules of the sectarian order, and who would not flinch in pushing that order, and the Lebanese in general, toward the precipice. Both men, in their disdain for Lebanon's past—at least that part of it clashing with their preferences for the future—demonstrated how illiberal too much yearning for revolution could be.

More personally, as I watched the 2006 war, I found myself repeatedly carried back to 1982, though my experiences were very different during each conflict. Nineteen eighty-two was my most durable memory of the nearness of the abyss in Lebanon. For many years, the year metaphorically bisected my own consciousness. There was before '82 and after, and for too long what came after often seemed only to have meaning, or usually no meaning at all, in the shadow of that summer and the wild feelings it released. Revulsion for what had taken place was tinted with almost exuberant incredulity at having made it through something so malignantly sweeping. Yet here we all were in 2006, once again imprisoned without warning in a new cycle of destruction.

On July 12, 2006, Hezbollah abducted two Israeli soldiers on the Israeli side of the border with Lebanon, in an operation that led to the death of three others and the injury of two more. The Israelis then suffered five more fatalities as they tried to save the abducted soldiers, then tried to save the soldiers killed trying to save the abducted soldiers. You could add the latter two to the blood tally, as they were almost certainly killed while or shortly after being captured. This rapid multiplication of bodies put Israel's government in bad humor, sharpened by an earlier abduction near Gaza of another soldier, Gilad Shalit, by Hamas. The next morning, on July 13, Israeli aircraft bombed the runways of the Beirut airport and began a blockade of Lebanon's seaports and most border crossings. Israel's armed forces, most of all its air force, hit targets throughout Lebanon, principally in Shiite-majority areas controlled by Hezbollah. The latest Lebanon war had begun, and it would last for thirty-three days, leaving over 1,200 people dead and turning hundreds of thousands more into refugees, living in schools, parks, public facilities, and the homes of other people.

As the conflict escalated, I was contacted by an American magazine to write a piece about what was going on. The editors had had the reflex of wanting to examine the war in the larger perspective of what life was like after the successful revolt against Syria the year before—a story about the rise and fall of hope among the Lebanese, who had believed their country was moving forward, however tentatively, as one wrote me. The way he formulated the argument was precisely how many Lebanese, including me, were characterizing their own predicament. Certainly, there were things unmentioned in that straightforward narrative. The widening rifts between those once united in the emancipation movement, particularly during and after the 2005 elections, a succession of unexplained bomb attacks, and the assassination or attempted assassination of journalists and politicians had already lowered our expectations months earlier. But as I looked back at what we had been through and were going through, the shades disappeared. There had been a moment of hope then and now there was carnage, and whichever way I turned things, the outcome of this war between Israel and Hezbollah had a very good chance of becoming a devastating blow to the Independence Intifada's accomplishments. I had never believed in the possibility of a revolution in 2005, but what I was witnessing around me had all the makings of a counterrevolution—an effort by Hezbollah to use the conflict with Israel to regain what the party had lost after its setbacks the previous year, and what Syria had lost.

Hezbollah would insist that its abduction of the Israeli soldiers was meant to secure the release of Lebanese prisoners held in Israeli jails, a pledge Hassan Nasrallah had earlier made and that the faithful later referred to as his "sincere promise." Among the prisoners was one Samir Quntar, the "dean of the prisoners" for having been imprisoned in 1979 after a military operation in northern Israel during which he had killed a child. That promise was part of Hezbollah's abduction plan, no doubt, and much later those affiliated with the party would still insist the only part of it. However, there were domestic and regional circumstances that made its timing more comprehensible. Lebanese leaders were then preparing for a new round of what was known as the "national dialogue," an effort by the politicians to come to an agreement on a host of issues over which they had differed after the convulsions of the previous year. The most divisive topic of discussion was the future of Hezbollah's weapons, which the anti-Syrian majority, now known as the March 14 coalition, wanted the party to surrender to the state.

In his turn, Nasrallah intended to push the state into adopting what he called a "defense strategy." His idea was to place "resistance" against Israel, but also against other perceived enemies such as the United States, at the heart of the state's concerns, with Hezbollah as the vanguard force advancing that agenda. By doing so, Nasrallah hoped to alter the context of the debate over weapons. If Lebanon became "a state of resistance," then there was no need to disarm Hezbollah, since the party was the highest personification of resistance. March 14 saw the offer for the trap that it was: a scheme to legitimize the unrestricted existence of an armed Hezbollah state in the midst of a less cohesive Lebanese state, which would thus see its tentative sovereignty aborted. However, Nasrallah was aware of the difficulties in his proposal. That's very likely why the capture of the Israeli soldiers was attempted when it was. The dialogue was about to address Hezbollah's arms in a forthcoming meeting, and Nasrallah must have calculated that a stirring accomplishment against Israel would strengthen his hand in the bargaining with the other politicians, even as he gave his dialogue partners assurances that there would be no conflict in Lebanon that summer.

Then there was the region. The Syrian president, Bashar al-Assad, had not swallowed his Lebanon setback in 2005, and the continuation of killings and bombings in the country was proof of this. In Iran, Mahmoud Ahmadinejad had been elected president in August 2005 and made hostility toward Israel and the United States much more a centerpiece of state policy than his predecessor had. In Iraq the Americans had successfully overseen a pair of elections in January and December 2005, but they were also losing ground to a mounting insurgency. And in January 2006, Hamas won the Palestinian legislative elections, before emerging as the most powerful force in Gaza. The seizing of Shalit just two weeks before the start of the Lebanon war, combined with Hezbollah's actions on July 12, created the impression that Israel was facing determined armed Islamists on two fronts. The final decision to capture Israelis from Lebanon was likely taken by Nasrallah himself. However, the secretary-general, a careful assessor of what the Soviet Union once called the correlation of forces, surely calculated in relation to the developments taking place around the Middle East. The abductions were there to put Nasrallah's Lebanese adversaries on the defensive and by extension bolster Iran's and Syria's interests against those of the Bush administration, which was backing the March 14 coalition. They also raised the heat on Israel at a time when Hamas was doing the same, to prove that the armed struggle was making headway. Nasrallah acted with the knowledge that Iran and Syria would be behind him whatever the outcome, and that any confrontation with Israel from Lebanon would be a convenient reminder that Iran effectively bordered Israel's north, whereas Israel was thousands of miles away from Iran.

When the 2006 war started, I was prompted to again pick up a book that I had first read during Israel's 1982 siege of Beirut, a now largely forgotten work by a Pole, Jan Karski, its title *Story of a Secret State.* It would help shape many of my thoughts on war and mass killing. During World War II, Karski had been an envoy of Poland's London-based government-in-exile to the resistance at home. He described the collapse of Poland, below an opening line written in sardonic contrast: "On the night of August 23, 1939, I attended a particularly gay party." Karski was later smuggled by the Jewish Bund into the Warsaw Ghetto so that he could report to the outside world on the atrocities going on there. As I read the book by candlelight for the first time in 1982, at the start of three months of a relentless siege and systematic bombardment, without any running water, electricity, or fresh food—the "Arab Stalingrad" as a Palestinian leader put it—I saw around me disintegration similar to what Karski had described. Beirut was not Poland or the Warsaw Ghetto, but people were people, many of them were being killed, and I read the book, quite unoriginally, and quite encouragingly, as an account of how people could win out against a nightmare. Yet Karski would later show that his nightmare had not ended. When he was interviewed by the French director Claude Lanzmann for his film on the Holocaust, *Shoah*, he would supply a dramatic highlight of the nine-hour marathon by repeatedly interrupting his on-camera interview because he could no longer continue describing what he had witnessed in the ghetto. When I later moved to Washington, I knew that Karski lived in the city and promised myself to look him up to thank him for his very useful book that had given me much to think about at a difficult moment. One evening I was returning by taxi from the airport and it began to rain. Two blocks from my home a man stepped out onto the curb waving at the car, anxious to escape the downpour. The driver sped on, and I recognized Karski. I stared, failing to tell the driver to stop. Maybe I wasn't prepared for the fact that that bullet of gratitude fired off in Beirut in the summer of 1982 would somehow hit less than a decade later at the corner of Connecticut Avenue and Porter Street NW. Or maybe I was not good at keeping my promises. But I never did thank Karski, regret my lethargy still, and will always regard his book as one of the finer expressions of how war rips the narrow membrane separating normality from an annihilatory void, and what a terrible mess is left to clean up when that happens.

There was no doubt in my mind on July 13, 2006, that Hassan Nasrallah had led us into such a void. With that indictment came an irony stretching back to 1982. Israel at the time had entered Lebanon to be rid of the armed Palestinian organizations, but it had also done so to bring a friendly president to power in Beirut. He was Bashir Gemayel, the head of the Christian Lebanese Forces militia—the same Lebanese Forces later led by Elie Hobeiqa, then by Samir Geagea—and Bashir's dream was to re-create a country in which Christians were again strong, in a state that was strong, with a large and strong army, to replace the Lebanon that had gone to pieces in 1975 when the civil war started. He had no great liking for Lebanon's sectarian contract, the National Pact of 1943, which he saw as a main cause of the country's weakness, with its reliance on encumbering balance. Yet Bashir was an anachronism. Even as he was trying to revive Christian fortunes, he couldn't quite see that it was the Shiites who had been roused by Israel, whose numbers were larger than Christian numbers, whose lands were occupied, and whose youths would soon mobilize against the occupation. Bashir, so crucial in bringing about the summer 1982 war with Israel, had helped release the Shiite genie from its bottle. He had sought to use the dynamics of conflict to reshape a Lebanese system for which he had no esteem, and in doing this he only softened it up for another group with little esteem for the system, one that historically had little say in the system. In acting as he did, Bashir displayed the same disdain that Hassan Nasrallah later would—Nasrallah, an outgrowth of Bashir's 1982 war, albeit against Bashir, eventually its most celebrated inheritor.

Bashir Gemayel and Hassan Nasrallah, so unalike, were yet so intimately tied together in the larger rhythms of Lebanese politics through their ways and wars—charismatic leaders whose views about Lebanon could only collide with the country's visceral pluralism.

Short and squat, a charging bull, Bashir was a linear politician in a country of contrapuntal ones. From the moment during the late 1970s when he had taken control of the Lebanese Forces, an amalgam of Christian armed groups that Bashir consolidated through violence or persuasion under his sole command, his ascendancy had followed a consistent path of accumulating power and eliminating or marginalizing all challengers. To this day he remains a hero to the Christians, a rare object of unity in a fragmented community, a fleeting, mental antidote to Christian decline. As Samir Kassir, not an admirer, once put it, "He was the first to rationalize the militarization of a segment of Lebanese society. . . . Bashir was an archetype for others to imitate; but he was poorly imitated." That is until Nasrallah, another linear politician, another aspirant to complete control over his community, later rationalized the militarization of the Shiites in a way the Lebanese forces never managed with the Christians. In August 1980, a month after Bashir had overcome a rival militia, establishing his total dominance in Christian streets, he and an entourage of men, including a senior army officer who happened to be then Lieutenant Colonel Michel Aoun, began planning to make him president within a two-year period. The plan came to fruition when Bashir, who had developed a close alliance with Israel, was elected on August 23, 1982, under Israeli guns. He was only thirty-four. And there he would remain. Three weeks later he was assassinated at one of his party's offices in eastern Beirut by a member of a pro-Syrian group. A prominent Lebanese politician later described to me how a senior Syrian military official called him that evening to break the news. "We had trouble getting him," the Syrian said.

In 1977, as a teenager, I had met Bashir in that same building, and his parting gifts to me were a signed photograph and an unexploded 120-mm mortar shell with stenciled Hebrew writing on it—a strange item to give a fourteen-year-old, and not particularly easy to smuggle into our apartment in a Muslim-majority neighborhood controlled by Bashir's enemies. The only other time I saw him, he was president-elect and had driven up to a building where I was staying in the mountains to meet with a parliamentarian living there. As I remember it, his car, which he drove himself, was an off-the-rack Honda, not the most secure vehicle for someone with many enemies. Bashir had the ways of a populist leader, his Arabic was colloquial, free of the evasive embroidery of most other politicians (in much the same way that Hassan Nasrallah's is), and his voice had the fervent ring of a teenager's. Yet he could be merciless when pursuing his objectives. Bashir and his followers were Christian nationalists impatient with the gesticulations of sectarian compromise. In a meeting shortly before his assassination with several of those who had eased his way to the presidency, Bashir repeated his intentions: He would respect coexistence with the Muslims, and added, "We can no longer govern with the men who were in power before 1975, or with the 1943 mentality. . . . A strong state for me is a state that is capable of protecting the Christian identity and guaranteeing the equality of all Lebanese. I am the president of the state and the leader of the nation. That is the real revolution. Without this revolution the war in Lebanon will have been in vain."

Picking through those words, you could see another of those revolts against a father, this time against Pierre Gemayel, Bashir's father, the leader of what was once the most powerful Christian political-military party, the Kataeb. The Lebanese Forces grew out of the Kataeb and was Bashir's instrument to transgress his father and his organization. His remarks to the comrades showed he was taking his private insurgency further than ever, because Pierre Gemayel was very much a man in power before 1975, and very much a man with the 1943 mentality, that of the National Pact. Bashir's revolt was also, perhaps, directed against his older brother Amin, a man so dripping with counterpoint that it is often difficult to get the point. Amin would be elected president after Bashir was assassinated, but he would prefer the circumlocutory political habits that his late brother, and Bashir's thwarted partisans, so detested—minus the political center of gravity, and the convictions, that would have prompted him to reform the pact of 1943 or, conversely, implement his brother's agenda.

Like Bashir Gemayel in 1982, Hassan Nasrallah in 2006 would enter into a war of hubris. But Nasrallah's war was also one of miscalculation, which he would spend a month trying to reverse, and from his success in doing so he would appear to bear out his own revolutionary destiny, or at least that of his party, whose humble servant he was. The lesson to all those who looked upon the formula of 1943 with sympathy was that sectarian compromise allowed less room for destructive vanity than the methods of the men of providence. In his book *Figures de Proue*, written in 1949, the French historian René Grousset described these dynamics best, against the backdrop of a Europe just emerging from the traumas of World War II, a consequence of Franco-German enmity: "If Europe in the end lost its place in the world, that's perhaps because for a century and a half, in periods decisive for its destiny, at the crossing of the roads, the land of Descartes and the land of Kant were abandoned to visionaries."

Hassan Nasrallah, too, has the flaws of the visionary, though his admirers usually look upon him through filters of hagiographic self-deception. Not much is known about Nasrallah other than what he has told a handful of publications over the years, which together serve as a terse official biography. All the versions present a similar story, and all leave almost everything about Nasrallah and his rise unsaid or unconfirmed.

Hassan Nasrallah was born on August 31, 1960, the eldest child of Abdel-Karim Nasrallah (none of the sources mentions his mother's name), a seller of fruits and vegetables. He grew up in the eastern Beirut shantytown of Karantina, the site of the nineteenth-century Quarantine area of the capital, later containing its slaughterhouse. During the 1960s and '70s, rural migrants settled in Beirut's eastern and southern suburbs to find work—or in the case of many Shiites to flee the insecurity in southern Lebanon, where Palestinian militants were fighting Israel. These were neighborhoods granting few favors, end stations for the destitute and marginalized, stretching in a downward loop from the Karantina, Burj Hammoud, Nabaa, Dikwaneh, all the way to the Palestinian refugee camp at Tall al-Zaatar overlooking Beirut, then south toward Shiyah, Ghobeireh, and Haret Hreik, the latter areas today Shiite strongholds. My recollection of Karantina, as we would speed by on Sunday outings, was of a wall on the highway above which we could see decaying structures, men sitting on the sidewalk outside—all unadulterated poverty. The demography of the eastern suburbs changed once the war started, as Shiites left the predominantly Christian areas or were expelled by Christian militias. Among those departing was Nasrallah's family, but also someone whose path Nasrallah would cross years later: Sayyed Muhammad Hussein Fadlallah, a cleric who for a time was described as Hezbollah's "spiritual guide." The accounts tell us that young Hassan was religious, that when others played or went to the beach, he would read Quranic texts; that he was devoted to the cleric who first mobilized the Lebanese Shiite community, Sayyed Musa al-Sadr. Nasrallah was even said to have tasted of the nectars of Martyrs Square before the war, but not those most other adolescents of his age might have sought out. Instead, he bought used books on religion from secondhand booksellers off the sidewalk.

With the start of the war, the Nasrallahs returned to their village, Bazouriyeh, in the southern Lebanese district of Tyre. Nasrallah would later tell an Iranian magazine that he became "less interested" in his village because it was "turning into an arena for the activity of intellectuals, Marxists, and especially supporters of the Lebanese Communist Party." There were almost no developed Shiite political organizations during the prewar years, and the young of the community tended, instead, to join Palestinian groups, the communists, or various Arab nationalist parties that recruited more on the basis of ideological commitment than sectarian identity. Nasrallah's aversion for "intellectuals" and "Marxists" suggested a premature suspicion of secular activism, but also of Shiite paths lying outside the confines of what Nasrallah (perhaps with expedient hindsight) considered legitimate forms of communal expression. Here were the origins of Nasrallah's totalistic approach to Hezbollah, his ambition to see the party fulfilling a role as a political, social, cultural, and religious overseer, but also, if more gradually, as virtually the exclusive representative of the Shiite community.

In the mid-1970s, however, Hezbollah was still years away. Many Shiites had gravitated to Musa al-Sadr's Movement of the Deprived, which by 1975 had established a militia known as the Amal Movement. Nasrallah joined Amal at the age of fifteen and became its representative in Bazouriyeh. Then began a new phase in Nasrallah's life. Thanks to a Shiite cleric in Tyre who gave him a letter of introduction to one of the very senior Shiite religious figures in Iraq, Sayyed Muhammad Baqir al-Sadr, Hassan was able to leave Lebanon to study in the holy city of Najaf. There he was placed under the charge of Sayyed Abbas al-Musawi, a Lebanese cleric from the village of Al-Nabi Sheet in the Beqaa Valley. Musawi became Nasrallah's teacher, friend, and in 1991, after Musawi was elected secretary-general of Hezbollah, apparently his main sponsor in the party. In 1978, Nasrallah fled Iraq, chased out by the agents of Saddam Hussein, and returned to pursue his studies in a religious school set up by Musawi in the Beqaa town of Baalbek. In recounting this experience, Nasrallah has little to say about the Israeli invasion of southern Lebanon in March 1978, which led to Israel's expanding its hold over the southern Lebanese border area. Considering the role Israel would later play in his political development, this absence is surprising. Is that because Nasrallah's attitude toward Israel was not fully formed at the time, or that many Shiites were still of two minds on the armed Palestinian groups controlling the south, for whose actions Lebanese civilians, mainly Shiites, were paying a heavy price? It's difficult to say, but Israel's invasion of Lebanon in 1982 ended Nasrallah's scholarly pursuits and began what would later become his dance of death with Israel. At the time, he was Amal's political representative in the Beqaa, but as Bashir Gemayel prepared to be elected president, Nasrallah and others more experienced than he broke with the movement because they accused the Amal leader, Nabih Berri, of seeking a compromise with Gemayel, and by extension with Israel.

Iran had, meanwhile, also entered the scene. The Iranian revolution of 1979 changed the ground rules of Shiite mobilization, announcing to the Lebanese community, as Musa al-Sadr had earlier, that there was a way out of Shiite irrelevance and that this way could be defined by an activist clergy. In August 1982, Ayatollah Ruhollah Khomeini met with Lebanese Shiite clerics and urged them to combat Israel's occupation. The arrival of Iranian Revolutionary Guards in the Beqaa at the same time helped provide an anchor for Shiite ferment. Hezbollah began taking shape, gathering individuals from a number of diverse political tendencies—the Amal Movement, the Daawa Party, the Palestinian Fatah Movement, and the Lebanese Communist Party, or more specifically the reborn Islamists among its members.

Despite his age, Nasrallah rose through Hezbollah's ranks in those years until, his sundry biographies inform us, two things of consequence happened. In early 1985 he went to Beirut as deputy to Ibrahim Amin al-Sayyed, who was appointed to take charge of the party's apparatus in the city. At the time, western Beirut had regressed to a state of nature, ruled over by gunmen, its nights a hood placed over forbidding, empty streets. Yet this relocation to the city represented a new morning for Hezbollah, coinciding with the release of its so-called Open Letter outlining its political program. Here was another case in which Beirut was a ticket to national consequence for men from the fringes, but with a twist: It was an entire movement now taking that path. Hezbollah, to gain in strength and legitimacy nationally and communally, needed to firm up its presence in the capital, and Nasrallah was one of those tasked to do this. He later took over from Sayyed, which allowed him to build ties with Hezbollah's rank and file.

And then Nasrallah asked to travel to Qom, Iran, to pursue his religious studies. Permission was granted, and the rumor at the time put this down to disagreements within the party, which Nasrallah has always denied. He didn't stay long in Iran, though something must have taken place there that advanced his career. The situation at home was deteriorating as Hezbollah and Amal entered into bitter fighting in southern Lebanon and Beirut's southern suburbs. By 1991, when Abbas al-Musawi became secretary-general, Nasrallah was elevated to implement the party's executive decisions, giving him great sway over its institutions and further strengthening his ties with cadres. And when Musawi was assassinated by the Israelis in February 1992, Nasrallah, although the youngest member of the party's supreme body, the Shura Council, and not Musawi's deputy, was named as his replacement.

As recounted this way, the story is that of a talented individual arriving from the very edges of Lebanese society to climb to the top rungs of Shiite power—Rastignac with a turban. But what are we not being told? How much can we verify? We're never told how the Iranians spotted this youthful visionary, or what the stages were in his fashioning; or who in the Iranian Revolutionary Guards or intelligence services facilitated Nasrallah's ascent, so that upon Musawi's assassination he was promoted over the head of Sheikh Naim Qassem, to this day Hezbollah's deputy secretary-general—always a bridesmaid, never a bride. We're never told much about what happened in the key years between 1982 and 1985, when "our youth, years, life and time became part of Hezbollah," as Nasrallah would explain to an interviewer. They were years of military training, recruitment, and organization, he would admit, but that tells us precious little about what his role was, and why it was Nasrallah, by no means a senior religious figure despite his desire to become one, who was later placed at the top of a political-religious-military organization. In part, this was Iran circumventing the traditional Lebanese religious hierarchy, as well as the Shiite political class, by empowering younger clerics of lesser prominence who would be more amenable to Iranian interests. The tactic was not very different than Musa al-Sadr's in the 1960s and '70s, when he promoted sometimes unimpressive Shiite clerics under his control to counterbalance more established ones not under his control; just as he used his popular base in Beirut's suburban slums to counterbalance those intellectuals and communists and other Shiites circulating outside the communal umbrella he was setting up.

And what does the scrubbed story of Nasrallah's rise really tell us about Nasrallah himself? It tells us *something*, none of it particularly surprising. We learn that he enjoys reading the biographies of Israeli leaders, for example, since it's useful to "know the enemy." However, it is a bit jarring that one of his biographical accounts, written in 1997, assures us he has just completed Ariel Sharon's memoirs, which the 2006 account in the Iranian magazine repeats verbatim. The information is there to be infinitely recycled, a decade apart. But we never learn, for example, what Nasrallah really felt when his eldest son Hadi was killed in a resistance operation in southern Lebanon in 1997, his body exposed by Israel's Lebanese militia allies for all to see. The heroic version tells us that Nasrallah was proud that his son had died a martyr, which may well be true, but there really must have been more to it than that. We don't know how the poverty that Nasrallah faced during his youth defined him or sharpened his passions and resentments. We don't know what he felt when he rode down to Martyrs Square to buy his secondhand religious books, if indeed that was what he did, but we might be pushed to ask if he allowed his eye to wander over that teeming, convulsive space, all latent desire in the effervescent lights of the movie posters and pastry shops and jewelry stalls, a space not his, but in truth not anyone's in its pursuit of more sensation and liberty. And what do these elisions and abridgments tell us about what Hassan Nasrallah thought on July 12, 2006, when he took Lebanon into a war that mortally wounded the already crippled emancipatory drive of 2005, but that also left far too many of his countrymen dead?

IT'S AN embossed photograph of Hassan Nasrallah that adorns the cover of a book on my desk titled *The Miracles of the Sincere Promise*, by Majed Nasser al-Zubaydi. The "sincere promise," as you might recall, was Nasrallah's pledge before the 2006 war to release Lebanese prisoners still being held in Israel. Over time, however, the term came to describe the 2006 war itself. But Zubaydi is less interested in the political and military aspects of the conflict than in how it relates to religion and the soul—for Hezbollah could not have achieved what it did, he writes, "without [the combatants'] faith in the [struggle] and the battle, which was the battle of Islam against unbelief, the battle of faith in its entirety against polytheism in its entirety." The book describes strange happenings, miracles, that led to what Zubaydi sees as Israel's defeat, and compares the war of 2006 to the Battle of Badr in which the prophet Muhammad defeated a superior army of Qurayshites, of unbelievers, a key stage in his rise to power.

That God and his prophet should have been deployed to handle Hezbollah's battlefield affairs was understandable; after all, this was the Party of God. But Zubaydi's book was only one of the more far-out interpretations of a war that was a maelstrom of interpretation, because the outcome could determine whether Hezbollah came out stronger or weaker. The miraculous was only slightly less present in a poll released a few days after the beginning of the fighting, when the Beirut Center for Research and Information, whose director had never hidden his sympathies for Hezbollah, published a survey showing that 87 percent of Lebanese supported Hezbollah's resistance against Israel. The figure was remarkable,

because there seemed to me to be quite a few people out there unhappy with what Nasrallah had provoked. But then these were
numbers, sacred numbers. "The words of liars/blush, but a statisti-
cian's/figures are shameless," W. H. Auden once wrote. I turned to
the poll question on the center's Web site, and what I saw was
the cause of what would become one of the most egregious examples of disinformation, conscious or not, during the month-long
conflict. The question was deceptively simple. It asked, "Do you
support the resistance's opposition to Israeli aggression against
Lebanon?" Since few Lebanese were about to openly support Israeli aggression, that 13 percent of respondents answered in the
negative was worthy of note. The hitch was the way the question
was worded, as it managed to transform a predictable answer into
a statement of approval for Hezbollah. The message made the
rounds, and foreign journalists who should have been more critical weren't, swallowing the hook whole. Lebanon loved the resistance, the statistics proved it, and the good word was beamed out
to an unquestioning world.

The truth was different, and more complicated. Nasrallah, as
he himself later acknowledged, had not expected the Israeli reaction to the abduction of its soldiers to be so ferocious. Caught between the choice of not admitting his mistake or admitting to it
and using that to denounce Israel's disproportionate response, he
chose the latter. Nor was this difficult to understand. The Israeli
bombardments created an appalling humanitarian crisis as hundreds of thousands of civilians fled areas of Shiite concentration in
southern Lebanon, in Beirut's southern suburbs, and in the Beqaa
Valley. The refugees moved to areas of Lebanon relatively safer
from the violence, mainly areas controlled by Hezbollah's political adversaries. The Lebanese displayed commendable solidarity
with the victims, even though formal and informal aid networks
were strained to the maximum. But it was equally true that the war
further divided them politically, exacerbating the polarization of
the year before, so that in the first days of the conflict a priority
of the prime minister, Fouad al-Siniora, was to manage tensions on
the ground between the different factions. If there were any doubts
about Hezbollah's 87 percent approval rating, Hassan Nasrallah

only hardened them. In an interview with Al-Jazeera a week after the war began, he chillingly declared: "If we succeed in achieving the victory . . . we will never forget all those who supported us at this stage. . . . As for those who sinned against us . . . those who made mistakes, those who let us down and those who conspired against us . . . this will be left for a day to settle accounts. We might be tolerant with them, and we might not." Nothing in that suggested broad support for the party's fight.

Without a clear plan, at least none any of us in Lebanon could discern, Israel resorted to that lowest common denominator of a tactic: compulsive bombardment. It bombed villages, particularly Shiite villages, Hezbollah-controlled neighborhoods in Beirut's suburbs, as well as Lebanese infrastructure, particularly highways and bridges, supposedly to prevent Hezbollah from rearming—a more difficult case to make when the bombs hit milk factories and television relay stations. Yet Israel was not going to release its abducted soldiers that way, nor was it going to defeat Hezbollah. That the attacks were largely carried out from the air, with Ehud Olmert's government showing no signs of preparing for a ground offensive until the final hours of the conflict, rapidly showed us that we were in a stalemate. Hezbollah fired thousands of rockets at Israel without interruption; Israel bombed Lebanon without interruption. What decisive victory could be fashioned from such a ruinous exchange?

However, the definition of victory was different for each side. Hezbollah grasped that by continuing to fire off its weapons, by showing that it had not been cowed, it could claim some sort of victory. This was a smart reading of how to play perceptions, and a necessary one. With the Shiites in the streets, Nasrallah could not add insult to their injury by displaying a faint heart, as this might have led to a violent backlash against Hezbollah for pushing the community into this mess in the first place. So Nasrallah, instead, pushed forward.

Israel, in turn, never seemed to define a clear objective in its operation. Initially, the chief of staff, Dan Halutz, promised to "turn Lebanon's clock back 20 years" if the soldiers were not released. However, the Bush administration, fearing that Israel might undermine the credibility of the Siniora government it supported, intervened to avert more widespread destruction, particularly of electricity and water stations. There was also Israeli talk of disarming Hezbollah, but the Olmert government soon saw that this was unachievable. The practical outcome was the pursuit of a blunt war of retribution against Shiites, destined to make the community recoil from war in the future. In that sense the Israelis were successful. While Hezbollah officials later insisted that the population encouraged the party to pursue "the choice of steadfastness," they also admitted there was considerable pressure on Hezbollah to resolve the humanitarian crisis; what they wouldn't say was that the party needed to resolve the crisis quickly before that defiant spirit dissipated.

From my vantage point in eastern Beirut, the war was different than what the victims were facing. We were kept awake by the Israeli jets at night; we heard the heavy bombs landing on Hezbollah's "security perimeter," the party's sanctum sanctorum in the Haret Hreik quarter of Beirut's southern suburbs, as if they were next door; we faced the power cuts and wondered where on earth Lebanon was heading. But this was nothing compared to what was happening elsewhere. Beirut's center was off-limits to Israeli bombs, we sensed, and across the street from my building a café named The Chase drew clients from all over. "We never close," a jaunty waiter told me, and though they did close, at midnight, that qualified as "never" in a mostly deserted neighborhood and capital. We momentarily had doubts as to our safety when Hezbollah hit Haifa, and knew those doubts would turn into certain danger if Tel Aviv were targeted. We also knew that whatever the dynamics of the war, unrestricted chaos was untenable for Israel and Hezbollah, unless it metastasized into broader regional chaos, which would make it untenable for everybody.

More difficult to stomach was seeing everything suddenly go to pieces, yet again, at the start of a summer when hopes had run high that Lebanon would build on the changes of the year before. It was after all "the tourist season," a notion that had over the years taken hold of the mercantile Lebanese imagination, whereby everything was somehow permissible outside the three months of summer when visitors, foreigners and Lebanese emigrants alike, flew in, spent money, and gave a resuscitative kick to an economy in perennial distress. That Lebanon's wars tended to occur in summer only reinforced the public's attachment to the idea. Now we were seeing the tourists, tens of thousands of them, fleeing the country, most of them on ships chartered by their governments since the airport was closed—fighting, crying, scratching for an exit, creating an impression among the Lebanese that once the foreign passport holders were gone, they would be left on their own. We were witnessing disintegration, and for me this was but another comment on the disintegration of what remained of the Independence Intifada. If there were still liberal spaces to be exploited, if we were to regain the initiative lost after the March 14 demonstration, if the national dialogue was to have any chance of pushing Hezbollah into a process in which the party would eventually hand in its weapons, the logic of war made that impossible.

It was no coincidence that Nasrallah, as the bombs fell, portrayed the war as an American and Israeli plot to disarm his party. It was a way of telling his domestic opponents, who had also wanted Hezbollah to disarm, who in the early days of the Israeli attacks had met at the American embassy with the U.S. secretary of state, Condoleezza Rice, that they were conspiring with the enemy. It helped little that Rice described events in Lebanon as "the birth pangs of a new Middle East." All that explained Nasrallah's threat issued on Al-Jazeera, but it also showed that the secretary-general had something more ominous on his mind: the intention to direct Shiite anger inward, against the March 14 coalition, because in so doing he could begin regaining what Hezbollah had lost politically in the post-Syrian system and deflect that anger away from the party for the rash way it had brought destruction down on the community.

Hezbollah was a victim of its own strengths. As the war began, there were those in March 14 who did not hide their hope that the party's power would be degraded. Nasrallah's comments to Al-Jazeera had not come out of the blue. One senior March 14 politician told me, "Nasrallah may emerge from the conflict with Israel stronger. To be cynical, for things to get better he must be

weakened further." That only echoed a more pervasive popular antagonism toward the party in some quarters, even as Shiite refugees
were viewed with sympathy. The contradictions were beside the
point. Hezbollah had led an entire country into a war, was strong
enough militarily to reject all calls from within Lebanon, and without, to disarm, and had a year before sided publicly with Syria after the murder of Rafiq al-Hariri. The party had created an
insurmountable problem that no one quite knew how to resolve,
so that there were those Lebanese willing to let Israel resolve the
problem for them, except that Israel didn't have the slightest idea
about what to do with Hezbollah either. Lebanon could neither
absorb a Hezbollah victory against Israel, nor a Hezbollah defeat.
A victory would reverse the gains achieved by the party's rivals
in 2005; a defeat would be felt by Shiites as that of their entire
community. Either outcome was certain to destabilize the political
system.

The war of 2006 took everybody by surprise, Hezbollah and Israel above all. It was a war of total improvisation. That is what
made it so stinging, but also so difficult to get a hold of. And just
as we were bracing ourselves for a longer conflict, it suddenly
ended, the killing aborted as abruptly as normalcy had been a
month earlier. Here was a war without sharp contours, compen-
sated for through higher levels of unfocused ferocity. However,
two men saw through the uncertainty and kept their head. As it
happened, they were on opposite sides.

The first was the prime minister, Fouad al-Siniora, for whom
the war was an opportunity to contain Hezbollah. Siniora had
been Rafiq al-Hariri's near-permanent finance tsar—like him, a son
of Sidon. All rounded angles and winks and nods as befitting a
man of the urban marketplace, unflappable, the former banker was
a natural choice as prime minister following the controversial elections of 2005. And yet I still remember how, with an absent look
and his hands in his pockets, Siniora seemed (and doubtless was
not) an afterthought among the mourners circulating through the
living rooms of Hariri's home on the night of his assassination. He
embodied a particular type of Lebanese Sunni, a believer in the
idea that Lebanon's depth lay in the Arab world, the conservative

Sunni Arab world. He saw himself as a quintessential Arabist politically and culturally, but an Arabism shorn of the radicalism of yesteryear, of any renovatory yearning; his Arabism was that of the courts and presidential palaces, with their old men, wedding cake furniture, and sealed windows, an Arabism of ornate compromises and weighty silences, of putrefying immobility.

But Siniora's natural suppleness did not translate into timidity or cowardice in the face of Hezbollah. He became the natural rival of the party in the summer of 2006, as the Sunni Arab regimes reacted with trepidation toward what they called Hezbollah's "adventurism" in starting a war. Siniora picked up their standard and presented a seven-point plan to fill the diplomatic vacuum. The plan had three items of particular significance: the dispatching of the Lebanese army to southern Lebanon, until then under Hezbollah's absolute control; the expansion of the United Nations force already present in the south, along with a toughening of its mandate so that it could bolster the army's efforts; and a return to the 1949 Armistice Agreement with Israel, as a way of avoiding future conflict in the border area. Siniora was rewarded for his efforts by an Arab League foreign ministers' meeting in Beirut in the midst of the blockade, which officially supported his plan. Here were the Sunni Arab regimes hitting back against Hezbollah, and more particularly against its sponsor, Shiite Iran, endorsing a formula that would limit Hezbollah's margin of maneuver. But the gathering was memorable for two other reasons: the hasty departure of Syria's foreign minister when he saw that his colleagues refused to adopt a Syrian position more favorable to Hezbollah; and Siniora's sobbing during his speech in the middle of a phrase defending Lebanon's Arab bona fides. That so insipid a passage should have brought on such emotion showed what the prime minister was all about—even more so if the tears were calculated. Hassan Nasrallah would later express his distaste for that moment, a visceral distaste betraying his understanding of what it meant in the context of the Sunni-Shiite standoff. "Tears don't liberate [land]," the secretary-general told a cheering audience. In an interview with me, Siniora offered this response: "[T]he impact of those tears on all the Arab world was greater than a thousand rockets fired on Israel."

Siniora's plan ultimately had major influence on a U.N. resolution—Resolution 1701—being prepared by the Security Council, and Hezbollah, with hundreds of thousands of Shiite civilians still in limbo, was forced to vote in favor of it in the cabinet. The party's leaders would never forgive Siniora for having outmaneuvered them, for having helped create an international framework limiting Hezbollah's freedom of action in southern Lebanon and restoring the army's presence there. But the other man who would keep his head during the 2006 war, Hassan Nasrallah, would take his revenge in a different way. When no one was looking, he declared victory, and the Shiite community, ravaged and demoralized, would declare victory with him. It was an odd outcome indeed, for most other Lebanese, ravaged and demoralized themselves, hardly sensed the zephyrs of victory. But Nasrallah had the passion of the Shiites behind him, and he had the guns. It was more than a victory, it was a "divine victory," Nasrallah would repeat again and again, whether we agreed with him or not. Everything about Hezbollah and its place in Lebanese society could be understood from that single, persevering claim.

If anyone can speak to the Shiite passion for Hezbollah, it is Luqman Slim, a Shiite activist whose home is only a stone's throw away from Hezbollah's security perimeter, demolished by Israeli bombs in 2006. But Slim is no friend of the party. He's the kind of person whom Hezbollah's critics, particularly those in foreign embassies, invite to their receptions to show there is a liberal Shiite alternative to the party. We first met at a café in Beirut's downtown area in 2005, when we and others were invited to chat with then Senator Joseph Biden. What makes Slim interesting is something else, intriguing for a former communist hostile to sectarianism. Today, Slim sees Shiite sectarianism as a reality to be faced head-on. He argues, "Let me take advantage of my Shiite-ness to be more effective in what I think will preserve Lebanese diversity and openness . . . and break the political monopoly of Hezbollah." This he has partly tried to do by publishing works on the Shiites by Shiites, the idea being to present a different reading of the community than Hezbollah's.

Slim's notion of reforming sectarianism by working through

the sectarian system itself is an approach that accepts the need to adapt to Lebanon's social reality in order to effect change, as opposed to falling back on the elegant utopianism of refusing to see sectarianism as anything but an aberration. However, for Slim, given his ideological antecedents, this conversion must have been difficult, a consequence of his perception that when it comes to pulling the strings of sectarianism, Hezbollah holds a decisive advantage. Slim was in the United States when the 2006 war started. He managed to fly back to Lebanon via Cyprus aboard a shuttling French military helicopter and returned to Haret Hreik. By then his residence had lost all its doors and windows because of the bombings. But did this make Hezbollah any less hostile toward him? "No," he responded. "In fact, they placed me on a 'dishonor list' during the war." Still, he remembered, neighborhood boys who sympathized with the party would come to his house to kill time and smoke water pipes.

Slim is a distillation of everything Hezbollah and Hassan Nasrallah have always disliked. He was once a leftist, is secular, and his father had leaned toward Bashir Gemayel. Yet what makes Slim uniquely odious to the party is that he and his family are of the house, of Haret Hreik, and were before Hezbollah was. The party can't expel him and his family from the quarter, so it makes life difficult for them. Shortly before I interviewed Slim, Hezbollah used its supporters to detain the car of the then French ambassador's wife (herself a Lebanese Shiite) after she had visited Slim's office. It was a way of saying that in the southern suburbs one talked only to Hezbollah. "A lot of Lebanese don't dare reject the blackmail Hezbollah is exerting on them under the pretext of resisting Israel," Slim noted. However, the party was a success story, I responded, why should Shiites revolt against it? He replied, "Hezbollah is a success story but a bad example of a success story. . . . Like many totalitarian parties it has managed to internalize fear in others; it has moved its oppression to the minds."

Whether Hezbollah can truly become totalitarian or not will be a function of how much Shiites continue to accept its authority. The community is traditionally pluralistic in its social and geographical makeup, in the formless structure of its religious hierarchy, a hierarchy without any hard and fast hierarchy, and in the community's intellectual diversity and cosmopolitanism, the result of considerable emigration over the generations. In its aspirations, however, Hezbollah is without question *totalistic*, an aspiration that being God's party only reinforces. As Nasrallah has so often insisted, Hezbollah is a political, social, cultural, and religious movement, but also, as the Lebanese scholar Ahmad Nizar Hamzeh has written, it "is first and foremost a *jihadi* movement that engages in politics, and not a political party that conducts jihad." The essence of Hezbollah is struggle, armed struggle, belying the arguments of those who believe the party can recycle itself into a political movement. Without the armed struggle, without weapons, Hezbollah could not exist, losing its very definition and its value as an organization working on Iran's behalf. And so, the party relies on the perpetuation of conflict as its life force, with its social and religious institutions, its schools and hospitals, even its participation in the workings of the state, serving as multiple walls within Lebanese society and the Shiite community to defend that option and the party's liberty to pursue it. Ian Buruma and Avishai Margalit, in their essay *Occidentalism*, have well described the interplay between violence and identity among groups, such as Hezbollah, who deem Western liberal democracy, or its lesser imitators (not least Lebanon's pluralistic system of sectarian compromise) to be corrupt and unheroic: "War is needed as a forge for a younger, purer, more vigorous community. Rebirth can come only from destruction and human sacrifice."

At no time was the power of this message more evident to Shiites, and even non-Shiites, than when Hezbollah compelled the Israelis to withdraw from southern Lebanon in 2000, in what was, that time, a far more palpable victory. However, the moment posed existential problems for the party, since "the resistance" risked being declared redundant. Until 2005, it was mainly Syria that protected Hezbollah's weapons, largely because the party's sporadic attacks on Israeli positions in a small slither of Lebanese land that supposedly remains occupied by Israel (though it is not recognized as Lebanese by the United Nations) also benefited the regime in Damascus, which saw Lebanon as a useful military pressure point on Israel in its negotiations over the future of the Israeli-occupied Golan Heights. After 2005, when the March 14 forces began pushing for Hezbollah to surrender its weaponry, the party's attitude became more defensive. As one Hezbollah official told me, "Hezbollah has fears and sensitivities with respect to Israel, and there are those who are afraid of Hezbollah's weapons. We need to find a middle ground."

The only problem is that no middle ground seems possible given how Hezbollah's role has changed since 2000. From a largely national movement initially focused on liberating occupied land, Hezbollah transformed itself into a more broadly defined "resistance" movement with regional ambitions in its support of armed groups everywhere—such as Hamas in the Palestinian areas or the Mahdi Army in Iraq—one which had to stay armed for as long as Israel endangered Lebanon. Yet as Israel, by its very existence, endangers Lebanon as far as Hezbollah is concerned, the party has effectively redefined the threat as open-ended, requiring the party's indefinite militarization. This is a convenient way for Hezbollah to retain, behind a pretense of national self-defense, a capacity to function in the Middle East on behalf of its regional sponsors and partners; but it also contains a self-perpetuating logic: If Hezbollah remains armed, Israel will continue to view the party as a threat, and will respond by continuing to threaten Lebanon, which will justify Hezbollah's retaining its weapons.

Among those who follow Hezbollah's fortunes, some tend to frown whenever its Iranian ties are emphasized. The reason is that this statement of the obvious somehow seems to detract from the essential authenticity of the party as a Lebanese phenomenon, and navigates too closely to what Hezbollah's enemies in the West say. Yet Hezbollah is without embarrassment a creation and an appendage of the Iranian regime, of its supreme leader and its security and intelligence apparatus. However, Iran has also, and quite skillfully, anchored the party, or allowed it to anchor itself, in the consciousness of Lebanese Shiite society and in a symbolism of communal adversity tailored to Lebanese realities. At the heart of this is the historical marginalization of Lebanese Shiites, their secondary status in the first four decades of post-Independence Leba-

non, their endemic poverty until not so long ago. From that sense
of alienation, from its harping on Shiite disaffection, Hezbollah
was able throughout the 1990s to build up its power base, a task
made easier by its liberation of the south from Israel, the vast social assistance and educational machinery at its disposal, and the
rising lack of credibility of the rival Shiite leadership in Amal.
However, the darker side of that populist strategy has been that
Hezbollah has further isolated Shiites from Lebanese society—a
psychological isolation from Lebanese history itself, from its political and sectarian system, which the party never ceases to condemn
even as it embodies its worst aspects: communal partisanship and
minority paranoia; but also physical isolation, through the party's
tight hold over Shiite-majority areas substantially autonomous
from the state's control in Beirut's southern suburbs, much of
south Lebanon, and the northern and western Beqaa Valley.

However, Hezbollah remains what it is in Shiite society, and
was able to benefit from this during the 2006 war, because in the
end it is perceived by many of its coreligionists as *morally* just. At
the core of this perceived moral goodness is the party's supposed
reversal of the Shiites' dismal history, its charitable works, its cour-
age in battle, the fact that for once the community is strong thanks
to Hezbollah's weapons, while other communities feel weaker in
consequence. There is malicious pleasure at work here, but also after 2005 a sense of regional empowerment thanks to the assertive-
ness of Iran and the Shiite rise in Iraq, to which, ironically, the
United States was a midwife. There is also the numbing recurrence
in Hezbollah's political culture of the ideal of martyrdom—
scaffolding for its sense of virtuousness, combining both valor
and suffering—building on the theme of martyrdom so central in
Shiite history. Yet as Paul Berman noted in his book *Terror and
Liberalism*, a cult of death can be the flip side to an ideal of total
submission, "submission to the kind of authority that liberal civi-
lization had slowly undermined . . . the ideal of the one, instead
of the many. The ideal of something godlike. The total state, the
total doctrine, the total movement." That helps explain how novel
a phenomenon Hezbollah is, a total movement in the least totalistic of Arab societies, and how those who describe the party as a

righter of historical wrongs inflicted on Shiites know only half the story.

One of the consequences of this, however, is that while Hezbollah dominates the Shiites, it is mistrusted by a significant portion of the Shiite intelligentsia. Not surprisingly, many of these opponents come from the political left and honed their political consciousness and instincts, no differently than Musa al-Sadr or Hezbollah did, in opposition to Lebanon's sectarian system. And yet quite a few of them subsequently came to accept the benefits of this system, even if they did not embrace sectarianism itself, as allowing paradoxically liberal diversity in their country and an alternative to Hezbollah's hegemony over Shiite minds and lives, their own lives. Hezbollah has filled a yawning gap left by the weak Lebanese state, but it has done so by fortifying the ideal of communal submission among Shiites and turning the Lebanese political system into an object of derision. As a consequence, after 2005 Hezbollah came to embody an antistate, blocking Lebanon's emergence toward some sort of normalcy once the Syrians withdrew.

The buttons Hezbollah presses may seem little different than those Musa al-Sadr pressed decades ago, when he first gave the Shiites a sense that their destiny was not perennial quietude. Both Amal and Hezbollah have fought to claim Musa al-Sadr's legacy, albeit in different ways—his use of social activism as a cornerstone of a Shiite political revival; his spanning of Shiite networks in Iran and Iraq; his resort to the mobilizing imagery of Arab and Palestinian nationalism; even his close ties to Syria's Alawite regime. But with Hezbollah there is an essential difference. Musa al-Sadr was not a man who pursued the ideal of submission, who had the means to impose the total movement (even if he might have had the urge), who reveled in his compliance with the total idea. He was not someone likely to tell a crowd, as Nasrallah did on May 26, 2008: "I am proud to be an individual in the party of *wilayat al-faquih*," a concept often translated as the Guardianship of the Jurist, most prominently associated with Ayatollah Khomeini and defining the nature of Iranian leadership, whereby the supreme religious leader, the jurist, also holds supreme temporal power. Here was Nasrallah candidly expressing his absolute loyalty, and Hezbollah's, to Ayatollah Ali Khamenei, Khomeini's successor as the absolute leader of Iran.

VERY EARLY in the morning on August 14, 2006, Luqman Slim left his house in Haret Hreik to see what was happening in the neighborhood. What he was about to witness was Hassan Nasrallah's rejoinder to Fouad al-Siniora. A cease-fire was to take effect at 8 A.M., and Slim noticed that already Hezbollah had put up posters declaring victory. More revealing, plastic tables and chairs had been placed at street crossings or wherever else people might gather, to show that Hezbollah was preparing to listen. There was much to listen to. The month-long war had ended and the party was about to absorb the Shiite response. A massive inflow of funds to compensate the victims, much of it Iranian, allowed Hezbollah to neutralize any potential anger early on, as did the promises of financial pledges from many outside states. Ali Fayyad, the director of the Hezbollah-affiliated Consultative Center for Studies and Documentation, would later tell me that "the war, which I don't want to defend, led to inflows larger than what was lost during the war." Perhaps, but Fayyad had an interest in playing down the losses, to underline that Hezbollah was less blameworthy than its critics suggested. A report his center released in November 2006 calculated losses from the war at some $500 million, between damages to business establishments and firms, vehicles, and agriculture. However, the study did not calculate indirect losses, environmental harm, infrastructure losses, damage to buildings, and long-term impact on economic confidence. That somehow seemed to be missing the point.

The point was that the Shiites had suffered terribly, as had many Lebanese, and the economy had taken a severe hit that could only further exacerbate years of slow growth rates and a mounting public debt. But what the war really told us was that Hezbollah's vision was irreconcilable with the vision of much of Lebanese society, and that included people who were politically on the same side as Hezbollah, without necessarily sharing its way of seeing the world. During the 1990s, Walid Jumblatt had neatly encapsulated this duality when he wondered whether Lebanon would become Hanoi or Hong Kong. That is, would it seek to become an international symbol of militancy and armed struggle, as represented by Hezbollah, or would it opt for the path laid out by Rafiq al-Hariri, who had sought to make the country a bastion of liberal capitalism and ecumenical permissiveness—a path recreating, often synthetically, an idealized Lebanon of the past? The enthusiasts of the 2005 Independence Intifada, for all their later divisions and shifting loyalties, more or less came down on Hariri's side. However, the 2006 war showed that one segment of Lebanese society disagreed—or more precisely that the party leading it disagreed, since when one looked closely, Shiites could be just as taken up by Hong Kong as anybody else, but were loath to betray their most powerful communal representative by overstating the point.

More intriguing was how Hezbollah's vision, Hanoi, was picked up on by quite a few Lebanese of the left, but also by individuals of the political left internationally who had the revolutionary itch, who were motivated, variously, by anti-Americanism, hostility toward Israel, or an abiding distaste for globalization. As the Hanoi-versus-Hong Kong dichotomy played out in their mind, the outcome very often was an embrace of Hezbollah's glorification of violence and a defense of its demand for total allegiance in the heat of battle.

Take the statement released in July 2006 in response to the Lebanon war and signed by nearly 450 intellectuals and academics, many of them Lebanese. The signatories expressed their "conscious support" for Hezbollah's resistance against Israel, "as it wages a war in defense of our sovereignty and independence, a war to release Lebanese imprisoned in Israel, a war to safeguard the dignity of the Lebanese and Arab people." They rejected the argument that Hezbollah had provided a pretext for the Israeli onslaught, since "the recent Israeli aggression is the latest in a long series extending back to the founding of the Zionist state and motivated by both historical ambitions vis-à-vis Lebanese territory and waters and by a racist supremacist ideology that denigrates the indigenous population, their culture, and their very existence." The statement condemned American support for Israel and affirmed the signatories' "utter rejection of the Lebanese government's decision to 'not adopt' the Lebanese Resistance operation, thereby stripping the Resistance of political credibility before the adversarial international powers. . . ." This referred to the Siniora government's refusal to endorse the abduction of the Israeli soldiers, of which it had not been notified beforehand. The statement also called upon the government to embrace the resistance "in various ways," and it concluded that "resistance is an intellectual act par excellence . . . [and] cultural and critical activity [is] an integral part of Lebanese national resistance, indeed of resistance to injustice anywhere in the world."

This was as clear a pronouncement on the desirability of the Hanoi option as Hezbollah was ever going to get; and as clear a denunciation of the vision of a Lebanese state averting war to pursue profit that defenders of the Hong Kong alternative were going to hear. It was difficult to convince many Lebanese that resistance was an intellectual act; after all, Israel and Hezbollah were not bombing each other with ideas. But there was something more disquieting at play here, which undermined the very notion of what ideas, and for that matter the intellectuals behind them, were supposed to represent. The thought process of the signatories, in its derogatory censure of any alternative path in Lebanon, was markedly illiberal, indifferent to the complex array of opinions characterizing the Lebanese consensus. This only showed the extent to which Hezbollah's logic led down a path to uniformity of opinion, the ideal of the one instead of the many.

Not surprisingly perhaps, it took a foreigner to express Hanoi best, though unintentionally, on the media outlet of the most forceful defenders of the Hong Kong vision. In early 2008, the Hariri-owned Future Television station interviewed the American academic Norman Finkelstein, who had written and commented extensively on the Palestinian-Israeli conflict. On his first trip to Lebanon in December 2001, Finkelstein had made a point of "publicly honoring the heroic resistance of Hezbollah to foreign occupation." In the Future interview, he spoke about the 2006 war, and remarked that "there is a fundamental principle. People have the right to defend their country from foreign occupiers . . . from invaders who are destroying their country. That to me is a very basic, elementary and uncomplicated question." Finkelstein compared Hezbollah favorably with the Soviet Red Army and the communist resistance during World War II ("it was brutal, it was ruthless"), though you had to wonder what Nasrallah made of that. Finkelstein then acknowledged that there were Lebanese who saw things differently. Armed resistance was the sole option against Israel, he maintained, "unless you choose to be [Israeli] slaves—and many people here have chosen that."

Those were fighting words. Lebanese lives and homes had been destroyed, and here was Finkelstein calling those who blamed the "resistance" for this state of affairs "slaves." But that wasn't the problem; the problem was the way in which the elevation of resistance to a fetish necessarily led to the abandonment of a universalist and humanist worldview and its replacement with categorical imperatives usually associated with the extreme right: blood, honor, solidarity, the defense of near-hallowed land. Here, too, was a show of blind faith in the service of total principle—the principle of all-embracing resistance—which meant abandoning the values of secularism, liberalism, and wariness of violence in the face of a religious, autocratic party pursuing a near-permanent armed struggle.

This jump did not surprise me. It was a natural conceptual succession when incorporating Hezbollah's mind-set, one that I had often witnessed among others in the Arab left, who had seen their ideals fall apart in a region where the fight against Israel had foundered, leaving behind despotic family-led regimes kept in place by layers of security agencies. In this astonishing exchange Finkelstein exposed better than most the intellectual path down which the party's ideas led. His was a postfact justification of Hassan Nasrallah's reckless provocation of war, the secretary-general's disregard of the likely consequences, his misreading of how Israel might retaliate; and it implicitly justified Nasrallah's refusal to consult his Lebanese partners before ordering the abductions, to even consider that they were part of the same national fabric as he—even if in the framework of a weak state allowing for pluralism. Finkelstein himself was of little importance; however, Hezbollah defended its war in much the same way the American professor did, with much the same condescension toward the rest of Lebanese society, and with the same unconcern for the wishes of those Lebanese who disagreed.

If Lebanon is a country of liberal spaces opened up by a weak state and the sectarian system's natural tendency to impose equilibrium, then Hezbollah may seem to be a giant bug in the ointment of that premise. After all, the wide margin of autonomy the party has earned may just be an extreme symptom of the weak state, with the result hardly a sturdier liberal order. That may be true if we leave aside the irony that Hezbollah consistently expresses its backing for a strong state while never mentioning that the only such state it would consent to is one that it effectively rules over. But the reality is that the party, because of its independence and its weapons, has also triggered the natural mechanisms in Lebanese society following from a desire to reimpose balance. And that's the problem. Hezbollah has managed to persuade Shiites that its disarmament would bring about the community's renewed marginalization. However, its insistence on retaining its weapons regardless of, even against, the anxieties of its countrymen has prompted its domestic adversaries to view their own struggle against Hezbollah, and alas against Shiites in general, in existential terms. Given the right circumstances, this may encourage them to arm as well, and in some ways that process has already started. The dilemma is straightforward. Either Hezbollah disarms out of respect for the national consensus, and by so doing relinquishes its reason to exist; or it refuses to do so, maintaining the Lebanese in a near-permanent state of civil dissonance, even if this is not necessarily expressed violently, without a valid national compact to unite them.

Lebanon's inability to manage that dilemma would emerge as the main source of domestic tension after the 2006 war, which left behind two Lebanons eyeing each other with suspicion. In the subsequent year and beyond, the country would remain irrevocably divided, never far from civil unrest. You could blame all sides for their miscalculations, for their frequent hypocrisy, and for their selfish pursuit of self-interest. But the essential source of destabilization was Hezbollah's view of itself, a view that could not be reconciled with even the loosest reading of the social contract governing Lebanon since Independence. This view Naim Qassem, Hezbollah's deputy secretary-general, would sum up in June 2008, when he insisted that the "resistance is not an armed group seeking the liberation of a piece of land. It is not an activity related to a circumstance that ends when its pretext ends. The resistance is a vision and a methodology, not just a military reaction." A vision and a methodology? Where was René Grousset to remind us about the damage wrought by visionaries?

With the 2006 war over, no one needed Grousset, however, to see that a party of visionaries—visionaries walking in the path of God—would refuse to sacrifice its life force to reintegrate into a Lebanese political system that its leaders despised. However, there was more to it than just Hanoi versus Hong Kong. The Shiites, no less than other Lebanese, were riddled with simultaneous and contradictory identities, and Hezbollah's world incorporated paradoxes no less than those of the other sects. The image of a Shiite Lebanon awash in turbans, chadors, and prayer beads was a caricature, one that could easily be dispelled by walking through Beirut's southern suburbs, or most Shiite communities. Secularism and religiousness, wealth and poverty, tradition and modernity, militancy and mellowness, Hanoi and Hong Kong—were present among Shiites as well, sometimes in the same families, even in the same persons. Hezbollah's genius was to draw from that diversity even as it sought to channel it and asphyxiate it with a worldview of total leadership, communal solidarity—or more accurately, communal defensiveness—a shared sense of historical oppression, admiration for human sacrifice in the battle against perceived evils, and an overbearing sense of moral self-righteousness. What Lebanon faced after the summer of 2006 would expose the dangers in all this—everything flowing from Hezbollah's conceit of having won a "divine victory" against Israel, when all we could see around us was senseless destruction.

4

Invisible City

And that blue is the sheen of a steel
It took white heats to anneal
                —Robert Conquest, "At the Rebirth of St Petersburg"

IN HIS IMPRESSIONISTIC 1972 film *Roma,* the late Italian director Federico Fellini has a scene centering on the construction of the Roman subway system. The digging opens up an underground gallery buried since ancient times, abounding with beautiful frescoes. However, as a group of characters admire the discovery, the frescoes begin to vanish because of their exposure to the air. Within minutes the apparitions are no more, dissolved mirages. Few scenes in cinema are more memorable in illustrating the evanescence of beauty.

A few years after seeing *Roma,* I happened to be in Rome to meet an old family friend who had been the architect of my great-grandmother's home in Cairo. Paolo Caccia Dominioni di Sillavengo was ninety-four at the time and had become something of a legendary figure for designing and laying out the Italian military cemetery at El Alamein, an endeavor that required him to live in the desert among the battle dead for years. However, it was his experiences in Lebanon that Caccia Dominioni described to me, particularly his building of what would become the Banco di Roma Building in Beirut's downtown area, next to parliament. In digging its foundations he had chanced on the remains of a Roman road running through the center of the ancient city. His ruins, too, would be only momentarily glimpsed, before being built over as Beirut modernized. The parallels with Fellini's film came to mind, but the message was rather different to me. What Caccia Dominioni recounted had less to do with the evanescence of beauty, though that was certainly a part of it; instead, it had everything to do with the evanescence of Beirut's identities.

In the aftermath of the summer 2006 war, Beirut would turn into a dangerous battleground for Lebanon's identities, particularly those emerging from the weeks of the Independence Intifada that the political divisions following only exacerbated. Up to the war, those differences had mostly been kept under control. Afterward, they would become more violent between the March 14 coalition and the Hezbollah-led opposition, including the followers of Michel Aoun who had participated in the anti-Syrian demonstrations of 2005, only to part with their March 14 allies over the parliamentary elections that year. The March 14-opposition rift would be consummated in a highly symbolic moment, when Hezbollah, along with its weaker partners, would descend on Beirut's old city center, the downtown area that Rafiq al-Hariri had been instrumental in rebuilding, to stage a sit-in lasting eighteen months, the intention being to bring down the government of Fouad al-Siniora, from which Shiite ministers had been withdrawn. That sequence of events, and the calculations surrounding it, would also tell us a great deal about Beirut itself, as a city and an idea—a place of resurrection through pragmatic compromise, that can be whatever you want it to be, whatever it needs to be, but which in this case failed to find any such compromise. That was because Beirut is often unable to reconcile its superimposed identities, making it an invisible city in many respects for allowing itself to often be without a durable, consensual center.

Beirut's Janus-like nature would also affect in the most fundamental way an important achievement of the Independence Intifada: the setting up of an international investigation and trial process to find the guilty in Rafiq al-Hariri's assassination and those that followed. The attempt at discovering hard truths would jar with the gelatinous ways of a city and a country where truth has always been hard to pin down. And because it was largely the Sunnis who wanted the truth and largely the Shiites, or at least their representatives allied with Syria and Iran, who had everything to lose from the truth; and because among Muslims Beirut had once been mainly a Sunni city, before Shiite migration had eroded that demographic predominance prior to and during the war—because of these realities, the currents released by the Independence Intifada would, by the end of 2006, transform themselves into the frightening prospect of Sunni-Shiite conflict. This would double as a fight over Beirut's character, a grueling fight for a city not anyone's for being everyone's.

The summer war of 2006 had been declared a "divine victory" by Hezbollah's secretary-general, Hassan Nasrallah. Yet what victory was this? Nasrallah had desperately little to show for it in terms of enhanced political power. A fortified United Nations force was now deployed in southern Lebanon alongside the Lebanese army (which Hezbollah had always tried to keep out of the south), under the mandate of U.N. Security Council Resolution 1701, making it more difficult for Hezbollah to fire on Israeli soldiers in the general border area. And while Hezbollah still controlled the south and rearmed with little difficulty thanks to weapons arriving from Syria, and through Syria sent by Iran, and while it rebuilt and expanded its military infrastructure north of the U.N. area of operations, the new situation, and the party's unwillingness to inflict new violence on a Shiite population in shock, for the moment neutralized the south as a battle zone. This was a frustrating outcome for a political-military organization whose sense of meaning derived from the perpetuation of armed struggle.

However, when it came to perceptions, Nasrallah managed to persuade his own Shiite community, as well as many Arabs delighted with seeing an Arab armed group standing up to Israel when their own governments couldn't be bothered to do so, that Hezbollah had won. Perceptions, in this case, were everything, and seemed only to be confirmed by Israeli soul-searching in which the Lebanon war was portrayed as a major setback, despite the calm imposed along Israel's northern border. There was also adroit manipulation of psychological dialectics in the secretary-general's playing the alleged victory off his community's misery and humiliation—ironically, misery and humiliation that he had triggered—before transforming this into vehemence against his adversaries, who would contest the victory. Nasrallah used that vehemence to further harden Shiite solidarity under his guidance when he picked a fight with the March 14 majority, with those whom he had accused during the July–August conflict of colluding with Israel and the United States against Hezbollah.

In late October 2006, Nasrallah declared that the opposition, which Hezbollah led and dominated, was entitled to transform its victory into a greater share of seats in the cabinet. He demanded that the March 14 coalition accept a "national unity" government in which the party and its allies held veto power. If this weren't done, Nasrallah warned, the Siniora government might face street protests in support of early parliamentary elections. Under the arcane rules of Lebanese cabinets, veto power, equivalent to holding a third of cabinet seats plus one, would have allowed Hezbollah and its partners to block key decisions they didn't like and prevent a quorum for cabinet sessions if their ministers stayed away, handing them substantial control over the governmental agenda. The March 14 majority rejected this, justifying its decision mainly on the grounds that Hezbollah intended to obstruct Lebanon's final approval of an agreement with the U.N. for the formation of a mixed Lebanese-international tribunal to indict those responsible for murdering Rafiq al-Hariri.

Nasrallah's demands, while they might have seemed valid given that he and his allies filled more than a third of the seats in parliament, represented in the context of the time no less than a coup attempt, an effort to build on the momentum of the summer war to alter the balance of power in Beirut. With a president, Émile Lahoud, and a speaker of parliament, Nabih Berri, who were close to Syria, Hezbollah's ability to shape the government's agenda would have placed the three top institutions in the state under Damascus's effective control. This would have meant a reversal of the gains of the year before, and while Hezbollah's veto power would have surely led to a watering down of the Hariri tribunal's authority, the party could have gone beyond that to influence the appointment of senior civil servants and security chiefs, and affect every other major government decision.

However, Nasrallah erred in ignoring the sectarian animosities his demands might release. Here, the secretary-general showed how little he understood the self-regulating nature of the Lebanese sectarian system. In threatening to take to the streets and impose new elections if his demands weren't met, Nasrallah abandoned the painstaking compromises the Lebanese were used to; and in wanting to dominate government decision-making, he provoked the wrath principally of the Sunnis, who legitimately or not, because the prime minister traditionally came from their community, saw this as an assault on their political prerogatives. Making things worse as far as the Sunnis were concerned were their doubts about Hezbollah's true intentions when it came to the Hariri tribunal, which was intended to shed truth about who had murdered their communal champion. There was little to reassure them. Hezbollah had claimed that it supported an investigation of Hariri's assassination, but only a year earlier Shiite ministers had temporarily "suspended" their cabinet participation after the March 14–led majority in government took domestic legal steps to establish the tribunal (though the Shiite parties denied, with little conviction, that this was the reason for their action). In early October, a few weeks before Nasrallah laid down his ultimatum for veto power in the cabinet, I interviewed Prime Minister Fouad al-Siniora. The tribunal was on his mind as he fired a warning shot at Hezbollah: "The tribunal was agreed upon [in a national dialogue between Lebanese leaders], and it's in no one's interest to make an issue of it." Siniora didn't say how Sunnis would react if the tribunal were thwarted, but his statement was infused with that thought.

On November 11, as it became plain that Nasrallah's demand for veto power was going nowhere, the five Shiite ministers in the government resigned, this time with no intention of returning. A sixth, Greek Orthodox, minister named by Émile Lahoud followed, but the March 14 government still retained the numbers allowing it to remain constitutionally in place. The ministers affirmed they were leaving because the Siniora government was no longer representative. However, the Hariri tribunal played a significant role in their decision. The government was preparing to vote on a draft agreement with the United Nations to create the tribunal, which Syria had told its allies it wanted scuttled. "The Syrians don't want to hear about the tribunal," one senior pro-Syrian Shiite politician told Walid Jumblatt privately, and while Jumblatt had an interest in saying this, nothing in the behavior of Hezbollah and its pro-Syrian partners proved the contrary. Amid signs that Hezbollah would soon begin street protests to topple Siniora, another assassination occurred, this time in an eastern Beirut suburb on the eve of Independence Day. The victim was a young minister with a familiar name: Pierre Gemayel, the son of former President Amin Gemayel and the nephew of Bashir Gemayel. In this time of assassinations, Pierre had been driving around in a South Korean rental, on the assumption that he would escape the notice of his killers in so unministerial a vehicle. He was shot several times through the car's side window, as was a bodyguard, died instantly, and left behind a wife and two small children. The March 14 sympathizers gathered in the tens of thousands at a church near Martyrs Square, as they had for Samir Kassir and for Gebran Tueni, in what was becoming a taxing refrain, all bouncing coffins and slogans.

On November 25, the government, having already approved the draft agreement with the U.N., formally approved the creation of the Hariri tribunal. Opposition parties declared the decision null and void by virtue of the Shiite community's not being represented in the cabinet. This was an interpretation that took Lebanese communal politics to their extreme. For while the political system was indeed based on sectarian compromise, it was never the intention of the framers of the constitution to create a system in which every major government decision had to be approved unanimously by the religious sects, nor that governments should fall if ministers from one sect happened to all resign at the same moment. Gemayel's assassination momentarily delayed the

Hezbollah-led protests, but only until December 1, when the opposition began an open-ended sit-in in the downtown area around Riad al-Solh Square, under the hill of the Sérail building where Siniora's offices were located. They pledged to pursue their action until the government threw in the towel.

In both reality and imagery the place and method of the sit-in was rich with meaning and paradox. Riad al-Solh Square was where Nasrallah had made his March 8, 2005, speech to the sympathetic multitudes, his intention being to intimidate the Independence Intifada into silence. In the contending, exclusivist imagery of those weeks, Riad al-Solh Square stood against Martyrs Square, which Hezbollah had left alone because that was where Hariri was buried and the party wasn't looking for a fight with the Sunnis over a body and a mostly empty space. But in December 2006, Riad al-Solh Square took on new significance. Being below Siniora's window, it was an ideal place to organize a grinding political altercation. There was also the fact that Solh himself had been the primary Sunni Muslim partner, along with the Maronite Christian president, in approving the 1943 National Pact, therefore a founding father of post-Independence Lebanon. Here were Lebanon's Shiites, for the great majority participating in the sit-in was Shiite, working to bring down a Sunni prime minister and his cabinet, gathering in a square devoted to the memory, in fact under the very statue, of the man who had negotiated on behalf of Sunni power in Lebanon.

As far as the Sunnis were concerned, that provocation was multiplied when they considered what the sit-in meant for the memory of Rafiq al-Hariri. As you walked through the protest site, a sprawling agglomeration of many dozens of large tents extending to the southern half of Martyrs Square (the army having blocked off the northern half, where Hariri's tomb is located), to the edge of predominantly Christian eastern Beirut, you could sense that for many of the participants their effort was blissful payback against that part of the city that Hariri had rebuilt. Here was the late prime minister's model neighborhood, peppered with luxury stores, trendy restaurants and nightclubs; here, too, was Hariri's version of the Beirut of tomorrow, with its manicured businessmen fueled by status and its beautiful people; and there were the Shiite youths, sitting on their plastic chairs outside dilapidated tents, smoking their water pipes and warily eyeing unfamiliar passersby, lords of their now-dead surroundings; there, too, were the Shiite families arriving from the southern suburbs, people once of the rural periphery, now of the urban periphery, aglow amid their momentary conquest, little displeased with the exasperation they had caused in a downtown area from which they had felt excluded. Few of them would have admitted that Hezbollah was an accomplice in that exclusion by creating an untouchable ministate within society, by slowly asphyxiating all Shiite expression outside the realms controlled by the party, and by heightening the sense of Shiite estrangement, even as the party helped Shiites enter the civil service and army so it could use them to protect its autonomy. The willful proletarianization of the downtown district by these particular Shiites, their thumbing of the nose at Hariri's legacy, at March 14, at whoever couldn't bear to see the downtown reduced to a shambles, was accompanied by Hezbollah's imposing its writ on what became part public protest, part military operation. Before long, people entering certain sections of the downtown covered by the tent city—for example to access their now-closed shops and remove merchandise—needed written permission from the party.

Interpretation of what was going on soon lost its stimulating nuances. Those opposed to the protests saw only the poverty, the dirt, and the social envy and resentment in what Hezbollah and its followers and allies were doing. They pointed to the irony that the Christians involved in the sit-in had pitched their tents next to a Christian quarter, rarely mingled with Shiite protestors, and before long had largely abandoned the tent city. Those sympathetic to the protest, in turn, played it up as an affirmation of multisectarian democracy, then earnestly described it as a social protest by poor Lebanese against a system benefiting only the rich. Both interpretations were sinister for picking up shards of fact and using them to prop up prejudices. That there was poverty and frustration in the tent city was undeniable, but that didn't tell us anything about how the sit-in was, strangely, an assertion of a Shiite right to be part of the city, of that part of the city where their presence now seemed so alien. If the protestors felt an urge to destroy what they pined for, then that was worth investigating, and it was a potent statement on the inadequacy of the integrative policies of the Lebanese state.

On the other side, the idea that the sit-in represented some sort of democratic archetype, an example of social justice at play, was equally blinkered. The sit-in was no more democratic than what had occurred a year earlier at Martyrs Square (and as a Hezbollah-staged operation it was far less spontaneous). The downtown area may have been a place of wealth, but all cities necessarily have such neighborhoods, and to extrapolate from that that the political animosities between March 14 and Hezbollah somehow denoted a conflict between rich and poor was nonsense. Shiites did not have a monopoly over poverty, particularly when compared to the Sunnis, whose rural periphery could be as crushingly destitute, if not more so, than that of the Shiites. Nor did being poor afford the protestors the right to economically bludgeon a prosperous area and put hundreds of equally disadvantaged service workers out of a job, as the sit-in did.

From a political standpoint, Hezbollah soon found itself a prisoner of the stalemate it had created. The nature of sectarianism made that inevitable. Fouad al-Siniora refused to resign, and there was not much Hezbollah could do about it. In the early hours of the sit-in there were fears the party would order its militiamen to storm the Sérail and force Siniora out at gunpoint. Militarily, this would have been a cakewalk for the party. However, it would also have provoked an outbreak of fighting throughout Lebanon between Sunnis and Shiites. And if that was not apparent enough, the most important call Siniora took soon after the protest began was from King Abdullah of Saudi Arabia. He told the prime minister that he was with him, before speaking to each government minister in turn, his way of saying that if Hezbollah chased them out, it would find itself in a confrontation with the Sunni Arab world. Then the delegations began appearing—from this Sunni district or that, from this March 14 redoubt or that—also expressing support for the government, daring Hezbollah to attack, slowing down the party's impetus. Yet Nasrallah only tightened the knot around his leg when, less than a week after the protests began, he threatened that if the government did not resign, the opposition would form its own government "with at its head a patriotic Sunni." Either the secretary-general was bluffing or he was greatly overestimating his capacities—strange for a man who had to broadcast that threat via television from the depths of a catacomb where he was hiding to avoid an Israeli assassination attempt.

That phrase represented a critical moment in the post-2005 period, one whose lessons Nasrallah would only imperfectly appreciate in the subsequent two years. The visionary had bared his teeth, but the dictates of Lebanon's sectarian balancing act nullified his efforts. Hezbollah's weapons allowed it many privileges, even that of establishing its own private territory, but under no circumstances could the party pretend to impose a legitimate Sunni prime minister, patriotic or otherwise, on an adverse Sunni community. This was egotism of the highest order, and Nasrallah wisely avoided following through on the plan when he realized what a Pandora's box it might open up in Sunni-Shiite relations. But the damage was done, and what it left behind was a volatile cocktail of emotions. To his followers, Nasrallah had once again discredited Lebanon's social contract. However, for Sunnis, that Nasrallah had failed to bring Siniora down only made them more confident that he was a paper tiger, even as his words persuaded them that his real goal was to crush the Sunnis and name their leaders. It was not surprising, then, that in the weeks after the start of the sit-in, there was a rise in clashes between Sunni and Shiite youths in neighborhoods strung along the line leading from Beirut's southern suburbs to the downtown area. Two days into the protests, a young Shiite from the Amal Movement was shot dead. Hezbollah had hit up against the Sunni refusal to bend to the party's demands, but what was ominously coming to the fore was civil conflict, the natural outcome whenever Lebanon's sectarian rules were disregarded. And in this dangerous game Beirut showed that it offered no real mechanism, or ethos, for the opposing sides to avert the worst.

This was foreseeable. Beirut was a city of fractures, and the events of 2005 had created a severe fracture in Lebanese society, one more unstable for being wrapped up in poorly informed intellectual absolutes. Broadly speaking, there were those on the one hand who welcomed the Syrian departure, not a few interpreting it as a golden opportunity to revive Lebanon's liberal cosmopolitanism, which had made Beirut a vanguard of Arab modernism. In their minds, Hezbollah was the antithesis of such an aspiration, a party that was autocratic and seemed to love death, when the essential Lebanese trait was to love life. It was no small irony that most of the political leaders of this group had once been allied with Syria and benefited from its Lebanese presence, but now, to protect themselves from the Syrian regime, which had proven itself adept at murder, they had allied themselves with a sympathetic United States. These were the aspirants of a Lebanese Hong Kong, against Hezbollah's supposed ideal of Hanoi, which the summer war of 2006 had revived.

On the other hand, there were the orphans of the Syrian order, whether Hezbollah or Syria's lesser partners (later joined by the Christian Aounists, who had welcomed the Syrian withdrawal before following their leader to the side of Syria's allies), who viewed the political project of their adversaries with suspicion, denouncing it as a scheme to push Lebanon into America's malevolent arms. However, the Shiite supporters of Hezbollah did not see themselves as opposed to modernism and cosmopolitanism. It irked them to hear the other side depicting them as retrograde, as people who had a passion for martyrdom. After all, the Shiite community was arguably more cosmopolitan through its extensions in the diaspora than the Sunnis, and the Shiites' vitality, that of a community on the rise after decades of social immobility, made them as friendly to modernism as others, perhaps more than most. And yet Hezbollah somehow did, in its rhetoric and symbolism, endlessly reiterate the absoluteness of the armed struggle against Israel, the merits of dying for the cause, while echoing tropes of the antiglobalization international left. For a time, Hugo Chávez was the most popular foreign leader among Shiites, polls showed, though most were surely drawn more to his anti-Americanism than to the man himself, who must have remained an enigma to them. When it came to Syria, there was no particular liking for the Assad regime, but what the Syrians had lost in Lebanon, Hezbollah might lose as well; and what Hezbollah lost, the Shiites would also lose. And these complicated thoughts, on one side of the divide and the other, became existential concerns contaminated by half-formed views about Lebanon and about the world in general; and since Lebanon's contaminated colors were sharper in Beirut, it was in the capital that these thoughts played themselves out, without resolution.

Beirut's real problem was its perennial inability to come to grips with truth and guilt—the two defining aspects of cities that wanted to escape their moral ambiguities. Those shortcomings undoubtedly made Beirut more fascinating a place, but they were inadequate when it came to absorbing the forces unleashed in 2005, when those faithful to the memory of Rafiq al-Hariri demanded truth and the imparting of guilt in his assassination, while Hezbollah sought to avoid both, and could point to the moral ambiguities that had always pervaded Lebanese society, and Beirut in particular, to justify its attitude.

When Hassan Nasrallah began his offensive against the March 14 majority, his objectives went beyond containing the repercussions on Syria of the Hariri tribunal. Syria didn't want the tribunal, and veto power in the government would have handed Hezbollah the means to carry out that request. But Nasrallah was also thinking of what the tribunal meant for his own party. The government's endorsement of the institution had the potential of becoming a silver bullet aimed at Hezbollah's heart, since it threatened to destabilize the regime of a country, Syria, representing the party's strategic depth, as well as a land passage for arms and much else arriving from Iran. There was also the matter of what Hezbollah knew about Hariri's murder and when it knew it. In the weeks leading up to the killing of the former prime minister, Hariri had been meeting with Nasrallah on a regular basis, mainly to discuss the summer 2005 elections. For the more dubious March 14 politicians this might have been a way of lulling Hariri into a false sense of confidence over his safety, to more easily eliminate him.

At the least, Hezbollah's vast intelligence capacities made it hard to believe that the party didn't know that Hariri was under mortal threat, then failed to inform him of this.

As Hezbollah initiated its protests against the Siniora government, Lebanon found itself a step closer to realizing what the anti-Syrian demonstrations of 2005 had demanded: justice. Whether their wishes would be fulfilled remained to be seen, but there was an ongoing investigation and now the tribunal was nearer to becoming a reality. That process had begun more than a year before with the appointment of the German judge Detlev Mehlis as first commissioner of the United Nations International Independent Investigation Commission (UNIIIC) mandated to uncover the truth about Hariri's assassination. Standing against Mehlis, and against his successors, were not only those opposed to discovering the truth and clarifying guilt, but also, more figuratively, Beirut itself, the battleground defining post-Syria Lebanon, whose spirit had always been about forgetting the past and living the moment.

I FIRST met Detlev Mehlis in December 2005, a few weeks before he ended his term at the head of UNIIIC. The commission, the rare fruit of rare unanimity on Lebanon, was established on April 7, 2005, under the authority of Security Council Resolution 1595. This was something altogether new for the international community: a United Nations investigation of a political killing. The resolution gave Mehlis broad powers, including access to all documentation, testimony, physical information, and any other evidence he and his team required. Further resolutions reinforced UNIIIC's mandate, granting it access to officials in Syria, including the president, Bashar al-Assad, whom Mehlis would seek to interrogate as a witness. Hariri's assassins had not bargained for this, particularly when several high-level political assassinations since the start of the civil war in 1975, including that of two presidents, had gone unpunished.

I had several times requested a meeting with Mehlis, and finally the person handling his media relations called me with the good news. Would I come up to UNIIIC's headquarters in Monteverde, a residential district not very far up the mountain above Beirut's eastern suburbs? The commission had rented a hotel, a charmless seasonal repository shaken alive with the prize catch of an international clientele. The surrounding area was isolated enough, its access controllable enough, so that a combined force of U.N. security guards and Lebanese army units could protect the investigators. Yet everywhere in the commission's routine was a fear of further assassinations. Mehlis would later admit that he had never gotten used to the tiresome security measures, so that even eating out at a restaurant became, quite literally, an unwieldy moveable feast. However, this caution proved to be justified: Only days after I met Mehlis, the parliamentarian Gebran Tueni was assassinated on a road taken daily by U.N. investigators. Mehlis would interpret the killing partly as a message to UNIIIC. In fact, one of the reasons he decided not to extend his mandate was that his security staff had informed him that it could no longer guarantee his safety after January 2006. If he wanted to stay on, he would have to conduct his work from Europe.

Mehlis's office was roomy, with a view of the mountain across the valley. To borrow from a Graham Greene novel, it seemed made and furnished for nothing but use. Other than a stuffed animal placed next to his computer, little suggested Mehlis had made the space his. The German was an atypical figure. A senior prosecutor at the Superior Prosecutor's Office in Berlin, he was familiar with Cold War–era Middle Eastern terrorism. Mehlis had investigated and proven Libyan involvement in the 1986 La Belle discotheque bombing in West Berlin, as well as Syrian involvement in an earlier bombing of the French cultural center in 1983. It so happened that a Syrian diplomat had transferred the bomb for that attack through the Friedrichstrasse train station, then a crossing point through divided Berlin. The diplomat turned evidence against his government, before asking for asylum in Germany as a consequence. "I can almost say he's a friend of mine today," Mehlis later told me when I visited him in his city. The commissioner was doubly bothersome to the Syrians in 2005; he knew their methods and could wade into brackish waters with shifty witnesses willing to cut a deal. Behind the translucent glasses and cherubic features, behind the overstated diffidence also, was a sharp mind and a tenacity that had allowed Mehlis to reach convictions in the La Belle case fifteen years after the crime. In our first meeting he was buoyant. Some weeks earlier he had gained Security Council backing, this time through Resolution 1636, obliging Syria to co-operate with his investigation, and he was about to interview several Syrian intelligence chiefs in Vienna. "The conditions we have are almost perfect. It makes our work easier. We are very happy," Mehlis said.

But the commissioner could not have been happy with recent developments in his case. Two witnesses he had interviewed were creating credibility problems for his investigation. The first was a Syrian man with ambiguous ties to his country's intelligence services who allegedly had prior knowledge of the Hariri bombing. He had just appeared in Damascus at a press conference stage-managed by the Syrian regime insisting he had been offered money by the Hariri camp to give false testimony to U.N. investigators. The Hariris denied this, and UNIIIC, in a December 2005 update report, went further in stating that it had "received credible evidence that, prior to [the witness's] public recantation of his statement to UNIIIC, Syrian officials had arrested and threatened some of [his] close relatives in Syria." As for the second witness, he was a low-level Syrian intelligence officer living in France who had pointed the finger at senior Syrian and Lebanese intelligence figures allegedly involved in the assassination. The information may have been true, or it may not have been, but the officer's reliability was questionable and the possibility that he had participated in Hariri's murder was such that he was soon declared a suspect, while some observers believed the Syrians had planted him to mislead and embarrass Mehlis.

Mehlis's reaction to both developments was serene. No, he did not feel that UNIIIC should just throw out the two testimonies. Liars could tell the truth, and the truth of what the witnesses had revealed would be determined by corroborating evidence. The commission's overall case did not rest on the information the two men provided, and if the witnesses had an integrity problem, that was probably because assassinations didn't tend to attract upright citizens. However, three years later Mehlis would imply that if someone was trying to cast doubt on the investigation, then the question was who? In the weeks before his departure, the German could plainly see what a minefield UNIIIC had to navigate through, one made more poisonous by the erroneous information or deliberate disinformation released almost daily by the pro-Syrian and anti-Syrian Lebanese media.

The problems Mehlis had with the Syrians had begun the previous October, when he released his first report on the assassination. The document was to serve as the backbone report for future reports. This distinction was important. Whereas there was a tendency after Mehlis's departure to see the latest UNIIIC report as the final word from the commission, Mehlis always viewed his October 2005 report as his main statement, which subsequent reports would update and improve upon. In emphasizing that point he was effectively saying that the assumptions in the first report were near-conclusive. In its October account, UNIIIC didn't mince words. Investigators determined that "there is converging evidence pointing at both Lebanese and Syrian involvement in this terrorist act." Syria's military intelligence had a "pervasive presence" in Lebanon, to the extent that four Lebanese security chiefs arrested on suspicion of involvement in the crime "were their appointees." Given this context and the "infiltration of Lebanese institutions and society by the Syrian and Lebanese intelligence services working in tandem, it would be difficult to envisage a scenario whereby such a complex assassination plot could have been carried out without their knowledge."

The report went on to present details of the investigation and the highlights of testimony by certain prominent witnesses. In so doing, UNIIIC affirmed a motive for the crime (Syria's fear that Hariri would challenge their authority in the summer parliamentary elections), and described escalating hostility directed against Hariri by the Syrians and their Lebanese allies. UNIIIC also established that the assassination was prepared over a period of several months and "carried out by a group with an extensive organization and considerable resources and capabilities." During that time, Hariri's movements were monitored and his itinerary "recorded in detail." For anyone who knew Lebanon, only the Syrians and those with them had the resources and capabilities that UNIIIC mentioned.

Of particular alarm to Syria's regime, however, was something that occurred when the report was released to the public. The second of Mehlis's unreliable witnesses had mentioned the involvement of senior Syrian and Lebanese officials in the assassination, including the brother and brother-in-law of Syria's President Bashar al-Assad. These men were pillars of the regime, and while few doubted that a Syrian decision on Hariri's removal would have involved them, it was now in a review of the witness's testimony in black and white under a U.N. letterhead. While the names were deleted in Mehlis's final version, the U.N. press office released the report as a Microsoft Word document. Journalists could access track changes showing the names removed in the final draft. This was awkward for Mehlis and for the U.N., although the conspiracy theorists argued the German had slyly ensured the Word version would be released in order to raise the heat on the Syrians. If so, Mehlis consistently denied it in subsequent interviews, including one I conducted with him in January 2008.

Mehlis's replacement, the taciturn Belgian Serge Brammertz, knew the German and had even sat in his garden near Berlin. Mehlis had recommended Brammertz to the U.N., among other candidates, feeling that he had what it took to lead a complex political investigation. Mehlis would later come to doubt his successor and the pace of his work, and in early 2008 he would publicly express those doubts for the first time, just as the Belgian was preparing to leave his post. But at the end of 2006, when Hezbollah staged its sit-in and the Siniora government formally endorsed the Hariri tribunal, those reservations were still unexpressed and the Syrians were still looking for ways to emasculate the tribunal from inside Lebanon. They failed to do so, but something more pernicious was taking place in the minds of many Lebanese: a gradual erosion in the sentiment that uncovering the truth about who had killed

Hariri needed to be a national priority, a means of ending political murder in the future. This could not be said of the Sunni community, or of the Druze followers of Walid Jumblatt, but beginning to fray was the resolve among Christians, whose unity of purpose with the Sunnis and Druze during the Independence Intifada had given that moment its particular energy. Michel Aoun had gone his own way, and as his political calculations changed and he allied himself with Hezbollah, he increasingly questioned the value of the investigation, going so far as to say on Lebanon's leading talk show in March 2006 that since a year of investigations had not reached conclusions as to the perpetrators, we might have to accept that Syria's regime was not responsible. Perhaps "fundamentalists" were behind the crime, he speculated.

This was hypocrisy. The U.N. investigation, far from reaching no conclusions, had largely substantiated Syrian involvement (involvement that Aoun, in earlier days, had proclaimed louder than most), even if Syria's intelligence services might have used a Sunni Islamist suicide bomber to carry out the crime it planned. But the details seemed unimportant. Aoun had deliberately broken with the Independence Intifada consensus on discovering the truth about Hariri's killing, and many Christians, even those with little patience for the general, shared his apathy toward resolving the crime. After all, plenty of Christian leaders had been killed in the past three decades, and no one had demanded the truth in *their* case. This was an ugly aspect of sectarianism rearing its head: communal selfishness, which, if it created spaces for pluralism, also, and with the notable exception of the February-March 2005 period, frequently thwarted constructive unity.

However, there was also something else in this breakdown of agreement over Hariri, with many Christians, but certainly not all, sharing the view of many Shiites, but certainly not all, that Hariri was a page best turned, since the anti-Syrian forces had won in 2005 and there was no need to push the nail all the way through the head of the Syrian regime. That something had to do with the personality of Beirut, Lebanon's hard disc, which mirrored the capricious ways of the Lebanese. Just as Beirut became a natural venue for the rifts in the winter of 2006 because it was a place all about evading unanimity, it had the makings of a place evading responsibility. Truth and guilt did not thrive in its erratic chemistry. The irony was that Rafiq al-Hariri was just as responsible for that aspect of the city's flightiness, for its amnesia, as were those uninterested in identifying his killers.

It was a ransacked Beirut that welcomed the end of the fifteen-year civil war in 1990. For those of us who had seen the city in its most pitiful hours, the recovery was a slow one. Almost two years into the postwar period, when I made my way home, Beirut was still a place roughly aborted, its lesions visible at every street corner, the roads soiled and rutted, the electricity supply theoretical and telephone communications hypothetical. Yet this was also a heroic place; there was splendor in its penury and renewal in its ruin. This was a city that had endured round upon round of destruction for over a decade and a half; that had been conquered by everyone but possessed by no one, its indomitability the subject of endless cliché, the most flattering of compliments. As I looked back on the war years, it wasn't the violence that I necessarily remembered most vividly, it was the valuable spaces that we had managed to create in between, our curiosity for what we could have in a place that had never willingly denied us what we couldn't. Few were the moments in which many of us felt as intellectually inquisitive as during wartime in Beirut, at one with a world outside that wanted us locked in. This derived from the essence of the city itself, from our own sense of dissidence. Only in the last two years before my temporary departure, in 1985 and 1986, did I feel that Beirut, or that part of it where I lived, its Muslim-majority western part, was losing to the void. Those were years when there were no rules but the rules of the gunmen, also when Hezbollah moved into the capital in earnest, now a part of Beirut but also suspicious of its potential for depravity. Christopher Hitchens has written of Beirut and other cosmopolitan cities this way: "There is . . . a reason they attract the ire and loathing of the religious fanatics. To the pure and godly, the very existence of such places is a profanity." Yet Beirut's profanity had for decades lured those Arabs escaping the stultifying austerity of their own cities. It seemed to best express the infatuation of the Lebanese with the worldly, so that even religion seemed a pretext for the material. By war's end, the city had absorbed the pure and the godly of Hezbollah. However, it had not converted them. That failing was why in 2006 the Shiite protest in the downtown that Rafiq al-Hariri had rebuilt was accompanied by an inability of the Lebanese to reach agreement over the Hariri tribunal.

Beirut's failure to midwife straightforward outcomes was foreshadowed by Hariri himself after 1992, when he became prime minister. His principal intention in rebuilding the postwar downtown, other than to turn it into an area of lucrative investment, was to make it an instrument allowing the Lebanese to forget the war. In the mid-1990s the internationally renowned sculptor Arman created a work to commemorate the Lebanese conflict. The sculpture was to be placed in the area that Hariri soon intended to start reconstructing. The final product, named *Hope for Peace*, was a narrowing tower in which Arman had inserted multiple stories of tanks and armored vehicles into cavities in the concrete, their cannons facing outward. Here were machines of war melted (coincidentally) into the single substance that Hariri intended to make the symbol of his new city, the city of the developer. Except for one detail: When the sculpture was completed, it was not placed in the downtown area at all. It must have been galling to Arman that his monument to the folly of war should end up, instead, outside the defense ministry in a Beirut suburb. It's not clear who banished the work, but one must assume that Hariri had the final say on the matter, since he had a final say on all matters related to the downtown. And one thing he apparently did not want was a monolith of rusting military hardware hovering over his showpiece neighborhood.

Hariri's plans for the old city center were angrily debated from the start, principally because at the heart of his project was money and property, but also a premonition of Beirut's future. When peace returned to Lebanon, the downtown area was a place of burnt-out buildings, minefields, and streets overgrown with a decade's worth of vegetation, some of its quarters inhabited by refugees, mainly Shiites, who had moved into structures only loosely habitable. In 1991, Hariri, through his Hariri Foundation, financed a master plan for the downtown area, commissioned by a state body known as the Council of Development and Reconstruction. The CDR would fall under Hariri's control before he became prime minister, turning into one of his main levers to direct Lebanon's reconstruction process. A second was Hariri's sway over a private property company, Solidere, created to develop the devastated downtown area. Faced with a Gordian knot of how to sort out property rights after a decade and a half of disarray, Hariri opted to cut through it by overseeing a process of widespread expropriation, giving property owners compensation or shares in Solidere. The constitutionality of the move was questionable, and the estimation of compensation in many cases was lower than market value or inconsistent. However, Hariri's project went ahead because of his power in the system and the absence of a realistic alternative given the near impossibility of settling property rights.

The Hariri-financed master plan was soon criticized by urban planners and others. Some saw it as being blind to developments in town planning elsewhere in the world, as favoring an urban area that would create difficulties of physical access and social integration, as creating an island of wealth and authority separated from the rest of the capital, or as rationalizing the tearing down of buildings housing a valuable part of Beirut's historical memory. In retrospect, the fears were only partly borne out, though the project has yet to be completed on its periphery. For practical reasons, Hariri altered aspects of the master plan; while Solidere's rehabilitation or reconstruction of old buildings proved a success, some will insist that the revived downtown is a passionless likeness of the past. Perhaps, but the debate over memory can be labyrinthine. One person's fond memory can be another's nightmare. The detail most people remembered, however, was that in just a few years Hariri oversaw the reconstruction of a charming downtown area, by any benchmark a remarkable feat. While the abuses involved were real, when visitors flocked to the area in droves starting in the early twenty-first century, Hariri had won that argument, the ends having justified his means.

However, that didn't change the fact that Hariri's ideal for the old city center left no room for wartime justice and guilt. In the new downtown there was almost nothing of the one epitomizing Lebanon's years of conflict. Solidere did offer a concession to the past early in the new century when it helped promote a "before and after" coffee-table picture book of the area, compiled by one Ayman Trawi and published with the assistance of a bank in which Hariri held a controlling interest. On one side readers were shown photographs of buildings or squares destroyed during the war years; on the other the same locations after Solidere had rehabilitated them. But what was this past except a mechanism to exalt the present? To Solidere, and to Hariri himself, the past was not something otherwise requiring regurgitation in order for Lebanese society to bring "closure" to its wartime traumas. As with the Amnesty Law of 1991, the Lebanese were better off not demanding retribution against the guilty, because the society would have been torn apart by that demand, for almost everyone—at least those in authority—was guilty. And yet the Lebanese still did remember, and this would be proven later on in 2007 and 2008 when their country lurched precariously toward a new civil war. Those old enough still could feel what it meant to enter a dimension of total conflict, to slip through the looking glass into a world of methodical collapse, a world in which Ayman Trawi would have had to publish his picture book in reverse. This points us to the greatest shortcoming in Hariri's mode of urban renewal.

As the opposition protestors took over Solidere's area in December 2006, they might have argued that since Hariri had never been overly concerned with retribution and justice when it involved the fate of Lebanese killed or maimed during the 1975–1990 war, they had no reason to be similarly concerned with retribution and justice on behalf of Rafiq al-Hariri or the others killed in 2005 and after. The argument would have been powerful, but incomplete. It would have required ignoring that Hariri's designated task after 1992 was to lead Lebanon out of its wartime mind-set; and it would have meant admitting that Syria, which many in the opposition defended after the Independence Intifada, was even less interested in memory than Hariri had been. However, where Hariri *could* have done much more, and should have, was in leaving mnemonic devices around the rebuilt downtown area, and Beirut in general, to show the wages of war. This would have helped reinforce and provide a meaningful backdrop to his reconstruction efforts.

The reality is that the war was quickly suppressed in Lebanese minds. That could be good news when demonstrating the national predilection for new beginnings, which is what Hariri wanted. Yet it was startling how little thought was given to remembering, even if people frequently did let their guard down. Not a museum was devoted to the war, even one that could play down political differences while showing how all had suffered in equal measure; not a monument was erected to the war dead or the disappeared, other than the Arman memorial banished to the Ministry of Defense complex; not an official day of remembrance was set aside to commemorate the start of the killings. Even among novelists, filmmakers, and playwrights the dearth of estimable works on the civil war was extraordinary—you could count them on the fingers of two hands. Why should this have mattered? Because Lebanon's pluralism, even if it meant the Lebanese could not agree on one interpretation of the war, let alone on matters of wartime guilt, would have allowed them to use these mementos to create personal narratives of the war years so that everybody could at least reach a level of common personal understanding of what had happened. Memory could speak, albeit dissonantly, but those in power were either uninterested or knew that too good a memory might prove to be their undoing.

Beirut's downtown area was the place where the adversaries of the Independence Intifada fought their most emblematic battles, but there was much more to the city than the downtown. And it was the larger city, with its complicated demographic and social realities, with its pluralism and the incompatible aspirations and drives this provoked, that defined the dissension characterizing Beirut after the 2006 war. Look over Lebanon's capital on any given day and it's not easy to imagine what it was like thirty-five years ago. When my mother and I stepped onto the tarmac at Beirut's airport in September 1970, we did so with some delay because Palestinian gunmen had taken over the tower in protest against the Jordanian army's offensive against armed Palestinian groups in Amman. I was too young to see in that event a premonition of the politics of the city I had moved to; but I wasn't too young to value Beirut as an object of desire. The city was smaller then, the empty lots numerous, and through the open spaces we could see much more clearly than today those elements lending totality to our lives: water, stone, and fire—the sea, the mountains, and the sun. The Mediterranean seemed more present for being visible from Beirut's deeper confines, its blues feeding into the smoldering sky—the subject of longing reverie many years on, not to say a cruel haunting from a time gone by. But the sun gone, in the winter months, the city could be as dank and frigid as a central European mud patch, even if this offered us fantasies of elsewhere. Ever more frequently in those years, politics swept through Beirut with a ferocity entirely new to us, as when tens of thousands of shouting mourners marched below our balcony after the death of Egypt's Gamal Abdel Nasser in late September 1970; or later on when social or political unrest repeatedly closed Beirut down, its boulevards locked behind bars of smoke rising from tires burned in anger. Things were happening, the city was changing, as was the Arab world. The spindly streets of our maritime outpost were arenas for the region's populist atavisms and utopian extremes. Beirut was too small and fragile to handle the dangerous traffic all around, yet also too daring and reckless to refuse it.

It was not until the war started in 1975 that those of my generation began understanding what it meant that our city was riding the tiger's tail. Beirut had expanded in the 1960s, accumulating many of its incongruities—rapid urbanization, more pronounced income disparities, and increasingly divisive ideological politics aggravated by the Palestinian Liberation Organization's transforming the city into its headquarters. As the war dragged on, it became a new kind of place. Its once-alluring spaces were filled out with unregulated construction, the city's new ugliness compounded by the demolition of many of its handsomest neighborhoods. People left the precarious center for the capital's periphery, and Beirut bloated, its extensions northward and southward along the coast, and eastward into the mountains, increasingly difficult to demarcate. For kilometers the city remained present, urban continuity preventing any clean break with its official boundaries. Quaintness was dissipating even as the city's temperament took on the hardness and viciousness, the insolence and resilience, that we never suspected it had in it.

Shaped like an inverted nose jutting into the sea, Beirut is geographically divided into fairly distinct areas of sectarian and social concentration. The city can be bisected by what was called during the war years the "green line"–a succession of avenues starting at Martyrs Square in the downtown area and cutting southward through the middle of Beirut before entering the largely Shiite southern suburbs. To the east of that line are predominantly Christian neighborhoods, to the West predominantly Muslim ones, but with a significant minority of Christians present. Within the western half of Beirut a further breakdown illustrates why the sit-in of December 2006 proved so volatile, as Sunnis and Shiites with sharply differing loyalties lived side by side. During the war years, many more Shiites began moving into what had been mainly Sunni low-income neighborhoods on the western edges of the "green line" (the middle class and upscale neighborhoods being located further to the west). This mixture was the result of natural migration in some places, but in others a case of refugees finding a new home amid conflict, or occupying buildings abandoned because of their proximity to combat zones. One such place was the western approach to the downtown, previously inhabited mainly by Christians, Armenians, and Jews, which Hariri was only able to begin rebuilding once the government had paid compensation to displaced Shiites so they would vacate the area. The process, divisive for being driven by conflicting financial interests, set the Shiites up, unjustly, as natural impediments to reconstruction, even as the refugees and their leaders did indeed take advantage of the corrupt compensation system to extract money from the state. The episode engendered ill will, hardly reflecting a city united in rebirth.

On the eastern side of Beirut, the pattern is reversed somewhat when it comes to income distribution. Near the old "green line" run mostly middle-class and upscale Christian quarters, with a small pocket of Muslims living on their westernmost edge. The further away one moves from the line, the more one enters low-income areas on Beirut's eastern periphery. These areas were mixed before the war, having a substantial Shiite Muslim and Palestinian population that either left voluntarily as the war loomed, or that was brutally driven out by the Christian militias after it started. While there is a high concentration of Armenians in some of the northeastern suburbs, Beirut's Christian suburbs reveal a recurring pattern, namely that they were often settled by individuals arriving from the relatively nearest rural hinterland. All these developments, particularly during the war years, helped fashion Beirut's demographic dynamics, which remain much the same today.

Lying below both halves of the capital are Beirut's mostly Shiite southern suburbs, the third distinct slice of the city, even if they are administratively separate entities.

The southern suburbs concentrate together a Shiite community as lost in bewildering inconsistency as other Lebanese sects. In February 2003, I attended a reception in the suburbs at the end of a conference organized by a German foundation in collaboration with a research center affiliated with Hezbollah. The restaurant where we met was in a recreational facility built by Sayyed Muhammad Hussein Fadlallah, a senior Shiite cleric who, like the much younger Hassan Nasrallah, had spent years in the eastern periphery of Beirut, before leaving at the start of the war. Fadlallah had been referred to as Hezbollah's "spiritual guide," a description that did not begin to explain his convoluted relationship with the party and its Iranian sponsors. As participants in the conference—Lebanese and Westerners—sat for a commemorative photograph in the limestone-bounded courtyard, a man next to me, a Shiite close to Hezbollah, said: "Can you believe we are in the southern suburbs." What he evidently meant was that Fadlallah's facility, with its pleasant restaurants and cafés, its stores and playing area for children, felt every bit as upscale as similar places in the trendier neighborhoods of Beirut.

I was taken aback by the phrase. In some ways it seemed to be-little the rest of the suburbs, so basic a part of Shiite identity in Beirut. I also happened to disagree, for while Fadlallah had indeed set up a rare and agreeable island in the midst of an overcrowded, mainly impoverished district, there was something about the southern suburbs that made such contrasts natural. This was no dour redoubt of religious conservatism; Hezbollah was domineer-ing, it was religious, and it was conservative, but you would be al-most as likely to see a young woman in a short skirt walking through the suburbs' streets as you would one wearing a head scarf; just as likely to hear about young men doing drugs and en-joying illicit sex as you would budding Hassan Nasrallahs reading their religious texts. This had little to do with open-mindedness on Hezbollah's part, though the party could operate in subtle ways. Rather, it resulted from an implicit contract between Shiites. Hezbollah earned wide latitude to define the community's politi-cal perspective, but that meant leaving individuals room to be themselves; it meant adapting to the complexity of Shiite society, with its intricate family relationships, geographical loyalties, and disparate solidarities. In aspiring to be totalistic—and over the years the party has limited the span of Shiite diversity—Hezbollah nev-ertheless had to accept that Shiites were children of a pluralistic or-der. Like all Lebanese, they could be receptive to the enticements of consumerism and just as easily fall for the profane and the allur-ing. In fact, my interlocutor had proved that point.

But even in the politics, you could sometimes hear of invigo-rating dissent. After the events of 2005 and the assassination of his colleague Samir Kassir, my Shiite friend Ziad Majed, a critic of Hezbollah and the Syrian regime who had been vice president of the Democratic Left movement, was forced to leave Lebanon for security reasons. However, he frequently came back on short visits, though never daring to sleep in his own apartment. One day in late 2008, Majed was invited to a morning political talk show, which happened to be playing on a television in a flower shop in the southern suburbs. A Hezbollah sympathizer entered and, see-ing Majed on the screen, began insulting him, calling him a traitor. The Shiite owners of the shop told the man to be more respectful, adding that they had no intention of selling him flowers. He left and returned with reinforcements to teach them a lesson. The florists, in turn, called in family members, who came down ready for a fight. Suddenly a quiet neighborhood found itself on the verge of a major brawl because someone had defended an individual distasteful to Hezbollah. Calm was restored, but the florists were still keen to meet Majed.

It was these elusive identities that Shiites took with them as they moved daily to the downtown area of Beirut and the Hezbollah-led sit-in. They moved through neighborhoods ripe for conflict in the wake of the Syrian withdrawal, through mixed Sunni-Shiite areas. These had been calmer when the wartime enemy was located across the "green line" among the Christians, but now they were being torn apart by the clashing allegiances of those with Hassan Nasrallah and those with Saad al-Hariri. This reality, accompanied by Hezbollah's playing on the Shiites' feeling that their destiny depended on Hezbollah's retaining its weapons, cut the community off from its own city, from the Beirut beckoning beyond the Shiite neighborhoods, where the stern promoters of tenacious armed resistance were anathema.

Yet there was an irony here. Hezbollah's only way of hitting back at its political enemies, themselves children of the city and whose murdered leader had been synonymous with the city, was to send its followers into the streets to somehow reaffirm the Shiite arrival in Beirut. That opened the door to several interesting possibilities. There was the possibility that the Shiites, or at least those siding with the opposition who had felt separate from the city, would exploit that moment and allow themselves to be drawn into the Beirut of more variety and sensation; that from their ruin of the downtown area an unanticipated intimacy would be born. There was also a second possibility, that with time, once the political discord had ended, the protestors would leave as they had come, inhabitants of Beirut but still not fully a part of it. And then there was a third possibility, the worst one of all: that the Shiites would find themselves in a no-man's-land of Hezbollah's making: drawn to the city and antagonistic to it; out to affirm their rightful presence in the city but also encouraged by their parties to do so by mistreating the city; responsive to the Beirut of myriad identities, but also caught up in an escalating fight to impose their own identity, or identities, on the rest. In the subsequent eighteen months, it was this last outcome that Beirut was made to endure, showing how little, perhaps, the Lebanese deserved so sensitive, so submissive, yet so spirited a bestowal.

5

The Crack-Up

Oh God, Oh God, this is the end, this is the end,
We were always frightened of the end, we
waited for it, and the end has come . . .
                    Elias Khoury, *The White Faces* (1981)

DAMASCUS, APRIL 24, 2007. The secretary-general of the United Nations, Ban Ki-moon, is sitting down with Syrian President Bashar al-Assad at the presidential palace in Damascus. For memory, the palace was built by Rafiq al-Hariri in the 1980s, when he was still a Saudi middleman in Lebanon's civil war and gifts to Syria's leadership were part of that embarrassment of riches a Saudi mediation effort entailed. Notes of the Ban-Assad conversation are being taken down by a U.N. official accompanying the secretary-general, and one month later they will find their way to the French daily *Le Monde*.

According to the leaked account of the meeting, Lebanon is the main topic of conversation. Of the country he was forced to withdraw from only two years earlier, Assad says: "In Lebanon, divisions and confessionalism have been deeply anchored for more than 300 years. Lebanese society is very fragile. [The country's] most peaceful years were when Syrian forces were present. From 1976 to 2005 Lebanon was stable, whereas now there is great instability." This instability, Assad continues, will only get worse if the special tribunal for Lebanon, the one being set up to identify and sentence those responsible for the assassination of Rafiq al-Hariri and others, is approved under Chapter VII of the U.N. Charter. Such approval is increasingly necessary because the political deadlock in Beirut, which Syria has helped aggravate, makes unlikely the institution's formal endorsement by Lebanon's parliament. (On May 30, the tribunal was established under Chapter VII, through Resolution 1757.)

Then, oddly, Assad warns that the tribunal "might easily cause a conflict that would degenerate into civil war, provoking divisions between Sunnis and Shiites from the Mediterranean to the Caspian Sea." Why the sudden mention of Shiites? Is this the Syrian president's underhanded way of suggesting that Hezbollah played a role in Hariri's assassination? The article offers no answer. Yet two years later that very idea would make its way back into public discussion of the assassination.*

More words are exchanged, until Syria's foreign minister, Walid al-Muallim, cuts in to say that the American ambassador to Lebanon, Jeffrey Feltman, should leave the country, and that he is prepared to offer him a vacation in Hawaii. Muallim, a rotund man with cascading terraces of fat, only permits himself that aside because his boss has just explained that the United States and France are playing a "destructive" role in Lebanon. In response to a suggestion from Ban that Syria and Lebanon establish diplomatic relations, Assad replies that this cannot be done with the Siniora government, which he considers illegal. However, if a government of national unity were formed as demanded by the Lebanese opposition, then it might be possible. Until now, Syria has always refused to recognize Lebanon diplomatically, for a variety of reasons related to Syrian interests, but mainly on the grounds that the imperial powers sliced the country out of a "Greater Syria" after World War I, leaving "one people in two countries," as Syrian officials later frequently explained. An hour and fifteen minutes later, Ban is preparing to depart, when Assad leaves him with this thought: "We are in the eye of the cyclone. You will, therefore, need to stay in contact with us."

Appreciate the ease with which the Syrian president issued

---

* See Chapter 7.

what were, quite plainly, threats in the presence of the senior representative of the international community. Perhaps that was why the exchange found its way into a foreign newspaper, as a self-evident illustration of the Baath regime's ways. It was also, and more importantly, an implicit affirmation that Syria, and perhaps not Syria alone, was involved in Rafiq al-Hariri's murder—since why else would Assad so fear a tribunal, especially one passed under Chapter VII authority? The brusque expression of Assad's belief that Lebanon was better off when he and his intelligence officers ruled over it must have shaken the courteous Ban, as the head of an institution that had passed successive resolutions to end that anomalous situation. We might also pause at the behavior of Walid al-Muallim, that of a civilian functionary in a system run by officers; or more accurately a Sunni functionary in a system run by Alawite officers, who overcompensated for his relative inconsequentiality by sounding like a hoodlum. Muallim's phrase would be remembered in January 2008, when a bomb attack against a U.S. embassy vehicle took place on the day that Feltman had scheduled a goodbye party ending his Lebanon mission.

Sordid as they were, the Syrian messages accurately reflected Bashar al-Assad's growing confidence in early 2007. Syria's allies in Beirut, above all Hezbollah, had not managed to overthrow the government of Fouad al-Siniora, but they had pushed Lebanon into a deadlock that could only benefit Assad, by showing that he held the keys to normalization. The Syrians were proving unrivaled merchants in carrion. Thanks to them and their local partners, Lebanon was cracking up, so that 2007 would be the start of a breakdown lasting until May the following year, which substantially reversed the gains of 2005. This period was characterized by escalating sectarian violence between Sunnis and Shiites, to a great extent a result of the tensions unleashed by Hezbollah's downtown sit-in. The violence could be more discerning, as when the assassination of members of the March 14 majority continued unabated. Lebanon's government and army would also enter into a three-month battle against militant Islamists in the Palestinian refugee camp of Nahr al-Bared, near the city of Tripoli, whose causes became, like much else, a matter of domestic disputation. Stand-

ing over all this was Bashar al-Assad, the man in the eye of the cyclone, sometimes pushing the Lebanese toward the precipice,
sometimes delighting in their flair for doing it themselves.

But more generally, 2007 was about Lebanon watching as its
paradoxical liberalism lost ground to consistent violence. What
many of us had feared two years earlier, that the Syrians would absorb the blow of their forced departure before patiently organizing
their counterattack, was happening. The Independence Intifada
was, perhaps, for only a brief moment an uninhibited popular ar-
ticulation of emancipation, but to many people it had opened a
window on countless potentialities, none of which included the resurgence of Syrian hegemony. This was naïve; it was a misreading
of Lebanon's importance to the Syrian regime and its ability to
punch above its weight regionally; but it also reflected the innate
positivism at the heart of Lebanon's liberalism, which jarred with
the inertia permeating much of the Arab world, itself a defining
feature, and a consequence, of the region's illiberalism. This positivism, we could see all around us, had taken a hit in the summer
of 2006, when Hezbollah carried Lebanon into an unnecessary war
against Israel, before Hassan Nasrallah insulted our intelligence by
declaring it a divine victory. Now, in 2007, what remained of that
positivism was in danger of permanently evaporating. While Lebanon still enjoyed its liberal spaces—which not even Syria could
plug up—it was the notion of a liberal whole that was being lost, of
a country moving in a cohesive direction, united in its pluralism,
able to light a consensual path out of decades of war and the Syrian presence.

In the streets of Beirut, Sunni and Shiites began fighting. This
seemed a contrived animosity for those who knew that relations
between the communities were little colored by timeless hatreds.
Lebanon's Shiites had been marginalized in the past, their newfound sense of entitlement behind Hezbollah was not surprising,
but their relations with the Sunnis had usually been peaceful. Lebanon was not Iraq; the Sunnis had not spent decades suppressing
Shiites, nor was Lebanon serious enough in its brutality, or its social structure flexible enough, to abide such a thing. The two communities had fought on the same side during the civil war, and

while there were Shiites who might have viewed Arab nationalism as a shorthand ideology for Sunni domination of the Middle East, their community could still be moved by Arab nationalist symbols and almost never defined itself *against* them, as did many Christians.

Rather, we were seeing something quite different, and quite familiar: Here were the consequences of Hezbollah's often expressed scorn for Lebanon's sectarian system—and, with that, its willingness to disregard sectarian self-restraint. The religious communities, or their representatives, generally avoided head-on collisions to advance communal agendas, and when they did, the results were often disastrous. Hezbollah could be receptive to the dangers of sectarian conflict with the Sunnis, but as the party's frustration rose over its inability to get rid of Fouad al-Siniora, it began pushing the envelope on what its adversaries found tolerable. The mood of mutual antagonism also came from a Sunni sense of vulnerability because the balance of Lebanese Muslim power was changing. The community thought it had prevailed after Rafiq al-Hariri's death, which it viewed, quite reasonably, as a Syrian effort to silence the Sunnis. The Syrians had been forced out of Lebanon and on March 14, 2005, over Hariri's grave, Sunnis had turned out in vast numbers to say that no one could silence them—least of all Hezbollah. But that was then. Hezbollah still held the guns and could draw on the antipathy of many Shiites toward whatever it asked them to be antipathetic toward. This mix—a Sunni sense of helplessness against Shiite sensitivities and weapons, Rafiq al-Hariri's still-warm body lying near where those deriding his memory had pitched their tents in December 2006, along with a government only nominally effective and a parliament unable to meet because of Lebanon's schisms—turned Lebanon's streets into the sole arenas for resolving political differences.

In late January, Sunni and Shiite youths engaged in running battles outside the Arab University of Beirut, nearly overwhelming the Lebanese army, which imposed an overnight curfew on the capital. Until then the clashes had mostly taken place after dark, in the innermost Sunni and Shiite neighborhoods. But now it was all out in broad daylight. Youths throwing rocks at each other, waving sticks and vandalizing cars, some men pulling out weapons and firing. Television footage showing Siniora at a conference in Paris welcoming over $7 billion in pledges to help the troubled Lebanese economy was interrupted by live feeds of what appeared to be the first instances of civil war. But just as the match neared the gasoline, the political leaders pulled it back. However, the anger on both sides was uncontainable. The television station of the Hariri movement later interviewed a young woman in a predominantly Sunni neighborhood. "Olmert is more honorable than Hassan Nasrallah," she repeated twice before the camera, referring to the then-Israeli prime minister. Nothing, it seemed, was sacrosanct anymore.

The Arab University rioting was an aftershock of a more far-reaching event that had taken place two days earlier, on January 23. Having failed to oust the Siniora government, Hezbollah and its opposition allies had decided to block roads throughout Lebanon with burning tires and sand berms, bringing the entire country to a standstill. The results were mixed. In areas where Hezbollah and the Shiites were strong, the closure was nearly complete. In predominantly Christian districts, however, the followers of Michel Aoun were unable to hold on for long, because there were not enough of them to enforce the decision, and too many people opposed to it. Revealingly, the plan was conceived by Hezbollah as a military operation, particularly its segmentation of Beirut and its encirclement of areas where March 14 supporters were strong. This would take on new meaning over a year later, when the party's militia overran western Beirut.

In the midafternoon I walked around with a friend to see what was happening. On the western edge of the Christian neighborhood of Ashrafieh, Hezbollah and its Amal allies had blocked what was once the "green line" dividing wartime Beirut. It was strange how the old reflexes were back, even if the objective was to isolate pro–March 14 Christian areas from Sunni ones. The army and the Internal Security Forces, Lebanon's police, were diverting traffic away from the barriers put up by demonstrators. This was justified for the safety of the drivers, but it also showed that the security forces had no plans to end this brazen challenge to public order. We stared as a bulldozer driven by an opposition member moved back and forth, piling sand and debris onto a swelling barricade while youths milled around shouting the driver on, as if a bit more junk would make a difference. The scene was almost comically nihilistic, but it seemed to have little effect on two policemen sitting on the side of the road, inanimate with boredom. "Why are you letting them do this?" I asked. "What do you expect us to do, shoot them?" he replied, amused by the stupidity of the question.

My friend and I then walked southward, reaching the Beirut National Museum crossing. Here the Aounists were in control, but the two or three we saw in the void of the large intersection, wearing their trademark orange, could have been scattered with a golf club. A middle-aged woman sat on a concrete divider, while a young man lifted a large rock, then aimlessly dropped it, before chatting with two Shiite opposition sympathizers dashing through on a scooter. Earlier in the day the Aounists had managed to close the coastal road cutting through the Christian heartland. Supporters of the Lebanese Forces, rivals of the Aounists, had opened the way by throwing stones at the protestors. There, as elsewhere, we could see on television that the army units surrounding the Aounists were in fact protecting them. People trying to get to work soon started complaining to local stations that the army was not allowing them to pass. There seemed to be more to this than management of a volatile situation; the army had many more officers sympathetic to the opposition than to March 14, and telltale signs of collusion were turning into an embarrassment.

That evening the Aounist collapse in the Christian areas and the fact that Walid Jumblatt's followers had opened roads in the Druze-controlled mountains southeast of Beirut left only Hezbollah as an effective opposition force on the ground, surrounding the western quarters of Beirut where Sunnis were concentrated. The Sunni mufti publicly warned that this had to end, while Jumblatt sent word to the army commander, Michel Suleiman, that if the barricades were not lifted, he would tell his followers in the mountains that he was being besieged in Beirut. Shortly thereafter, by all accounts because of Iranian intervention, the protests suddenly ended. The bulldozers that had been worked so avidly to put up barriers would now, before the night was out, take them down again. Tehran, realizing that a Sunni-Shiite clash was imminent, had called Hezbollah off. However, in the anxious hours of the evening, there were those in March 14 who must have wondered what would happen if the protests continued for several days. If the army would not restore order, would it defend the government once the tables tilted decisively Hezbollah's way? In the late afternoon I had called Siniora's media advisor, Aref al-Abed, and asked about the mood at the Sérail. Abed was careful not to criticize the army but said that the prime minister had spoken to the military leadership about its performance in places. That both the mufti and Walid Jumblatt felt a need to escalate their threats later on suggested that Siniora's efforts had not been entirely successful.

With the opposition's blocking of streets and the consequent Arab University rioting, which began because of a fight between students of different political allegiances, two opposing dynamics were developing: Hezbollah and its allies were building up toward a state of controlled disorder to gradually undermine the credibility of the Siniora government. But since it's never easy to control disorder, particularly in so tense an atmosphere as the one then prevailing in Lebanon, what they were actually doing was laying the groundwork for uncontrollable civil conflict. Hezbollah was reluctantly realizing that its options were limited. By pushing too far, the party risked an internal Lebanese war that might well swallow it up, neutralize it in the fight against Israel, and alienate the Arab world's Sunnis, making Hezbollah less effective a force on behalf of Iran—which itself must have seen few advantages in all this.

Syria's leadership, in contrast, may have perceived the rewards in a new Lebanese civil war, since it expected to be the one invited to pacify Lebanon. Chaos would show how ridiculous was the belief that a sovereign Lebanese state could be viable. That was the meaning of Bashar al-Assad's conversation with Ban Ki-moon. The Syrian president also knew that a disintegrating Lebanon would be unlikely to carry through effectively with the Hariri assassination trial, because the tribunal was to be a mixed institution, with Lebanese judges as well as international ones. No Lebanese judge would readily accuse Syria if his or her own government lost its sense of purpose, even less so if it were disinclined to antagonize a Syria resurgent in Lebanon.

Where the Syrians were more constrained was in understanding that their preferred outcomes were not necessarily Iran's. Conflict in Lebanon could turn against Hezbollah and the Shiites, and the Iranians did not seem eager to go down that road, nor did this seem necessary when Hezbollah's military might allow it to push the Lebanese system in the directions it wanted. Hezbollah would probably not win a civil war, since sectarian Lebanon disallowed straightforward finalities, but it could easily defend itself against the March 14 majority, which though it enjoyed American support did not have American soldiers in the streets. So here was Lebanon caught up again, with Sisyphean recurrence, between the priorities and interests of regional and international actors, which its domestic disagreements facilitated. It may have seemed difficult to make a compelling case for Lebanese pluralism in light of that situation, or to point to the advantages of a sectarian system that seemed so naturally to breed discord. However, it was the dictates of sectarianism that had made Hezbollah hesitate on the night of January 23, when the party and Iran debated whether to push their advantage and pursue the strangulation of western Beirut. When faced with the likelihood of war, they had backed down. The sectarian rules bred a weak system, but the consequences could be daunting when these were ignored. Hezbollah, grudgingly, heeded the lesson, for now.

WHAT STAYED in my mind long after the opposition's decision to block roads was that preposterous scene greeting my friend and me at the museum intersection. The middle-aged woman sitting on the concrete divider; the young man not sure what to do with his rock. You could take seriously the Hezbollah or Amal youths in such situations—they had engaged in protest actions before; but these people? These Christians didn't have the temperament of insurgents, nor did most other Aounists, who turned out only in small numbers to close roads on that January day—to Aoun's irritation.

The breakdown of 2007 was also intimately related to developments in the Christian community. The circuitous path of Michel Aoun following his return to Lebanon, after almost a decade and a half of exile in France, greatly reduced the momentum of the emancipation movement against Syria after 2005. For many years it was the Christians who had been the cornerstone of opposition to Syria, and during the postwar period it was the Aounists who had become the strongest and best organized of the Christian groups. However, when Aoun turned away from the March 14 majority, the Christians found themselves divided, and Syria's Sunni and Druze adversaries were without an effective Christian partner to consolidate a post-Syria Lebanon. This divorce would cripple the anti-Syrian alliance, and then would threaten it when Aoun formalized his relationship with Hezbollah through a joint document signed early in 2006, ensuring the party would no longer be isolated nationally.

Aounist bitterness was explainable, even if his movement's about-face after 2005 was far less so in handing Syria and its allies an opening to reimpose their will in Lebanon. The Aounists were among those who had taken the hardest knocks during the years of Syrian hegemony, when the rest of Lebanon had paid no attention to their predicament. For them, Rafiq al-Hariri was the Lebanese face of the Syrian order, someone who would side with Damascus against his own countrymen if it meant preserving the stability of the system and his interests in it. Against the Aounists' vision of a country whose primary foe was Syria stood the looser ways of Hariri, for whom urbane co-optation was always more attractive than confrontation. His postwar reconstruction effort, the Aounists could see, was a giant pot of gold in which everyone had a share— Lebanese and Syrian officials above all. It was very corrupt, obscenely so, they insisted, which is why Hariri's killing presented the Aounists with a dilemma. Suddenly, the man they had detested was elevated to the status of sacrificial lamb for Lebanon's liberation. It was good news that the Sunnis and Druze had joined the Christians against Syria, but it also drew the limelight away from Michel Aoun, who, though he hadn't liberated anything, had persisted against Syria when no one else had. Yet there was Aoun, during the first months of 2005, in serious danger of becoming an afterthought in exile, his onetime enemies at the forefront of the Independence Intifada that might finally liberate something.

Subtle readers of Lebanese resentments, the Syrians quickly picked up on this. Before Aoun's return to Lebanon, envoys flitted between Paris, Damascus, and Beirut to discuss the conditions of his homecoming. The Assad regime detected that Aoun could be turned into a weapon against the Hariri camp and Walid Jumblatt. Throughout the weeks of anti-Syrian demonstrations after Hariri's assassination, when a Syrian withdrawal looked increasingly likely, Aoun displayed visible discomfort with his newfound allies in Beirut. He sensed that they were looking to cut him off in the run-up to parliamentary elections. That was very much a possibility, as Aoun's influence over Christians was bound to shake up a status quo in the anti-Syrian camp with which Jumblatt and Saad al-Hariri were comfortable, as it allowed them to call the shots. But on the side of Jumblatt and the Hariris, as well as that of the Lebanese Forces, there was a fear that Aoun had reached an arrangement with Syria that might undermine their gains. They were little reassured when Aoun returned in May 2005, after the legal accusations against him and his followers were hurriedly dropped by the pro-Syrian Lebanese authorities. The president, Émile Lahoud, facilitated Aoun's arrival, even providing him with a security detail. This seemed to bear out that, whether Syria had made a deal with Aoun or not, it had certainly launched him as a missile into the anti-Syrian camp. It was all very hard to pin down, mirrors reflecting mirrors, but it made inevitable the outcome the Syrian regime had prepared for: a split between Aoun and his transitory allies in the emancipation movement.

That split, followed later by the agreement between the Aounists and Hezbollah, would reveal that Michel Aoun, otherwise a most erratic man, was thinking in a linear way. He had never hidden his ambition of becoming president, and with one year left on Lahoud's mandate Aoun had reason to hope. He was, after all, a Maronite with communal legitimacy, which the elections of 2005 had demonstrated. The only thing was that, linear or not, his plan to reach the top involved a counterintuitive calculation that he could do so against the March 14 parliamentary majority (and in Lebanon parliament elects the president). How would he make this work? By allying himself with Hezbollah, and its arms, but, more important, by changing his attitude toward Syria and Iran, whose allies in Lebanon could then be counted upon to assist Aoun against Saad al-Hariri, Jumblatt, and the Lebanese Forces. Aoun's strategy suggested he was preparing for some form of Syrian restoration in Lebanon, alongside substantially greater Iranian influence, which was not unreasonable given how difficult it was for March 14 to maneuver politically. It wasn't clear who was using whom—Aoun using Syria, Hezbollah, and Iran against March 14, or they using him against March 14; but everyone was using someone against March 14, and the Syrians showed great talent in using the Lebanese against each other to reverse what had happened in 2005.

To understand what was taking place, you had to know something about Michel Aoun himself, his political instincts and his character, and what that said about his Maronite community in general. Aoun had entered the political scene publicly in 1988, when he was army commander. The mandate of the president of the time, Amin Gemayel, was expiring, and the wartime divisions meant there was no agreement over a successor. So Gemayel handed over to Aoun, asking him to form a military government as prime minister. This broke with tradition, since Aoun was a Maronite, not a Sunni, but a similar arrangement had worked out well at a moment of presidential crisis in 1952. However, instead of waiting for everyone to agree to a new president, Aoun decided to save Lebanon, and very likely to impose himself as president. He entered into a conflict with the militias in 1989, particularly the Lebanese Forces, over their illegal ports, before declaring a "war of liberation" against Syria. In mid-path, however, he again turned his guns on the Lebanese Forces, provoking months of internecine carnage as the Christians went at each other, obliterating their onetime unity that had kept the Syrians out of their districts. On October 13, 1990, the Syrians moved their army against Aoun. He fled to the French embassy and was later allowed to depart to France. Aoun had brought on a Christian catastrophe, but he had also managed to feed off of a part of the Christian public's exasperation with the Syrians and with the rule of the Lebanese Forces, and its yearning for a return of the Lebanese state after years of wartime disarray.

During Aoun's bout with the Lebanese Forces, in October 1989, Lebanese parliamentarians were invited to the Saudi resort of Taif to agree to reforms that would serve as the basis for constitutional amendments helping to end the country's long conflict. The so-called Taif Accord redrew the contours of Lebanese politics, taking much power away from the Maronite president and transferring it to the council of ministers, presided over by a Sunni prime minister. The Shiites were also rewarded when the term of the speaker of parliament was extended. Aoun rejected the accord, on the grounds that it was vague in setting a deadline for a Syrian withdrawal from Lebanon. However, there seemed to be a more visceral motive for his refusal, one that also helped explain why the Aounists were so ambivalent about Hariri after his assassination. It was that Taif was viewed as having broken the Maronites' back politically. Once the war ended, Hariri was the ostentatious incarnation of Sunni resurgence at the Christians' expense, thanks to Taif, while Aoun's exile personified their regression. Aoun's rancor was compounded by the fact that Hariri had left behind a legacy of reconstruction, corruption or no corruption, while Aoun had left behind only ruins. And Hariri's rise reminded Aoun, perhaps too uncomfortably, that he, Aoun, was greatly responsible for having shattered Christian power through his war against the Lebanese Forces, so that in the zero-sum game of his mind Aoun felt that what Hariri had gained he himself had lost.

In the spring of 1996, I first visited Aoun outside Paris in the tiny hamlet of La Haute-Maison, east of the Euro Disney amusement park. A detachment of gendarmes guarded the villa where he was staying, though the bucolic emptiness all around suggested a Borgesian labyrinth far better at keeping intruders out. I sat for two hours with the general and had come as a friendly disbeliever. Aoun's war against the Syrians had failed, but he was almost alone in still speaking against Syria. It was difficult to take this unsystematic populist very seriously, even if many would later regret not taking him seriously. He was someone who had surrounded himself with deferential devotees, for whom he had no visible empathy. In public Aoun gave the impression of being a narcissist, in love with the sway he held over his crowds, who could speak in impressionistic yet impractical injunctions, inclined to take his most unreasonable ideas seriously. Nevertheless, he was an astute reader of the Christians' gut fears, but also of the bitterness of those most socially vulnerable among them. This came from being a man of the social fringes, where those fears were most pronounced, Aoun's family having moved to Beirut's southern suburbs from the south—much like the Shiites later. Aoun's rise had been through the army, not descent from a prominent political family, explaining his aversion to the prominent families, and even more his desire to join their ranks. There was a devouring dissatisfaction to the man, the spite of someone who felt the deck was stacked against him—who would move his followers by explaining how the deck was stacked against them—alongside the peasant suspicion of someone avid to protect his measured gains.

On my two visits to La Haute-Maison, I found Aoun personally amiable, even unassuming, in the privacy of his borrowed home. When the sun's rays blinded me on one occasion, he stood up to close the curtain. His aim was off as he pulled the curtain the wrong way, but few Lebanese politicians would have troubled themselves with that effort. It was my first visit, however, that gave me insights into the general. A considerable amount of time was spent discussing current Lebanese politics, particularly the forthcoming parliamentary elections that year. Aoun was outraged because of the legal accusations leveled against him by the pro-Syrian government. He was most animated when speaking in the first person; the private and public Aouns were hopelessly entangled, so that politics were for him entirely subjective. When I asked what Aounism was, he replied: "It is Man!" I wasn't sure what he meant by that, nor, I suspect, was he, since Aoun only really saw his movement as a continuation of himself. Perhaps he was that man, or Man. Until then he had failed to organize his followers, and when I asked why, he gave me a response that could be interpreted in two ways: "So they end up with the Syrians?" Aoun could have been telling me that by setting up a structure, his followers would be easier to arrest. However, when he later described his concern that some Aounists, to get into parliament, might cut a deal with the Lebanese state at election time, I realized the general had little trust in his partisans, explaining his hesitation to organize them. A structure would create new interests and rivalries, which Aoun could not control from afar. So instead, for a time, he safeguarded his personalization of the Aounist movement, its full absorption into himself.

As I heard him speak, then and later, it became clearer to me that Aoun was as much a follower as a leader—a follower who, doubtless, could place himself at the front of the line and bark out the instructions and push the right emotive buttons, but only because these were the buttons he himself responded to. The demagogue was a dupe for his own demagoguery. Aoun was no original; he was far wilier than he was given credit for, but usually for no net gain, and he had little of the creative innovation that true leaders have. His rhetoric was invariably directed *against* something, but when it came to being *for* something, Aoun lacked precision, was devoid of deep conviction, and could alter his views with maddening variability depending on the dictates of his quest for power. Yet the man was also an emanation from the depths of Lebanese society, Maronite society in particular. Worse, he was an emanation from a Maronite society that felt itself at the end of its historical rope.

Christian perplexity, an illusory sense among Aounists that the relationship with Hezbollah might revive Christian fortunes—in particular those of the Maronites—against the Sunnis, was one explanation for the presence of Aoun's followers in Lebanese streets in January 2007. But it explained little else. How strange it was to see a Christian political movement that had always described itself as a defender of the law and the state, one particularly popular among professionals and an economically shaky petty bourgeoisie, for whom order and secure employment were the highest of values, caught up in an insurrection to bring down a representative government by forcibly preventing the Lebanese from getting to work. No less strange was Aoun's alliance with Hezbollah. Here was a party with a militia stronger than the Lebanese army, yet Aoun had sided with it, even though Hezbollah continuously defied the authority of the state that Aoun had once fought the Christian militia to reassert. But Aoun was not deterred by inconsistency. He was making a presidential bid, and only if the government of Fouad al-Siniora fell and was replaced by a government in which the opposition held veto power might he impose himself once Émile Lahoud's term ended. He would then become the savior of the Christians, of Lebanon itself, as he had always wanted to be—like Bashir Gemayel and Hassan Nasrallah a man of destiny, levitating above the shady rituals of the Lebanese political game, a revolutionary man, someone (if all must be said) far too good for the society he would sacrifice time and effort to refashion.

You had to pity the Christians, the Maronites particularly, for abandoning themselves again after 2005 to the men who had contributed most to their woes. Aoun stood on one side, with the opposition, while Samir Geagea, the Lebanese Forces leader, who had fought Aoun before being imprisoned in 1994, was on the other side with March 14. In the middle, their loyalties less well-defined, was a floating mass of Christians, neither here nor there, responsive to arguments on both sides, mistrustful of both sides, a destabilized minority buffeted by siren songs all around, but generally more dubious of the March 14 majority for being plainly dominated by two non-Christians, Saad al-Hariri and Walid Jumblatt. Many Christians had not wanted to notice, hard as it was to accept their diminishing national role, but Lebanon was now largely defined by its Sunnis and its Shiites, with the Christians (estimated, loosely, at a third of the population) trying to find a place for themselves in this arrangement between Muslims. The Taif Accord had formalized that reality, though it had also maintained Christian and Muslim parity in parliament. However, even that parity, Christians sensed, was only a by-product of Muslim goodwill, not deep conviction; or, more cynically, it was a mechanism whose re-tention was necessary to avoid destabilizing Sunni-Shiite relations. This was hardly reassuring for the future, and the Christians were hardly reassured.

Like many from the wartime generation, I had witnessed the steady process of Christian decline from up close, having grown up in a Westernized urban Maronite environment, though my family on my mother's side had come from the rural Kisirwan. I felt great empathy for this obstinate, irrepressible mountain community, with its natural inclination for pluralism too often discolored by disputation. There was something affecting in the Maronites' tendency to begin grandiose projects they could never finish. Every Maronite, it was said, could imagine himself a president or a patriarch. Rare was the rebuilt village church destroyed during the war that hadn't been conceived as a soaring basilica, yet that stood half-completed, a concrete atrocity, its funding having long run out. In this overconfidence was an explanation for the community's successes, its buoyancy when facing new undertakings. Here was the excess of the mountain, so unlike the parsimoniousness of Lebanon's urban sects, with their merchant ways. These traits had, together, made modern Lebanon, in fact could now be found conjoined in many Maronites themselves, for what was the history of the community, indeed what was the history of most Lebanese communities, but a long migration toward the city, then beyond into more multinational embraces?

One could understand a great deal about the Maronite community by looking at the pragmatism in its religiosity. When it came to religious practice and doctrine, the church could oscillate between mulish obscurantism and expedient adaptability. This was a Mediterranean creed typically unfettered by doctrine, where notions of guilt were pulverized by a devotion to form infused with oriental superstition, a proclivity for gold, high ceremony, and ephemeral spirituality. It was all mercifully blithe, the boundary between good and evil hazy, clergymen frequently more louche than the sinners. A confession, a good deed, or just a candle lit in the Virgin's name could buy one a dispensation from heavenly annoyance. The absence of self-reproach explained Maronite litheness, as did the community's pervasive faith in miracles (a faith

reinforced as the community lost its relative importance), its conviction that the divine might gamely intervene in the most tedious
of daily affairs. Just as there was no clear dividing line between
good and evil, there was no clear dividing line between the temporal and the divine, which lent the Maronites a sophistication free
of neutralizing cynicism. For if God and Jesus and the Virgin Mary
and the saints were circulating about, ever ready to do you or me
a good turn, then nothing was impossible.

The Maronites were not a community that many loved, being
so often at discordant angles with their Arab surroundings. They
were an odd exception to the Muslim majority in the region, odder
still for having helped govern modern Lebanon when Christians
in other Arab societies were afforded, at best, secondary political
roles. In its heyday most Maronites had little taste for Arab nationalism, the ideology of the postcolonial Arab world, though it was
Christian publicists in the early twentieth century who had helped
set its intellectual foundations. This estrangement also brought on
the disapproval of many a righteous Westerner alighting in the
Middle East burdened by postcolonial guilt, wounded by the in-
justices inflicted on the Palestinians, or simply impatient for cultural ruptures in his or her fantastic Orient of the imagination. For
many of them, throughout the post–World War II decades and
into the years of the Lebanese civil war, the Maronites were four
times guilty: of obtusely resisting the Middle East's future by re-
buffing Arab nationalism and reaffirming their ancient communal
identity against the luminous possibilities of the modern Arab
man; of looking back on the years of the French Mandate with
mitigated approval, and later transferring that feeling to a more imposing replacement, the United States; of having betrayed the Palestinians, whom the Maronites fought during Lebanon's civil war,
but whose cause they began doubting before then when the PLO
made Beirut its headquarters; and of trying to imitate the ways of
the West, of imagining that the West still thought in terms of pan-
Christian solidarity, while trying too hard to earn Western esteem
instead of asserting their cultural distinctiveness as Arabs.

Ultimately, the Middle East's destiny would confirm the worst
of Maronite misgivings. Arab nationalism would disintegrate into

the most debilitating authoritarianism, making the evils of colonialism seem almost tolerable in comparison; the Palestinian cause would stagger through inconclusive decades without resolution, so that the Maronite impulse to avoid paying a domestic price for the Palestinians' misery would become widespread in the region; and in a world of expanding globalization, imitation of the West would become something common, as would its opposite: the reaffirmation of primary identities in heterogeneous societies.

The Maronites' foresight would do them little good. They could take solace in the fact that Lebanese society, with its alluring combinations, with its Christian influence feeding off of Muslim influence, made their country appreciated among Arabs in search of a temporary vacation spot or place of exile, one culturally familiar but also uninhibited enough, lively enough, even Western enough, to provide welcome relief from their own more staid societies. But was that saying very much? In a small way maybe it was, an appreciation of Lebanon's liberal uniqueness to the outsider; however, in the long term where did that leave Lebanon, and the Maronites and Christians in particular? The cliché of a mosaic society only went so far. As Christians gasped for the oxygen of political relevance in the post-2005 period, pulled by one side or the other in Lebanon's Sunni-Shiite divide, they sensed that they had little say in their own future. They had once led in Lebanon, and their most prominent wartime leader, Bashir Gemayel, had tried, for a moment in 1982, to rebuild a strong state in which Christians would recapture a choice role. However, Bashir had had no time to see that he was just a player in a founding moment of the Shiite community. Michel Aoun, almost twenty-five years later, would lean on the Shiites to lend a hand to the fading Christians. Yet he, too, was an anachronism, another example of Maronite overconfidence, another half-built church with its funding having run out. There was no reason for Hezbollah to help the Maronites get what they wanted politically, namely returning to the presidency the powers it had lost at Taif, nor did the Shiites see any benefit in entering into a conflict with the Sunnis to counteract the Maronite sense of loss. Aoun's siding with Hezbollah and the Lebanese Forces' siding with March 14 gave the Christians a salutary leg in each camp, protecting them from the excesses on either side. Yet that was only a fine illustration of a minority hedging its bets, an admission that the Christians were at the mercy of forces outside their control.

ON THE morning of May 20, after returning from a trip to Chicago, I turned on my television set to see that heavy fighting had broken out in and around the northern city of Tripoli, particularly in the Palestinian refugee camp of Nahr al-Bared, a few kilometers to its northwest. In the early morning the Internal Security Forces had surrounded a building in Tripoli to arrest members of Fatah al-Islam, a Salafist jihadist group with possible ties to Al-Qaeda, which had recently appeared in Nahr al-Bared. Allegedly, the men had robbed a bank in a nearby town. Shortly thereafter, in another neighborhood, Fatah al-Islam militants fired at police, then barricaded themselves in a building. The group's combatants also came out of Nahr al-Bared and murdered soldiers still asleep at a military post, while later an army convoy came under fire south of Tripoli. A government minister would tell me he had gone to the cabinet session that day without a definite idea of how many soldiers had been killed, nor had Prime Minister Fouad al-Siniora. They both gasped when learning from the army commander, Michel Suleiman, that 27 were dead, as well as an unknown number of civilians.

For three months the Lebanese army would besiege Nahr al-Bared, destroying it in its entirety. When it was over, 163 soldiers had been killed and several hundred others wounded. This was a high toll for a military institution that had few effective combat units. Fatah al-Islam and its allies in the camp lost 222 men, according to Lebanon's defense minister, while 202 were captured. Interpretation of what had happened would soon overtake the event itself, feeding into the antagonism between the March 14 coalition and the opposition.

My return to Beirut had been marked by two things that

summed up for me where the emancipation movement of 2005 found itself. While in a Chicago taxi on the day of my departure, I heard a radio segment quoting a former National Security Council staffer named Flynt Leverett, who had authored a book on Bashar al-Assad. Leverett had often criticized the U.S. government's isolation of Syria, and in the segment he made the point that the Bush administration had "romanticized" Lebanon's "Cedar Revolution." The winds were shifting in Washington, mainly because of the administration's setbacks in Iraq, and those like Leverett were gaining ground in the debate over Lebanon and Syria. These were political realists who believed that Syria had more to offer the United States than March 14 did, and who had no interest in Lebanon's sectarian democracy, which they dismissed as a sham. The thing was that Leverett and those like him were tone-deaf to the valuable innovations of the Independence Intifada: the spontaneous protests demanding a Syrian departure and justice for the murder of Rafiq al-Hariri; the arrest of four security and intelligence chiefs under popular pressure; and the end of Syrian rule that had devastated Lebanon's constitutional institutions. It would have been lost on Leverett to suggest that in abandoning these gains, the United States would have abandoned a part of its liberal self.

As if to show what was really at stake, on the night the Nahr al-Bared battle began, a bomb exploded outside a fashionable Beirut shopping mall across the street from our apartment. This was the latest in a succession of bomb attacks after the Syrian withdrawal and seemed to be related to the fighting in the north—at least that was the impression those responsible wanted to create. I ran through the mall's parking lot, heavy with smoke, and stood above where the bomb had gone off. The device had been placed near the mall's outer wall, setting vehicles on fire and killing a woman in a nearby building. The damage was substantial; however, like most of the other bombs detonated at night during the previous two years, this one was meant to heighten fear, not provoke a bloodbath. The mall was popular with tourists, and the explosion, just before the start of the holiday season, made it more

likely that Lebanon would again be a place to avoid that summer—
something that could hardly suit a government struggling to create
an ambient sense of normalcy.

In the north the Lebanese army began employing artillery,
tanks, and helicopters against Nahr al-Bared, now emptied of most
of its residents. Much was left unsaid about the specifics of the battle, not least the ambiguous relationships between the army and
the Syrians, and between Fatah al-Islam and Sunni Salafists and Islamists in north Lebanon. These ambiguities fed the domestic political split, as each side—March 14 and the opposition—used Nahr
al-Bared to discredit the other, amid exclamations of unanimity
behind the army.

For the March 14 coalition the events in Nahr al-Bared were
another Syrian effort to destabilize Lebanon. Spokesmen for the
majority pointed out that Fatah al-Islam had emerged from a pro-
Syrian, anti–Yasser Arafat group based in Damascus named Fatah
al-Intifada, and that it appeared to have benefited from Syrian
backing when its militants entered Lebanon. They drew attention
to the fact that the apparent leader of Fatah al-Islam, Shaker Absi,
had been released early from a prison in Syria, indicating that the
Syrians intended to use him in some capacity. These suspicions
were reinforced when, five days after the fighting began, Hezbollah's leader, Hassan Nasrallah, declared that there were two "red
lines" in the current situation: there should be no attacks against
the Lebanese army, and the army should not enter Nahr al-Bared.
This seemed to be proof that Nasrallah was protecting Fatah
al-Islam. However, he was also only restating an old Hezbollah
principle—that the Lebanese state should not deploy in Palestinian
refugee camps, as this could lead to the disarmament of Palestinian groups and create momentum for the disarmament of Hezbollah. The army was displeased with the statement, and ignored it.
However, the incident illustrated Hezbollah's tenuous acceptance
of even the very basics of state authority and sovereignty.

Not surprisingly, the view of the opposition was diametrically
opposed to that of March 14. For opposition spokesmen and
media, events in the north were the result of collusion between
the Sunni Future Movement of Saad al-Hariri—backed by Saudi

Arabia—and Fatah al-Islam. In this narrative, the Future Movement had built bridges to Palestinian and Lebanese Sunni Salafists, including Fatah al-Islam, in order to combat the Shiite Hezbollah. The Lebanese army, therefore, was the victim of a perfidious triumvirate of Hariri, the Saudis, and Fatah al-Islam, with Hariri working through the Internal Security Forces, commanded by a pro-Hariri officer from Tripoli.

As ammunition, the opposition pulled out an article published by the American journalist Seymour Hersh in the *New Yorker* of March 5, 2005. Hersh had traveled to Beirut, where he benefited from the assistance of his friend Michel Samaha, a former minister and one of Syria's more resourceful paladins, who first introduced him to Hassan Nasrallah in 2003. In his piece Hersh argued that the United States, in order to contain Iran, had engaged in a major realignment in the Middle East, which involved "the bolstering of Sunni extremist groups that espouse a militant vision of Islam and are hostile to America and sympathetic to Al Qaeda." In Lebanon this "redirection," as he termed it, involved cooperation "with Saudi Arabia's government, which is Sunni, in clandestine operations that are intended to weaken Hezbollah, the Shiite organization that is backed by Iran." Hersh wrote that the Siniora government had "allowed some aid to end up in the hands of emerging Sunni radical groups in northern Lebanon, the Bekaa Valley, and around Palestinian refugee camps in the south." One source he quoted, a British former spy, told Hersh that when Fatah al-Islam splintered away from Fatah al-Intifada, "I was told that within twenty-four hours they were being offered weapons and money by people presenting themselves as representatives of the Lebanese government's interests—presumably to take on Hezbollah."

The narratives on both sides were flawed, even tendentious. Hersh, in particular, overstated his case, wading into the convoluted world of Lebanese Sunni Islamist politics with simple ideas and an undue reliance on hearsay. This was heightened by the type of journalism Hersh practices, in which he allows himself to channel the views of others, with little on-the-ground investigation to confirm his assertions. For a better-informed account of what happened, one should turn to the work of a French scholar, Bernard

Rougier, who published an article on Fatah al-Islam in September 2008, after repeated trips to north Lebanon to speak to Salafists and others familiar with what had happened. His was the first real attempt to step back and look at the events of 2007 from its many angles.

For Rougier, "[t]o explain Fatah al-Islam in terms of 'manipulation,' whatever its origin, detracts from an understanding of [associated] social and identity-related dynamics that were largely autonomous—which still doesn't mean that this or that side didn't try to exploit these for its own self-interest." Fatah al-Islam, he wrote, did indeed grow out of Fatah al-Intifada, under the auspices of its secretary-general, Abu Khaled al-Amleh. Following the 2006 Lebanon war, Abu Khaled, who was based in Syria, had wanted to establish a branch of Fatah al-Intifada that could fight Israel effectively, on the Hezbollah model. Shaker Absi, a Fatah al-Intifada officer just out of a Syrian jail, was tasked with setting up the unit. He proposed that the fighters go to Iraq to combat the Americans, and there he reportedly joined up with Abu Musab al-Zarqawi, the head of Al-Qaeda in Iraq. Upon returning to Syria, Absi was caught up in a discussion between different groups in Syria close to Al-Qaeda about whether to organize a jihad against the Syrian regime, or, alternatively, to move to neighboring Lebanon or Iraq. Abu Khaled persuaded Absi to go to Lebanon and train his men in Fatah al-Intifada camps along the Lebanese-Syrian border. From there the militants entered the northern Lebanese Palestinian refugee camps. Unable to set up their headquarters in the smaller camp of Baddawi because of resistance from other Palestinian groups, they moved to Nahr al-Bared, where, in September 2006, Absi announced Fatah al-Islam's creation.

The new group was led in a collegial fashion, Rougier continued, through three committees—a political, a military, and a religious committee—and attracted different clusters of militants from all over the Arab world. A heterogeneous structure was developing around a nucleus of jihadists who had fought in Iraq, before moving to Lebanon through Syria. "[T]he group managed, thanks to the additional contribution of Lebanese and Palestinian volunteers, to be recognized as a legitimate interlocutor by most of the religious forces in north Lebanon." This transformation, Rougier underlined, transcended Lebanese or Palestinian politics, developing in the context of a transnational call for jihad. Absi had contacts with Salafists in Nahr al-Bared, Rougier wrote, "who, in turn, legitimized the presence of Fatah al-Islam in the camp, in the hope of becoming their source of religious reference and weighing on the domestic equilibrium." While these Salafists were part of a broader northern Salafist constellation, which included Lebanese ostensibly "on the same side" as Hariri's Future Movement in Lebanon's polarized sectarian politics, Rougier dismissed the idea of organized collusion between Fatah al-Islam and the Hariri camp. Fatah al-Islam, he wrote, also had ties with Islamists close to Syria and Hezbollah, and must have been regarded by the Hariri family as a competitor for Sunni support, even as the group, in turn, surely regarded the Hariris as "Westernized" and "impious."

Rougier is a careful scholar, fluent in Arabic, which gives him added insight into his sources. His account was more thoughtful than anything presented by March 14 or the opposition during the Nahr al-Bared battle. It also tended to be backed up by the reporting of others, for example the knowledgeable journalist Hazem al-Amin of the daily *Al-Hayat*, who has followed the tentacular relationships between Sunni Islamist and Salafist networks in the north. That didn't mean that everything Rougier's sources revealed was true, but from my own visits to Tripoli, I saw the intricacy of the Islamist and Salafist landscape, and the double and triple allegiances many of these groups simultaneously entertained. Nor are all northern Salafists jihadists; indeed, only a minority advocates violence in the name of religion.

Against the version presented by March 14, Rougier affirmed that there indeed had been contacts between Fatah al-Islam and Lebanese Salafists, who under different circumstances collaborated with the Future Movement. He also implied a more roundabout, but also deniable, connection between Syria and Fatah al-Islam, contradicting those who saw a direct command relationship between the two. Against the version of the opposition, and of Seymour Hersh, Rougier pointed to the ties between Fatah al-Islam and pro-Syrian Islamist groups in Tripoli. More important, he highlighted the suspect creation of Fatah al-Islam under the very nose of Syria's intelligence services. It is indeed virtually impossible to imagine that Abu Khaled al-Amleh and Shaker Absi, both members of Fatah al-Intifada, could have organized their group in Syria, could have benefited from Fatah al-Intifada bases near the Lebanese-Syrian border, and could have sent militants back and forth between Syria and Lebanon without the knowledge, therefore the tacit approval, of their Syrian intelligence contacts.

What emerges, therefore, is a more complex story than the one rival Lebanese alliances were peddling, which also helped to better illustrate Lebanese realities in 2007. That the Future Movement oversaw a conspiracy to arm Fatah al-Islam against Hezbollah was both unconvincing and has never been proven. However, given the elaborate networks of Sunni solidarity, particularly at a time of tension with Hezbollah and the Shiite community, there certainly were points of contact between northern Salafists, Fatah al-Islam, and individuals liaising with the Future Movement or under its broad umbrella. This was facilitated by the fact that Future likely sought to avoid a confrontation with the Salafists then, so as not to divide the Sunni community. The movement happened to be more a disorderly amalgam of parallel Sunni interests after the Syrian departure than a tight organization. Its leadership was inexperienced in the tangled ways of the north, where Syria had always held the reins tightly, fearing that Lebanese Sunni activity might affect its own Sunni heartland cities to the east. Therefore, the Hariris' choices, buffeted by the competing demands of their diverse Sunni constituencies, were at times careless ones, implying a deeper relationship with militant Islamists than was really the case. Complicating the picture was that the Internal Security Forces (particularly its intelligence arm, the Information Department) was close to the Future Movement and had infiltrated northern Salafist groups, so that what might have appeared to be complicity could have been a means of keeping tabs on their activities.

There seems little doubt that Syria, at the very least, did not prevent Fatah al-Islam from establishing itself in Lebanon, when it did not actively assist the group. However, as Fatah al-Islam grew beyond the core of its initial founders into a more complex organization, attracting jihadists from around the Middle East, it is conceivable that the Syrian attitude changed. That is the view of the well-informed former head of Lebanese military intelligence, Johnny Abdo, who told me that as the Nahr al-Bared fighting intensified, Syria helped the Lebanese army against Fatah al-Islam. In exchange for this, the army evacuated from the camp militants more closely affiliated with Syria. It is difficult to confirm this version, but Abdo still has many informants inside the army and is an advisor to the Hariri family, so his argument merits consideration, particularly when many in the March 14 coalition were affirming precisely the opposite.

Nahr al-Bared was an essential moment for post-Syria Lebanon. It was the first time that armed conflict had broken out inside the country after the Syrian departure, and it struck at the heart of Lebanese domestic contradictions, as well as Lebanon's relations with Syria and its predisposition to venting regional rivalries. It was also a crisis that the Siniora government managed to weather, showing that its capabilities were not as depleted as many assumed, nor those of the Lebanese army, which had earlier displayed worrisome diffidence in implementing the law. But most of all, the events in the north exposed the ways Syria sought to create openings to regain a prominent place for itself in Lebanon while also adjusting to the reality of a neighboring country no longer under its direct control.

Syrian deceitfulness notwithstanding, the Assad regime seemed genuinely concerned about the vacuum it had left behind across its border in northern Lebanon, the stronghold of Lebanon's Sunnis. For the regime, that border was the soft underbelly of Alawite rule, a natural line of contact between predominantly Sunni areas of Lebanon, Syria, and Iraq. The Assad regime could not readily abandon northern Lebanon to its foes, particularly the Hariris, which they feared might give their backers, the Saudis, a leg up on Syria. Against this backdrop, an organization like Fatah al-Islam could serve concurrent purposes. It could split Lebanon's Sunni community, between those with Fatah al-Islam and those against; it could tarnish the Hariri camp for allegedly linking its fortunes to a Salafist jihadist group, which would also alarm the non-Sunni allies of the Future Movement; and it could push Lebanon's Sunnis into a confrontation with the Lebanese army, undermining the emergence of a capable Lebanese state, for the Siniora government, the Syrians knew, needed the army's goodwill to remain in place. It was, once again, about Sunni power and how to contain it. That had been a canon of Syrian rule over its neighbor for decades, a principal reason why the Assad regime had always mistrusted Rafiq al-Hariri. But it also represented Syrian acknowledgment that the upshot of the Independence Intifada was that it had turned Sunnis into a bulwark of Lebanese resistance to Syria, largely because of the Sunni terror of a Syrian comeback, so that by breaking Sunni unity and discrediting Sunni leaders, Damascus would be better able to regain some sort of a say in Lebanon.

Three months after the Nahr al-Bared fighting began, it came to a sudden end. In the early morning of September 3, the last militants in the camp tried to flee in three groups; most were gunned down or captured. Absi was not found, despite a short-lived report that he had been killed, which a DNA test soon disproved. Later, Lebanese officials declared that he had escaped a day earlier, with disagreement persisting over how he had managed to do so. Johnny Abdo contended that the army had allowed him to flee in an under-the-table arrangement with Syria, to end the fighting. Others doubted this story and believed that Absi escaped to Baddawi and was later smuggled out of Lebanon. Whatever the truth, Fatah al-Islam's trajectory only accentuated the dark zones prevailing on all sides in the political struggle over Lebanon's future. However, it was above all a reminder of Bashar al-Assad's intentions when he told Ban Ki-moon in April that Lebanon was most peaceful when Syria's army was present there. The Syrian president sought to prove this by hook or by crook.

Then there were the assassinations. On the afternoon of June 13, I happened to have coffee with a friend of mine, Bassem al-Shabb, the Protestant parliamentarian from Beirut and a member of Saad al-Hariri's bloc. We said our goodbyes and I headed down to my newspaper. On television was a new scene of destruction. A bomb had exploded in western Beirut near the Sporting beach club, killing Walid Eido, a Sunni representative from Beirut and Bassem's colleague in the Hariri bloc. Eido had been on a daily outing to the Sporting, near where the assassins, wise to his routine, had picked him off. I called Bassem to express my sympathies: "We probably won't be seeing each other for a long time," he groaned, preparing himself for what would turn into months of forced seclusion for March 14 parliamentarians.

The anti-Syrians in parliament explained the killing as part of a scheme to slowly cut down their slim legislative majority. A presidential election was nearing, and March 14 and the opposition profoundly disagreed over how to interpret the constitutional clauses governing the vote by parliament. March 14 interpreted the constitution in such a way that it allowed them to elect a president by a simple majority if, on the first ballot, a two-thirds quorum was not present. The opposition rejected this, justifying what was clearly its intention to boycott parliamentary sessions—and therefore deny a quorum—in the event both sides failed, first, to agree to a president. By killing parliamentarians, March 14 representatives insisted, the Syrians and their local allies were trying to deny them the possibility of mustering even that simple majority. This arcane constitutional discussion would take on importance in subsequent months, but it perhaps only partly explained why Walid Eido had been eliminated. There was a much simpler reason for killing March 14 figures. To keep the survivors indoors and prevent them from engaging even in rudimentary politics on the ground that would allow them to firm up their influence.

Memories could be short, however. Only three months after Eido's assassination, a bomb in an eastern Beirut suburb killed another parliamentarian, Antoine Ghanem. He had just returned from a trip when he decided, unwisely, to visit a friend. Again someone was waiting. Ghanem had never been the most charismatic of politicians—many people weren't even sure what he looked like when the news broke. This was a man from the old school, a sixty-four-year-old lawyer with thick glasses and Edward G. Robinson lips. His Arabic, on the occasions he spoke publicly, was formal, anesthetizing. Yet Ghanem's relative anonymity made his end more pitiful. He personified the diminishing marginal returns of Lebanon's killing machine. Ghanem was a son of the aspiring middle class, a member of the Gemayels' Kataeb Party, respectable, close to the center of Lebanese life in Beirut, but rather like the Christian quarter of Tahouita where he was born, not quite there. All the better-known politicians attended his funeral, cutting through undulating applause as they entered the church, surrounded by chic bodyguards, so that Ghanem seemed almost an accessory at his own funeral. The mourners came from the unfashionable neighborhoods, with their oversized crosses framed by open shirts, their daily toil so remote from the hard political lesson that Ghanem's killers wanted delivered. These were not people who had often been asked to decide anything, so what was expected of them from Ghanem's elimination? Here was a funeral too far, without new meaning, therefore without very many emotions, except for those displayed by Ghanem's family and friends; without even the aesthetic appeal that could freeze a mental frame and render the event meaningful. If any killing could be deemed superfluous, this was it.

Shortly thereafter, I left for a vacation in France. We seemed to be in an interregnum before the end of Émile Lahoud's term in late November. For a few blissful weeks the country was out of sight and out of mind, with one exception. While in Paris, I contacted Detlev Mehlis, the former head of the United Nations commission investigating the Hariri assassination. Mehlis was beginning to have deep misgivings about the investigation run by his successor, Serge Brammertz. In an email to me in late November, he summed up his views following several exchanges between us. Mehlis wrote that he did "not see any trial in the foreseeable future." This he described as a "realistic assessment" of the situation, stemming from the fact that, since early 2006, no new suspects had been identified and "[n]o visible new elements seem to have been added" to the case. Mehlis also revealed that most of his senior investigators "had been asked to leave," and concluded that "the perspective does not look good to me, and it seems that out of political reasons a lot of people [outside Lebanon] want it exactly like that. I see no desire to return to the original pace of the investigation." Mehlis later clarified that his own investigation was "half done" by the time Brammertz took over, six months after it had started, implying there was no justification for the delay. In another email, Mehlis had criticized Lebanese journalists for cutting Brammertz so much slack, including me. I asked him whether he would be willing to go on the record with his doubts. At the moment, Mehlis replied, he preferred not to, since it would involve reproaching just about everyone involved in the investigation and tribunal process, including the United Nations. "That would be a little too much criticism for almost everyone, right?" he wrote.

There may not have been much hopefulness left inside Lebanon, but the international effort to resolve the Hariri murder was a different matter. The U.N. investigation was supposed to be taking place outside the country's exposed political boundaries, and in statement after statement March 14 politicians made the point that the Hariri tribunal was unavoidable, that justice could not be stopped. Now Mehlis, the man who had once incarnated that certitude, was, at least privately, tossing a big stone into the puddle of high expectations. It was a fitting coda to a bad year that was not even over yet.

6

The Crack-Up Continues

SOON AFTER MY arrival in Washington, D.C., in the summer of 1985 to study for a master's degree, I received word that a friend of mine, Richard Salem, along with his sister and uncle, had been kidnapped in West Beirut. Richard had been a teenage comrade, and there was a time when, with a cousin of mine, we spent every Saturday afternoon at a Beirut movie theater. Several weeks before his abduction, shortly before my departure, Richard and I had said our goodbyes. By then we were seeing relatively less of each other. Yet for years after I had heard of his disappearance, I would dream that he had been released, only to awaken to the nightmare that he had not. The three were never heard from again, though Richard's mother, until she died in May 2009 after being hit by a car, continued to believe her children were alive, and left their clothes folded in their closets.

A somehow-related memory is that of seeing my mother on television, injured in the car-bomb explosion that killed Lebanon's president-elect, René Mouawad, on November 22, 1989. I had just turned on the nightly news in my Washington apartment, and there she was, bleeding from her forehead, holding up a hand to block the camera, knowing, she later told me, that I would be watching. Minutes before Mouawad's convoy appeared, she had been standing across the street from the point of the explosion, detained by a Syrian soldier who had checked her bag for security reasons. "What's inside?" he had asked. "A bomb," was her response. The two had laughed.

Back in Beirut during the 1990s, I rediscovered a corroding photograph of Richard and me in a friendly tussle on a balcony, his face completely covered by a ski mask. Soon thereafter I attended a play written by the Lebanese novelist Elias Khoury and staged by the actor Roger Assaf, titled *The Memoirs of Job*. The theme of the play was wartime memory, and it contained a scene in which the face of a kidnap victim under interrogation was hidden by a ski mask. Khoury had based his character on a composite of several people who had disappeared during the war, including Richard and his sister.

One evening, I happened to see Khoury in the street and offered him a ride home. As we were driving by the scene of Mouawad's assassination, I told him my mother's story. He was duly impressed, or pretended to be, by the surreal coincidences the story yielded. However, he more than reimbursed me through the connection he provided between my snapshot of Richard and his own play.

After the civil war ended, it was almost possible to enjoy such instances of disquieting happenstance. But in May 2008, Lebanon entered into a brief domestic war that reminded us of what the savagery between 1975 and 1990 had really been about. Those who lived through the war felt themselves again being pulled toward the abyss as the bottom was hit in Lebanon's three-year experiment to break free from Syria and strengthen the liberal impulses in a society free of violence. Hezbollah and its Amal allies overran western Beirut, while Hezbollah opened a front in the mountains against the Druze. When all was over, the results were ambiguous, a bit of this balancing off a bit of that. However, the militias mainly of the Shiite community had brought war out of the chest and oiled it along with their guns. It would take the efforts of several countries in the region, and of the Lebanese themselves, to avert new civil conflict that might have segued into a broader Sunni-Shiite conflict that nobody in the Middle East wanted.

In November 2007, I returned to Beirut from vacation, two weeks before Émile Lahoud's presidential mandate was to end. The French humorist Alphonse Allais once wrote that "to leave is to die a little, but to die is to leave a lot." After nine years in office, Lahoud was finally leaving, his political death a certainty, and the hope was that Lebanon would finally be able to live a little. Here was the man whose efforts to impose a centralized militarized system after 1998 had backfired against both him and Syria, and whose forced extension in office had brought on the crisis of 2004. For those two shipwrecks alone Lahoud deserved our undying gratitude. But the more substantial question was, who would replace him? While I was away, there had been efforts to answer that question, but to no avail. The March 14 majority and the opposition had failed to agree on a candidate, which meant parliament would be unable to achieve the required quorum to elect a new president. On the side of March 14, two candidates had been put forward as the coalition's favorites in the event it decided to use its simple majority to bring a president in without a consensus. However, offering up two candidates effectively neutralized both, and the plan went nowhere because the opposition would have taken it as an act of war. The opposition, in turn, declared its support for Michel Aoun, but other than the Aounist faithful this endorsement was so tepid, so ambivalent, that it only established how little Hezbollah trusted Aoun with power. However, the opposition gained more from a vacuum. Hezbollah ruled in the streets, which meant it could raise and lower the pressure on March 14 at will, while a void at the top of the state gave the party—and with it Syria and Iran, even if they pursued separate priorities—more leverage to impose its conditions on any new president.

This deadlock accelerated the search for a candidate acceptable to both sides, and attention turned to the army commander, Michel Suleiman, who had adroitly navigated through political minefields during the previous three years. His name had been raised by the Egyptians in one mediation effort; he was also known to be appreciated by the Saudis, the Russians, and the Maronite patriarch, but it was the fear among many March 14 politicians that Syria would also welcome him, since it had appointed him and might be tempted to use his influence over the armed forces and security agencies to contain the likes of Saad al-Hariri, Walid Jumblatt, and Samir Geagea. That may have been true, but there was also a protocol to Syrian power that had to be respected. In the past, whenever Damascus had promoted Lebanese, it had obliged them to earn the favor first by compromising themselves, so that Syria alone could bestow its authority on them and also act as the final reference point.

However, something unforeseen was in the air when, on November 13, some ten days before Lahoud was to depart, I made telephone calls and sensed that the mood in the Hariri camp was shifting toward Suleiman. That evening, I visited Walid Jumblatt to get a better sense of what was going on. He said he was unhappy that March 14 had failed to back the election of a former minister who, though he was in his eighties and had once declared that he would lie down in the street to prevent Syrian tanks from leaving Lebanon (he hadn't), was better than no president at all. I raised the issue of Suleiman and described the apparent attitude change in the Future Movement. "Everything points to Suleiman coming, no?" I asked. Jumblatt did not answer, but he had surely gotten wind that Saad al-Hariri was preparing to take everyone by surprise on the presidency; or had he? A week later a Future parliamentarian spoke for Hariri and his bloc in announcing they would welcome a constitutional amendment to bring Suleiman into office. An amendment was required (although it was never voted upon) since the army commander, as a senior civil servant, was otherwise not allowed to stand for election.

By then Lahoud had bid Lebanon farewell, with a speech that many misunderstood as a declaration of a state of emergency. When one parsed the verbal convolutions, however, it was empty talk. The opposition had wanted the president, in his final act, to take executive decisions that would politically impair March 14. In fact, Lahoud, who would soon lose the protection provided by presidential office, had no intention of angering those states supporting the majority, particularly the United States. The president quietly contacted foreign embassies to assure them that he would go just as quietly. It was a fitting finale for a mendacious man, but Lahoud had fulfilled one end of his bargain with Syria and the opposition: He had done nothing to facilitate the choice of a successor to fill his now-empty office.

Saad al-Hariri's endorsement of Michel Suleiman was a gamble. In its simplest form, the idea was for March 14 to be responsible for bringing the army commander to power so that he would be beholden to the majority. This would create a dilemma for the opposition: It could either accept Suleiman, therefore comply with the majority's choice; or it could oppose him, earning the general's animosity and that of part of the army, while undercutting someone close to Syria, all to maintain a debilitating and unpopular political vacuum. There was also a more fundamental rationale, namely that by backing Suleiman, March 14 would be able to garner Maronite Christian support while weakening Suleiman's main rival for the presidency, Michel Aoun, denying Hezbollah a credible Christian partner. Aoun had miscalculated. Had he remained at equal distance between Hezbollah and March 14, he would have been uncircumventable as a candidate. Instead, by siding with one against the other, he became someone whom the majority sought at all costs to stop. However, Suleiman was an unknown entity. Even Hariri's Christian allies needed convincing. Samir Geagea had spent eleven years in a cell at the defense ministry, seven under Suleiman, and was not pleased that Hariri with Walid Jumblatt and Fouad al-Siniora had agreed to the choice between themselves, without consulting him. However, it was Syria that seemed most hesitant. It was not personal with Suleiman. Damascus considered him among the most desirable of candidates. It was just the conditions at that moment that were a problem. Syria didn't like it that the general was to be elevated by its enemies. It didn't like it that the Christians might unite around Suleiman, when the post-2005 situation had, as far as the Syrians were concerned, so advantageously divided them. And finally, Syria didn't like it that a new president, if smoothly elected, would establish that Lebanon was normalizing without Syria, and that the era of Lahoud was truly over.

Syria paid a price for its temporary intransigence, but a small one indeed. In the weeks before Lahoud's departure, the French president, Nicolas Sarkozy, decided to engage Bashar al-Assad over Lebanon, hoping that Syrian acceptance of an election would open the door to better Franco-Syrian relations. The French felt there was "the possibility of an evolution" with Damascus. As far as Sarkozy was concerned, his predecessor Jacques Chirac had been too close to the Hariri family and the March 14 coalition to pursue creative diplomacy on that front. Sarkozy seemed motivated by several things. He wanted France to be more of a player in the Levant and the Middle East, and what better way than to deal with Syria, which was destabilizing most of its neighbors? Sarkozy was also encouraged in this by the emir of Qatar, who had won an attentive ear in Paris and had good relations with Assad. But there was also something else in Sarkozy's reversal of policy: a yearning to erase the legacy of Chirac, for whom he had an aversion. By November, relations with Syria were being run out of the Elysée Palace, where Sarkozy handed the matter over to Claude Guéant, his most senior advisor. The French effort was the first breakdown in the Franco-American partnership that had facilitated passage of Resolution 1559 as well as subsequent Security Council resolutions on Lebanon. Sarkozy's readiness to bring Syria in on the Lebanese election contradicted the spirit of Resolution 1559, which had called for a free and fair electoral process in 2004 "without foreign interference or influence." However, these matters carried little weight with the French president, who, as was his impetuous way, had already rushed ahead to the then with Syria, without waiting to see what might happen in the now.

Assad was more patient. As French envoys traveled to Damascus and Beirut in November, the Syrian president did nothing to break the Lebanese impasse, nor would this have made any sense. Assad was in the driver's seat and knew that the lack of progress in Lebanon only made him more indispensable. Without a president, the country was especially vulnerable to his ultimatums, augmenting Assad's chances of bringing in a new president—perhaps Suleiman himself—on his own terms, as well as imposing a balance of forces in a new government that would allow Syria's allies to veto decisions they were unhappy with.

The French had hit up against a wall of Syrian interests without foreseeing how Assad was likely to react. It was a shoddy diplomatic performance. Since Sarkozy was the one wanting to open a channel to Syria, Assad rightfully concluded that he needed Syria more than Syria needed France, which meant that if Syria rejected French mediation now, Sarkozy would try again later. And anyway, how important *were* the French to Syria? Assad was pleased with a European hand after two years of isolation, but Paris was just a passage to better ties with Washington. Because the Bush administration was unwilling to reconcile with Syria, the Syrian president could take his time with France. Sarkozy did have some pride left. When the Syrians continued to block the Lebanese election, he temporarily suspended his mediation effort and managed to publicly utter his displeasure. That was the derisory toll that Syria paid for obstructing Lebanon's presidential election, and for violating the essence of Resolution 1559.

Michel Suleiman had the stain of Saad al-Hariri's approval to wash away. The army commander would spend months playing down that troublesome embrace. But with all the talk of whether he would take office or not—and his chances rose when the Arab League began a mediation mission in early 2008 to have Suleiman elected—very little was said about why, again, Lebanon was preparing to elect a general as president. Between the outgoing Émile Lahoud, Michel Suleiman, and Michel Aoun, we were dodging berets, when Lebanon, throughout its years of independence and until 1998, had only once had a general as head of state, in an Arab world awash with military leaders. Rare were those in March 14 who expressed displeasure with Suleiman. One of them, however, was Carlos Eddé, the head of the venerable but by then much-depleted National Bloc. He vowed to leave the majority coalition if the army commander was elected, and for all his troubles he was treated as an eccentric. Yet Eddé was an aficionado of military history, and more than most knew the egocentricity of the army officer, particularly in a society like Lebanon's where constraints on military power were not developed. Eddé hadn't liked Lahoud, didn't like Aoun, and had deep reservations about Suleiman, who hailed from the same district as he. Whatever the practicality of his position at that moment, it was consistent, when other March 14 politicians had veered like champion skiers in their views of the army commander.

One of my friends, Najib Khazzaqa, once offered this insight into Lebanon's military, from his years as a journalist and, before that, as a Lebanese member of the Palestinian Fatah movement. We were driving toward his hometown of Zahleh in the Beqaa Valley one day, his white walrus mustache shuddering in the wind, when Najib remembered an incident from the war that had taken place nearby.

"In the army the officers are hungry and it's the wives of the officers who are the officers," he declared loudly.

"How so?" I asked.

"This is what officers do. They marry a woman who brings in a regular salary, let's say a schoolteacher. The woman wants her husband to be promoted because that means she will be promoted. The wives of officers admire officers higher in rank than their husband, and they know that their husband needs that officer to be promoted. So sometimes they have to make, well, sacrifices. The problem is when the sacrifices become pleasurable."

"I see."

"During the war I protected some officers at the Rayyaq airbase near here. We placed one of them in an apartment where he was safe—at the time I was with Fatah, and I was told by Abu Jihad to make an ID card for him. A friend and I would go and visit him and his wife. We played cards once and won some money off of them. The wife told us, half-jokingly, 'When this war ends, you two will be the first ones I hang.' I thought about what she said, and then I understood. For her, the army was supposed to represent power, and during the war the army, like her and her husband, had fallen a long way. Mark my words, the wives of officers are the officers."

I would have a chance to confirm Najib's itinerant wisdom time and again in talking with officers. Wives aside, the military suffered from an incongruity that he had well illustrated: Here was an institution enjoying broad popular approval, for being so rare an object of national approval. This tended to heighten Lebanese expectations in the army's capacities that it could not usually meet, particularly when it was laden down by an officer corps often governed by and playing to the vicissitudes of politicized advancement. This gap between reality and expectations generated uncertainty about the army as a symbol of authority, and insecurity among the officers. After all, what was authority in a society in which state institutions mirrored sectarian realities and tended to be weaker than communal leaderships? And what was power in postwar Lebanon, when the army and its intelligence branch had become appendages of Syria? The perversity of the relationship was best illustrated by a single convention: Officers attending training courses in Syria, and they were more frequent after 1990, were expected during their exams to fill out an introductory page in their notebooks with tributes to the Syrian president. The price of refusal, and some refused, could be a stalled career.

This was the world that Michel Suleiman came from. He had been chosen by Syria in 1998 to take over command of the army from Émile Lahoud, when he was chosen to be president. Lahoud's predecessor, Elias Hrawi, had requested, in his final meeting with his Syrian counterpart, Hafez al-Assad, that the outgoing commander of his Presidential Guard get the nod as commander. Ghazi Kanaan, the head of Syria's intelligence network in Lebanon at the time, was asked by Assad for an opinion. He didn't say no, but he didn't say yes. His mind had already been made up. He ruled out Hrawi's choice, considering him, with a second favorite, too close to men whom the Syrians mistrusted. That left Michel Suleiman. He would coordinate closely with the Syrians over the years, managing with little visible difficulty the house of many mansions that is Lebanon's armed forces. However, the general was no innovator, whether in his relations with Syria or much else, no *révolté*; he wasn't about to question the status quo, since he was himself its product.

Still, Suleiman could walk between raindrops. His talent for doing so was apparent after the assassination of Hariri, when the army was at the center of all the contradictions it had dredged up. Three of the four generals arrested for their suspected involvement in the crime came from its ranks, and it was the army that tried to prevent demonstrators from reaching Martyrs Square two weeks after the killing, only to back down to avoid bloodshed. Suleiman was a prisoner of conflicting agendas. Émile Lahoud would doubtless have liked him to suppress the demonstrations, while Suleiman also had to consider Syria's and Hezbollah's preferences. However, he had realized that he would be the fall guy for the killing of unarmed civilians. In the end, he had read the situation correctly, remaining impartial. Suleiman must have also sensed that this would increase the odds of his becoming president one day. So, in late 2007, the army commander was the last one left standing, not for the first time, acceptable to all, trusted by none, itself a badge of honor. Yet Suleiman still had many hoops to walk through to be fully accepted by Syria, and he would spend several more months counting how many.

One of the first was the assassination on December 12 of Brigadier General François Hajj, the chief of military operations and a close friend of Suleiman. This was not the easiest of crimes to interpret. Hajj, who came from the southern town of Rmaysh, was said to sympathize with Michel Aoun, as did many senior Christian officers. He was also regarded as a favorite to succeed Suleiman as army commander and had played a significant role during the Nahr al-Bared fighting. Aoun suggested that Hajj's killing was really directed against him—perhaps his way of compensating for the fact that all those murdered since 2005 had opposed him and, more important, had opposed Syria. More likely, Hajj was killed as a warning to Suleiman, and to March 14, that it was the Syrians who would bring in Lebanon's next president and army commander, not Saad al-Hariri and Walid Jumblatt. Hajj would later be declared a "martyr" of the independence struggle against Syria by March 14, but the majority's parliamentarians who attended his requiem mass were booed by younger officers as they entered the church. Suleiman got the message and continued his balancing act: There was no love lost between him and Aoun, who, he knew, wanted to be president in his place, but Suleiman was not about to alienate the pro-Aoun Christians in the military on whom he relied; and, though surely embittered by the loss of his comrade, he was also not about to point a finger at the likely culprits and spoil his election chances.

AT AROUND this time, I received word from Detlev Mehlis that he would grant me an interview, to coincide with the three-year anniversary of the Hariri assassination on February 14. Mehlis did not mention it in his email, but he also planned to break his silence now because Serge Brammertz was preparing to leave the U.N. commission. Mehlis later told me he felt some responsibility for having recommended Brammertz in the first place, which is perhaps what he meant when he wrote me: "I think I owe this to the Lebanese and to 'my' UNIIIC team." He would grant one interview to me, and one to a German publication, he added, and that would be that. I received a go-ahead from the *Wall Street Journal*, for whom I had done interviews in the past, and flew to Berlin in mid-January 2008.

Mehlis picked up my wife and me from our hotel on the Friedrichstrasse and drove us out to his house in a Berlin suburb. After lunch at a nearby inn, we sat down for the interview in the interregnum before a four-course dinner that he and his wife had prepared for us and some friends. This fastidious German seemed anything but a fastidious German. A *bon viveur*, generous, armed with the irreverence that tends to differentiate Berliners from most of their countrymen, he came from a generation for whom the Cold War was a neighborhood concern—in Mehlis's case literally, for the old wall had been only a block away from his home. It wasn't so much a craving for order that seemed to inhabit him as the awareness of the proximity of disorder—that what you wanted to keep away might be there behind the door. The crimes that Mehlis was best known for solving—the La Belle discotheque bombing, the bombing of the French cultural center in West Berlin—fit into this category. Here was his city transformed into a mailbox for political messages from the outside, the perpetrators abetted by the communist regime over the border, the victims addendums to make the messages more terrifying. That's what made Mehlis apt for the Hariri case. The line between order and chaos had dissolved in an instant on February 14, 2005, and it took someone familiar with the suddenness of chaos to get the point. Mehlis was a natural investigator, a job that in some ways resembles a natural shopper. Some people will inspect all varieties of an item before deciding which one to buy, and then they will count their change afterward. Mehlis had done all that during his time in Lebanon; he had even reached firm conclusions. But now, in his minimalist living room, he wanted to tell me that Brammertz, who was unfamiliar with chaos, had been shortchanged, or had shortchanged the rest of us, and that bothered him to no end.

I started by asking Mehlis why he regretted having left the investigation when he did, as he had earlier explained to a newspaper in Frankfurt. "From what I am hearing, the investigation has lost all the momentum it had [when Brammertz took over] in January 2006. Had I stayed on, I would have handled things differently," he answered. Among the things he would have done, he said, was to continue informing the Security Council and the Lebanese public about his ongoing investigation, whereas Brammertz's reports had been terse and uninformative. Wasn't this justified by the secrecy of the investigation, I asked. Mehlis was dismissive: "I don't accept the concept of the 'secrecy of the investigation,' nor is it a judicial principle that I know. For me, as a German, the notion of a secret investigation sounds ominous." When I suggested that Brammertz had identified "persons of interest" in the crime, therefore that perhaps progress *had* been made, Mehlis replied: "Unfortunately, I haven't seen a word in his reports during the past two years confirming that he has moved forward. When I left, we were ready to name suspects, but [the investigation] seems not to have progressed from that stage. There is no judicial term that I have ever heard of called a 'person of interest.' You have suspects, and a 'person of interest' is definitely not a suspect. If you have identified suspects in a case like this one, you don't allow them to roam free for years to tamper with evidence, flee the country, or commit similar crimes."

Particularly irksome to Mehlis was the fact that Brammertz had reopened the crime scene for analysis, only to confirm Mehlis's original findings. "I wondered what he was doing," he said. "We already had Swiss, French, and German expert opinion indicating that the explosion that killed Hariri was beyond doubt an above-ground explosion. By reopening the crime scene he cast doubt on the credibility of the investigation that I had led. He also wasted valuable time and manpower." Yet Brammertz had continued to enjoy support at the Security Council, suggesting that his low-key style had been appreciated at U.N. Headquarters. In light of this, was there meddling from Secretary-General Kofi Annan's office in Mehlis's work? "Annan made it clear to me that he did not want another trouble spot. I respected this, but he also respected my point of view," the German replied. "The U.N. did not interfere in my efforts and had no leverage over me, as I was not after a position in the organization"—a dig at Brammertz, who was preparing to move to a U.N. court, the International Criminal Tribunal for the Former Yugoslavia.

I brought up again the case of the two Syrian witnesses Mehlis had questioned, whose testimonies had partly discredited the investigation. One had recanted in a Damascus press conference; the second was a suspect. "In such crimes you cannot be choosy about whom you are dealing with," he answered. The two had provided information "which we could sometimes corroborate with information received elsewhere. . . . Maybe the witnesses were there to discredit the investigation, but that can help us determine who wants to discredit the investigation." While the tribunal had been established under Chapter VII authority several months earlier, Mehlis said he did not expect a trial to begin "within the next two to three years, unless the investigation regains momentum." Would the tribunal still go forward? "Definitely, no one can abolish this tribunal," he replied; "I may not be happy about the time frame, but am deeply convinced the case can be solved and will be solved." It was an optimistic conclusion, but in light of what he had said earlier, it sounded halfhearted, an effort to end on a bright note for all those who had believed things would turn out better— at least in the way he himself had.

The Canadian Daniel Bellemare, Brammertz's replacement, would show that he was on the same wavelength as his predecessor. Brammertz had played a significant role in Bellemare's selection, had briefed him before he began working, and both shared an understandable view, often repeated, that they had to be judges even more than investigators, since the evidence they were uncovering had to persuade a court of law. But somewhere in that insistence was implicit criticism of Mehlis, who had offered Bellemare this bit of advice in our interview: "Concentrate on the Hariri case itself; don't try to write a history book. . . . Analysis can never replace solid investigative police work." The new commissioner proved as tight-lipped as Brammertz. After his arrival I spoke with his then spokesman, Ashraf Kamal, who said that Bellemare intended to be more accessible. That was excellent news, I replied; would he indulge me with an interview? Kamal called me back to say that Bellemare would not be talking just yet. I hadn't expected a different answer, but that absence of expectation was itself a sign of a problem. No one was asking for secrets; just for the Canadian to update us on where his investigation stood in a way that was more compelling than all those outstandingly evasive reports put out by the U.N. commission.

Later on, I would get a better sense of why he may have been so reticent. When he began his work, Bellemare is said to have told his Lebanese counterparts that he hoped that within six months he would be more advanced in his investigation than he was. This was, in its bland way, a significant statement. By then the U.N. investigation had lasted for two and a half years, not to mention the initial Fitzgerald inquiry, so that for Bellemare to express his "hope" that he would have more information within half a year was a telltale sign that Brammertz had not moved as quickly as everyone assumed. Indeed, before his departure, the Belgian commissioner reportedly explained to the Lebanese that there was not much new in his file on the case, but also that one more year was needed to conclude the work. This seemed a contradiction, for if he did not have much in his file, how could he set so explicit a deadline—a deadline incidentally, never met? A more comprehensive picture was necessary to get a better sense of how much, or how little, Brammertz had progressed. The rare information surfacing usually came from sources speaking off the record, or on deep background. But some of the skeptics were significant individuals in Lebanon's political or judicial hierarchy. There were also those Lebanese politicians with a deep interest in the case who defended the Belgian, saying that whereas Mehlis had set the groundwork for the investigation in Syria, Brammertz was sometimes better able to get information out of the Syrians, whose relations with the German had become acrimonious. Mehlis had had a different strategy, one that involved using Syrian reluctance to cooperate with him to force the Security Council to clarify his mandate; Brammertz's role was to put to advantage what Mehlis had gained, in order to widen the wedge of information.

At least that was the theory. However, while you could hide many things, you could not hide time or words. As the months came and went, as the commission's mandate was extended again and again, and as the UNIIIC reports told us the same things again and again, the idea that everything was on track became thoroughly unpersuasive. The nadir was surely reached on March 29, 2008, when Bellemare, in the tenth report of the U.N. commission, and his first, assured us that "[t]he Commission can now confirm, on the basis of available evidence, that a network of individuals acted in concert to carry out the assassination of Rafiq Hariri and that this criminal network—the 'Hariri Network'—or parts thereof are linked to some of the other cases within the Commission's mandate." The Lebanese had not waited for almost three years to hear this proclamation of the obvious, one repeated time and again in earlier reports. Worse, Bellemare confused readers by carelessly using the term "criminal network," suggesting a Mafia hit, when he implicitly endorsed the view of Brammertz and Mehlis that Hariri's murder was political, if only by virtue of being linked to subsequent killings and crimes in Lebanon that were undeniably political. Alongside this, more information was emerging from individuals other than Mehlis expressing unhappiness with the Brammertz mission, as well as their growing doubts about Bellemare, who had never investigated a complex political crime of this nature. The Belgian had hired an inordinate number of analysts, getting rid of investigators, which Bellemare sought to later reverse, although inexperienced holdovers from the Brammertz years with little expertise in criminal investigations remained in place. An analyst could perhaps link the tooth of a bomber to a part of the globe where he had resided, or identify where paint at the crime scene came from; but only an investigator could arrest suspects, compare testimonies, play suspects and witnesses off against one another, thereby casting light on the process and hierarchy of decision-making in the crime itself. The fragments of criticism told an incomplete story. Yet when you placed them against a backdrop of doubts expressed by Mehlis (who had worked on such cases and had an interest in seeing Brammertz and Bellemare vindicate him), as well as privately by senior Lebanese officials; when you looked at the repeated extensions requested by Brammertz and Bellemare, the time-wasting in reopening the crime scene, and the commission's ever more laconic reports, it became difficult not to conclude that the momentum had indeed been lost between 2006 and 2008, and that this might ultimately have a harmful bearing on the future trial process.

On the day before the Mehlis interview was to appear in the *Wall Street Journal*, there was another assassination in Beirut, this one more obviously linked to the Hariri investigation. Captain Wissam Eid had just turned off a highway near the eastern suburb of Hazmiyeh, when a car bomb placed at an intersection destroyed the car he was in. Eid, a thirty-one-year-old Sunni officer in the Internal Security Forces, hailed from the northern Lebanese town of Deir Ammar. He had been working closely with the U.N. commission, playing a key role in analyzing communications intercepts. The day before his murder he had reportedly spent four hours with the U.N. commission. A judicial official later recalled that Bellemare did not believe there was a link between the meeting and the killing, a view with which a Lebanese judge involved in the case disagreed, believing that Eid had made a breakthrough. Perhaps, but the Canadian commissioner surely understood better the connection between Eid's elimination and his own efforts. The assassination seemed to confirm two things. First, that for all the signs that the momentum in the investigation had been lost, there was continued progress on some fronts, in this case the Lebanese side of the investigation, which explained why Eid's removal became so urgent. Second, and more disturbing, that there were those inside Lebanon's security establishment keeping tabs on this progress, before passing it on to those wanting to thwart it. Eid was the second security official killed after François Hajj, albeit for different reasons. Since the involvement of Syria or its local allies seemed a near certainty in both crimes, the killings could, in part, be read as warnings directed at the army and the Internal Security Forces that there was a price to pay for efforts to break free from their past collaboration with Syria and Hezbollah. Sovereign security was the backbone of any Lebanese state hoping to emerge from under the detritus of Syrian rule. Eid's fate, like that of Hajj, showed that this transformation wouldn't be smooth.

DURING THIS period, war never seemed very far away. Lebanon was without a president, and its streets were the scenes of almost daily brawls between Sunni youths loyal to the Future Movement and Shiite followers of Hezbollah or the Amal Movement. The army and the security forces were exhausted, and it was all the more difficult for the military leadership to act decisively when their commander was the anointed presidential nominee and had to calculate how each move would affect his electoral chances. However, the army remained united, the exception in a society that had not been so vehemently divided since the end of the civil war.

As things appeared to disintegrate, it occurred to me that this must have felt something like what the Lebanese went through in the lead-up to the war in 1975. Here was a government whose legitimacy was being challenged by a powerful segment of the society; here, too, was the existence of an armed group overseeing a state within the state, Hezbollah having replaced the Palestinian Liberation Organization in that role; and the army, as a microcosm of the divided society, seemed powerless, authorized only to act as a referee and separate the combatants before the next flurry of punches.

However, Hezbollah was preparing for an escalation, along with its allies. Early in the new year, unusual types of demonstrations began taking place. People affiliated with or mobilized by Hezbollah would stage the demonstrations against some aspect of government social policy, then move rapidly to different areas of western Beirut. Something was going on, suggesting a broader mobile protest effort, one with quasi-military overtones. You didn't hold maneuvers to spontaneously express social beefs. Nor, throughout this period, were opposition spokesmen silent about their intentions. Already, a year earlier in January 2007, in the run-up to the day when the opposition closed roads throughout Lebanon, they were using the imagery of a coup to make their point. In an article published at the time in the Hariri-owned *Al-Mustaqbal* newspaper, the journalist Qassem Qassir provided interesting insights into the opposition's thinking. Qassir was a Shiite who had once hosted a show on Hezbollah's Al-Manar television station, before his differences with the party ended the relationship. However, he still had good contacts inside Hezbollah and still lived in Beirut's southern suburbs. Qassir's sources explained that the opposition had numerous "scenarios" to overthrow the Siniora government, among them "a repeat of the February 1984 intifada." That intifada was a military uprising carried out during the war years by Walid Jumblatt and Nabih Berri against the regime of Amin Gemayel, leading to the takeover of western Beirut by Jumblatt's and Berri's militias and their lesser allies. It said a great deal about Lebanese politics that Jumblatt and Berri were now on opposing sides of the political spectrum, and that Jumblatt was aligned with Gemayel. I had spent much of that terrible February '84 day huddling in the corridor of our apartment, hearing rocket-propelled grenades and tank shells exploding outside the building, so for that example to be resurrected almost two decades after the war's end was disheartening. It showed that the opposition was certainly thinking of using its weapons to overthrow the March 14–led government, even if in early 2007, when Qassir's article appeared, it had prepared a range of nonviolent options short of that.

However, by early 2008 those options had been greatly reduced. Having been unsuccessful in dislodging the government, Hezbollah had decided to impose a state of continual instability. The demonstrations were one aspect of this strategy; another was the party's continued refusal to order its representatives to parliament to elect a president, thereby perpetuating the vacuum at the head of the state. A further convulsion of sorts occurred in late January 2007, when Shiite demonstrators fought with the army in the neighborhood of Shiyah during one demonstration. It degenerated into gunfire, leading to the death of three people, including an Amal official. The episode represented a major challenge to Suleiman, and the protests may have been a trap by the opposition to deflate the army commander. He responded to the incident by setting up an inquiry and detaining several officers, though it remained unclear who had fired first. The incident, like so much else in Lebanon, was swept under the rug, purportedly because there was evidence the official had been accidentally killed by an opposition gunman. However, Suleiman had no interest in pressing the point, nor was Hezbollah looking for a quarrel that might break the army apart, to no one's advantage.

On the side of March 14, the intentions were less destructive than Hezbollah's, but political imagination was sorely lacking. The standoff allowed little room for Fouad al-Siniora's government to do very much, and the government did not do very much. It was unclear, however, who benefited from the ongoing immobility. Was it the Syrians? To a large extent yes, since it raised their stock both regionally and internationally to end this state of affairs; however, the Syrian plan was obstruction, nothing less but also nothing more. The Assad regime could create a vacuum, but it could not fill it. And if it could not fill the vacuum, then its ability to revive its levers of power in Lebanon was wanting. Did Iran benefit, and with it Hezbollah? Again, to a large extent yes; but open-ended discord, particularly when it pitted Sunnis against Shiites, was not something the Iranians wanted to see escalate, particularly when they were looking for ways to run out the clock before the Bush administration left office. For the United States and the so-called moderate Arabs, Lebanon was a disquieting example of Iran's ability to project itself in the Middle East—and Iranian sway over Hezbollah had decisively surpassed that of Syria since the departure of Syrian soldiers in 2005. There was not much Damascus could do to prevent this: Its allies were weak, and Hezbollah alone had the weapons and means to defend Syria's Lebanese stakes. Stalemate became the lowest common denominator for all sides. Syria and Iran had time on their side, as did their local devotees, but that was only another way of saying that the Siniora government could not easily be removed. Those in the majority could take solace in this, but then what? Politics were frozen, and in such situations there is a natural tendency to hold the government more responsible.

Equally bothersome was the news that the Future Movement had brought in young men from rural northern Lebanon to help protect Sunni neighborhoods, alongside Sunni youths from the city. These were the "Sunni militias" that Seymour Hersh had mentioned in his *New Yorker* article, without explaining who or what they were. In fact, there was no evidence of an organized Sunni militia, only of usually unarmed young men working as part of private security companies under the Future umbrella. That did not mean, however, that weapons were not circulating in Sunni quarters. As Muhammad Barakat, a young Sunni active in defending the lower-income quarter of Tariq al-Jadideh later described it to a pro–March 14 Web site, a delegation from the quarter asked Saad al-Hariri to supply them with arms, but he refused, saying that only the army and the Internal Security Forces should have them. This had the contrary impact of pushing people to buy personal weapons on the market, since the security forces were unable or unwilling to challenge the better-armed Shiite groups. As the situation deteriorated between Sunni and Shiite areas, kidnappings and beatings of each other's youths escalated. There was an alarming rise in the frequency of armed clashes, even if nobody ever seemed to get hurt. Barakat wrote, "We didn't have a united military command . . . we took orders from nobody, we decided and executed on the basis of our emotions."

Barakat perhaps overstated Saad al-Hariri's passivity. Hariri flatly denied to me that he had purchased personal weapons, but there is some information, including from politicians within

March 14, that the Future Movement had done just that, but that its leaders never distributed them. The reality is that Hariri's followers were haphazardly structured and poorly led. A militia, as many a former Lebanese warlord will admit today, takes years, expertise, and training to build. Hariri's partisans had none of these, let alone Sunni blessing to organize for war. For example, Farouq Itani, a Tariq al-Jadideh resident who had served in a Sunni militia during the civil war, a real one this, recounted how youths in the quarter began discussing arming themselves in early 2007 as tensions in the streets rose. However, there was disagreement over such a measure, and no organized effort was put in place to arm the community on a large scale, even as young men like Barakat became more belligerent. Here, it seemed, was another case of the Hariri camp caught in a quandary: on the one hand resisting efforts to establish a militia; on the other failing to decisively intervene to prevent the surreptitious militarization of segments of the Sunni community, so as not to lose Sunni sympathies. Nor did it help that the security companies organized by the Future Movement themselves sent confusing signals. On the positive side, these created structures helping control youths who, left unrestrained, might have become troublemakers; but such entities could also become embryos of paramilitary organizations replacing the ineffective security forces; and so, they were also equivocal expressions of where the Hariri camp stood on the role of the army and the state in protecting civilians.

There was a dangerous fuzziness here: The strong suit of the majority was its claim to represent the state against Hezbollah's antistate. However, too quickly the dynamics in the streets appeared to be overwhelming an often-disoriented Future Movement, which wanted to be seen as defending its own, but not in such a way that this would undermine national institutions. This irreconcilable duality—irreconcilable because the state was in no position to take measures against the heavily armed Shiite militias, let alone consider disarming them—would endure until the outbreak of fighting in May.

The spark that led to the miniwar of May was provoked, perhaps not surprisingly, by Walid Jumblatt. During the previous months the Druze leader had sharpened his criticism of Hezbollah. February 14, the commemoration of Rafiq al-Hariri's assassination, came shortly after the assassination in Damascus of a senior Hezbollah operative, Imad Mughniyeh. Hezbollah was planning a memorial of its own in Beirut's southern suburbs on the same day that the followers of the March 14 majority were gathering at Martyrs Square. With opposition tents still pitched at the southern end of the square, a continuation of the protests begun in December 2006, a high fence guarded by the army dividing the two perimeters, Jumblatt had goaded the party. Mughniyeh was killed by the Syrians, he said. "They're eating each other," he had shouted with an impudent twang.

In late April, Jumblatt held a press conference to denounce the treatment of a French socialist official who had been detained by Hezbollah for taking photographs of Beirut's southern suburbs from his car. The party was a "state within a state," Jumblatt declared, which was of course true, though given that he and most of us had long known this, it seemed a case of the Druze leader exploiting the incident for domestic gain. Relations between the political alignments were at their worst in months, and complicating the matter was that, in the ongoing maneuvering, some opposition figures began floating a quid pro quo to allow a presidential election. They offered to go ahead with one in exchange for acceptance by March 14 of the law that had governed the 1960 parliamentary elections, which favored the opposition. The law broke down the constituencies in which March 14 held an advantage, while leaving Shiite constituencies as one, so that Hezbollah's electoral weight remained as potent. The majority saw this as a trap, another thrust to be parried in a contest leading nowhere.

However, it was Jumblatt who shook the political scene off its axis when he played a key role in forcing the government to take two measures on May 6 that were bound to lead to a confrontation with Hezbollah: the dismissal of the head of security at the Beirut airport, Wafiq Shouqair, who had allegedly failed to dismantle cameras operated by Hezbollah filming the airport runway from outside the facility, which March 14 leaders feared would facilitate attacks on their aircraft; and a decision to legally investigate a private Hezbollah telecommunications network set up around Lebanon. Shouqair's removal was designed to reduce Hezbollah's sway over the airport. But action against the telecom network, reportedly laid out by Iran, was far more important to the party, as this was the central nervous system bolstering Hezbollah's autonomy, allowing its officials to communicate with less risk of eavesdropping. This perhaps made sense against Israel, but it also allowed the party to implement domestic military or political actions away from prying eyes.

It took the Siniora government much of the night to approve of these two decisions, with the prime minister and two ministers alone initially opposing them as a case of needlessly picking a fight with Hezbollah. However, Jumblatt threatened to withdraw his ministers from the cabinet if he didn't gain satisfaction. According to the Druze leader, Saad al-Hariri "was [also] for the acceleration of the two decisions," and helped convince Siniora to go along with them. Jumblatt would later justify his actions by saying that if the government couldn't take such decisions, then what was it good for? Hezbollah's telecommunications network was indeed a glaring violation of the state's sovereignty, as was its implicit control over the airport. However, March 14, and Walid Jumblatt in particular, had long been aware of the network and had no illusions whatsoever about whether they could come and go through the airport without Hezbollah knowing about it. What had brought things to a head?

That question has never been properly answered. It's the view of some in March 14 that Jumblatt fell into a trap set for him by the head of Lebanon's military intelligence service, General Georges Khoury, who gave the Druze leader the information about the airport cameras, knowing he would react virulently. Some argue that this was because Khoury hoped that the ensuing clash, which Hezbollah was bound to win, would open the door to Suleiman's election, allowing Khoury to replace him as army commander. This seemed too intricate a scheme by half, and others in the majority were more circumspect about the causes, even if they all believed that Jumblatt had made a mistake.

I later asked Jumblatt why he had done what he had, and

whether it was true that he had fallen into Khoury's trap. He answered that he didn't believe Khoury was the person responsible for the trap he had indeed fallen into. "To this day I'm confused about what happened." This seemed disingenuous. Of course, Jumblatt could make mistakes. However, for someone as well informed as he was, who knew that Hezbollah was preparing an operation on the ground and was looking for an excuse to launch it, this kind of error was out of character. One possible explanation is that March 14 had, or believed it had, international assurances that it would emerge stronger from a confrontation with Hezbollah, then miscalculated. Jumblatt hinted at this in a conversation. Another is that Jumblatt intentionally precipitated a conflict in May 2008 for reasons of his own, perhaps preferring it to one later on when March 14 would be weaker, because the Bush administration by then would have left office. Yet when I asked Jumblatt about this theory, he dismissed it as "suppositions."

On May 7, pro-opposition labor unions called for a general strike to protest work conditions. This was really only a façade for Hezbollah and Amal to force the government to back down on its two decisions. The next day Hassan Nasrallah made a speech demanding precisely that, and directed his anger against Walid Jumblatt, who, he said, was the effective head of the government, not the "employee" Siniora. To touch Hezbollah's telecommunications network was to touch the resistance itself, Nasrallah warned, recalling that he had told Jumblatt "any hand that touches the resistance and its weapons will be cut off." The gunfire then began. In a coordinated operation, Hezbollah and Amal attacked Future Movement offices throughout predominantly Muslim western Beirut (they stayed away from the mostly Christian eastern neighborhoods), and by that evening had taken over that half of the capital. Future, with no organized or trained forces to resist such an onslaught, was routed. This seemed the start of a new civil war, but when I called a parliamentarian from Tripoli, Mosbah al-Ahdab, with this assessment, he seemed dubious, even though the situation in his own city was worsening. Everyone was calculating, and while a war was what we had, the politicians seemed to be thinking beyond war to the dictates that would ensue. I had failed to see that all the ingredients of war were present but one: March 14 had neither the will nor the military means to engage in a prolonged battle. The Sunnis were angry, they had some weapons, but this had not translated into a systematic program of militarization, despite what Future's enemies were saying. Jumblatt wisely told his followers in Beirut to keep their guns in the closet and let the wave pass. His home was surrounded, as was that of Saad al-Hariri, but the opposition could not cross the Rubicon by killing both men.

From just across the old green line those of us living in the Christian areas could hear the explosions very clearly. The contrast was surreal. There were the detonations of rocket-propelled grenades, while only a few hundred meters away was normal life, or as normal a life as could be in the shadow of rocket-propelled grenades and errant bullets. When this phase quieted down on May 9, a curtain descended on western Beirut. Opposition militiamen attacked Hariri-owned media outlets, closing down a daily newspaper and burning a television station. Hezbollah's crack forces handed over the streets to the less-disciplined Amal Movement, while the Syrians, wanting their pound of flesh, instructed a militia under its orders to take over those quarters where it had been present during the war years.

Fronts were opening elsewhere, in the city of Tripoli, between Sunni and Alawite neighborhoods, in the central Beqaa Valley, within mixed Sunni-Shiite villages, but most intensely in the mountains southeast of Beirut overlooking the city, which were under Jumblatt's de facto authority. Hezbollah combatants took a strategic hill above the Druze-controlled towns of Aley and Bayssour known as Hill 888, by infiltrating from one of the two Shiite villages in the area. Their aim was to control access in and out of the Druze Mountains from the capital, but more immediately to tighten the noose around Jumblatt's neck and teach him a lesson. At the same time, Hezbollah sent motorized units into the Druze-controlled Shouf Mountains to the east, which overlooked the party's strongholds in the Beqaa Valley.

Khodr Ghadban, who was at the operations center of Jumblatt's Progressive Socialist Party during the fighting in Aley, later described what happened. It was instructive that Ghadban, a Druze from Aley, had helped man the PSP tent at Martyrs Square after Rafiq al-Hariri's assassination, only to find himself manning the front three years later. He recalled that Jumblatt had urged his followers to avoid skirmishes, but the Druze were not the kind to roll over when they felt their homes were at risk. The villagers angrily demanded weapons from Jumblatt's representative on the ground, Akram Shehayyib, a parliamentarian. However, Jumblatt avoided full-scale mobilization, even as he made sure that Hezbollah gained no military advantage against him. The Druze managed to dislodge Hezbollah from Hill 888, imposing a status quo around Aley, though the bombings continued for one more day. In the town of Shoueifat, near the coast, Jumblatt's followers and those of his rival, Talal Arslan, joined forces to repulse a thrust by Hezbollah, killing a senior military commander. Arslan was in the opposition, but Druze tribal solidarity had taken over. Hezbollah also suffered a setback in the Shouf, when a convoy was surrounded by armed villagers before being allowed to return to the Beqaa.

On May 14 apprehension in the mountains was still high when I drove around with my friend Nicholas Blanford, a correspondent for the *Times* of London and the *Christian Science Monitor*. There were four of us, including a photographer and Nick's fixer, a Shiite who lived in the southern suburbs. After a run through western Beirut, its main thoroughfares still cut by opposition militiamen, we headed for Aley, before descending to the Shiite village of Qomatiyeh. We had heard that the army had deployed between the Shiite and Druze areas, but there was not a soldier to be seen anywhere. Entering Qomatiyeh, we were met by a funeral procession for a young Hezbollah member. His name was Suleiman Jaafar, and according to a judge from the village with whom I spoke, he had been shot by a sniper while driving his car. The Druze had come down to burn the vehicle, before executing Jaafar when his comrades had tried to rescue him.

Photographs from that day are still on my cell phone, and what they show is a commemorative poster of a young man with teen-idol looks, sporting a weeklong beard and gelled hair. He was buried under the banner of Hezbollah, but what did Hezbollah really mean to a youth wanting to look stylish, in a mountain village like this one, with his sister crying nearby, under an indulgent sun and the languid Mediterranean below? The people around us weren't burdened true believers; they were, for the most part, mild rural Shiites trapped in a situation over which they had no control—much like the Druze in the nearby village of Aitat, against which a new combat line had formed. The judge was worried. An educated man who looked like a cerebral playboy, a curiosity for still living in Qomatiyeh when he owned an apartment in Beirut, he had local stature to communicate with those of local stature in other villages, therefore knew the dire consequences of being on bad terms with the Druze. He had been unable to drive to his court in Tripoli, fearing the Sunnis would want to exact revenge for what had happened in Beirut. The judge didn't oppose Hezbollah—probably he had benefited from its support in the byways of judicial politics; yet as we spoke, I sensed that his deeper fear was that the rough seas plied by the party would submerge this gentle place with its gentle inhabitants, whose problems he enjoyed helping resolve.

From Qomatiyeh, we drove upward, past the Christian village of Souq al-Gharb, during the war a notorious battlefront between the Lebanese army and Jumblatt's militia, through the second Shiite village in the area, Keyfoun, and on into the Druze village of Bayssour, around which the fighting had been intense for control of Hill 888. We stopped in a sandwich shop for lunch, and I began chatting with a young Druze, asking for his estimates of casualties. He seemed pleased that his side had gotten more of theirs than their side had gotten Druze—confirming what a young Hezbollah combatant we met in Qomatiyeh had told us. The Druze knew their mountain and could be unforgiving in its defense. But the lugubrious mathematics of death were getting to all of us. What a sad country this is, I thought, convinced that the Leviathan of war could no longer be stopped. But I was wrong. The Druze had won this round, but their areas could not sustain war for very long. Jumblatt later reminded me that even during the civil war, when his men had expelled the Christians from the mountain, many Druze had left for Syria. The economics of victory had proven severe; the Druze were mostly impoverished, living off agriculture yielding limited profits. The more numerous Christians were a major source of the mountain's wealth. Now, Hezbollah was reminding Jumblatt that two of his doors out of the mountain, the one leading to Beirut, the other to the Beqaa, could be closed at will. The party didn't need to win this round militarily to get that message across. And it worked: "I didn't want another exodus," Jumblatt later said. However, he could take satisfaction in that he had not been humiliated. Hezbollah had learned that its large advantage in weapons meant little if its men entered districts controlled by the other religious communities.

Beirut was a different matter. Hezbollah's hubris, and more generally that of many Shiites, took on the tones of sectarian-tinged *Schadenfreude*. A friend in the party would later sum up this mood in a moment of candor: "We beat the crap out of them, and no one could do a thing about it," he said. The Sunnis felt humiliated, and that was precisely the aim of Hezbollah and its allies. Worse, the Sunnis now mistrusted the Lebanese army, which had not only failed to stop the opposition's offensive and done little to limit its worst excesses, for example the torching of the Hariri television station, but had remained silent when certain units collaborated with Hezbollah and Amal gunmen in some neighborhoods. If this was a Hezbollah and Syrian test to see if Michel Suleiman could be trusted, or, conversely, an effort to prevent his election, the army commander passed with flying colors, because within days he was president.

Almost nobody, in Lebanon or outside, wanted to see a sectarian war between Sunnis and Shiites. The Siniora government reversed its two decisions affecting Hezbollah, with Jumblatt now leading the retreat, and the Arab states, usually so slow off the mark, rapidly endorsed a Qatari initiative to bring the Lebanese leaders to Doha to hammer out a deal. There was a revealing subtext here. In the past it was the Saudis who had mediated Arab disputes, not the diminutive Qataris—the Venetians of the Gulf for pursuing policies of amoral dexterity in defense of their narrow interests. But the Saudis had taken sides in Lebanon and were on bad terms with Syria and Iran, so the go-between task devolved to Qatar, which got on with everybody. From the outset, it was understood that Suleiman would be elected once a package deal had been reached, which meant that Michel Aoun's presidential ambitions would end (though, ever confident, he reportedly flew to Doha persuaded that an accord over the presidency would break down). After several days of negotiations, the participants agreed to a final document that was vague enough so that both sides could claim some share of the success. A presidential election would take place immediately, a national unity government would be formed in which the opposition would hold veto power, and the 1960 law would be adopted for parliamentary elections in 2009. The Lebanese also agreed to a dialogue "on promoting the Lebanese state's authority over all Lebanese territory," a roundabout way of addressing Hezbollah's weapons; and they agreed "to abstain from [using] weapons and violence to record political gains."

Who had won the round? There were those in March 14 who insisted the opposition had. The election law favored the Shiite parties, the opposition had finally won veto power after eighteen months of trying, and while Suleiman was elected after the politicians returned from Doha, he had almost sold his soul for this to happen. There was truth in the assessment, but the intangibles told us more. For starters, what was the practical payoff of the Shiite degradation of Sunnis, and of Beirut itself? As Saad al-Hariri implied in a moment of disenchantment, if Hezbollah wanted to break the Sunni moderates, fine; let it face the extremists. He would later say that he had never thought that Hassan Nasrallah would take the risks he did and bring Lebanon to the verge of civil war. "The people who saved the country were us, because we didn't react. Let me be frank. Had I stood up and . . . asked every [Sunni] man and woman to come and defend Beirut, what would have happened?" The masks had fallen, and Hezbollah, which had insisted that it would never turn its weapons on fellow Lebanese, had done precisely that. The premise that the party was the vanguard of a national resistance against Israel, or against America, or against neocolonial hegemony, or whatever, collapsed, as did its claim of providing a realistic state project for Lebanon. From now on, Hezbollah's legitimacy would come out of the barrel of a gun.

As for Suleiman, while his loyalties and ability to maneuver remained a matter of considerable doubt, the vacuum at the head of the state had finally been filled. Aoun, the source of so many problems in his quest to be president, had failed, and now there was a Christian leader less likely to replenish his reservoir of goodwill by manipulating Christian rancor against the post-Taif order. Suleiman's election, whatever the president's merits or demerits, took Lebanon a step away from the past. I had always been a pessimist about Syria, never believing that it had surrendered its desire to return its tanks and soldiers to Lebanon. Yet for the first time since 2005, I sensed the Syrians were losing their grip on a certain way of running Lebanon—the old way. This was an election whose results Damascus could accept; Syrian preferences were being reimposed in some form; but the complications and collisions allowing this contrasted starkly with the effortlessness of Syria's hegemony in the past. Moreover, to retain credibility, Suleiman would have to consider the worries on all sides. He could not rule as a Syrian minion in the way that Lahoud had. More important, the May events had shown that the potentiality of war was locked into every head, and that whether it was Hezbollah or Iran or Syria trying to impose itself through force, the next time this might be met with heavier arms, the consequences uncontrollable.

Then there was Beirut itself. Opposition militiamen had demonstrated their talent for defiling a versatile, accommodating city, but that only confirmed their ignorance of how to take advantage of it. This wasn't Hanoi against the Hariris' Hong Kong; it was the South Bronx—a gang protecting its turf. Some Sunnis reacted with odious chauvinism to what had happened. Beirut was not a city for everyone, a Hariri parliamentarian later said; it was a city only for its own. She meant it was a Sunni city, with no place for Shiites. Such statements entirely missed the point about Beirut's multiple identities, but they provided a good measure of Sunni bitterness. They were also a sign of frustration with the inability of the Lebanese to answer a simple question: Which Lebanon would win out between two apparently irreconcilable projects—that of Hezbollah or that of a sovereign Lebanese state, ramshackle to be sure, but still a state? In late May, sensitive to that question, but also wanting to outline a basis for safeguarding his weapons, Hassan Nasrallah declared that Lebanon was not caught between two choices, Hong Kong or Hanoi. He pointed out, "The resistance, in the spirit of the martyred leader Rafiq al-Hariri, tried to say: 'We imitate no one, not Hong Kong and not Hanoi, and we do not follow models; we Lebanese manufacture models.'"

Yet what an aberrant model it was that Nasrallah wanted the Lebanese to manufacture. After all, his ideal—that of an independent armed force like Hezbollah with close ties to regional powers like Iran and Syria, living alongside a Lebanese state that would not trespass on its territory—had made the May fighting possible. However, Nasrallah could be irony-proof, and this was even more flagrant in August when he made another speech, stating, "We are no aliens to Beirut; we are an integral part of the capital and we wish all the best to Beirut and its residents." This was said in a spirit of reconciliation to the Sunnis, also of justifiable affirmation. But it also showed that Nasrallah had failed to register the mood on the day the Siniora government revoked its two decisions in May, leading the opposition to dismantle its barricades in western Beirut, end its sit-in in the downtown area, and reopen the road to the Beirut airport, which Hezbollah had closed the day the strike action began. As opposition supporters folded their tents and returned to the southern suburbs, many Lebanese breathed a collective sigh of relief that *they* were clearing out, that things were back to normal and the ordeal over. Within hours people began flooding into the downtown, marking with icy contempt what those responsible for the area's eighteen-month agony had done. Yet how disconcerting that Hezbollah had relegated its supporters, and Shiites in general, to the category of trespassers in the city. The party had violated something in Lebanon's sectarian contract, and although the post-Doha language was about amity, it was too much to ask of those Lebanese who had been brutalized in May, who had seen opposition militiamen roaming the streets outside their homes as masters over their lives, that they should not themselves one day yearn to speak in the vernacular of the Kalashnikov.

7

The End of the Beginning

These opposed ambitions bring about one of three results;
a principality, a free city, or anarchy.

Machiavelli, *The Prince*

Above Beirut's northeastern suburbs, overlooking the dust-
bin of Nahr al-Mott, the River of Death, really no more than
a dead river, is Roumieh prison, whose lingering aestheticism, the
work of reputed Lebanese architect Pierre Khoury, betrays an ambition, once, of wanting to create a modern penitentiary. In early
2009 the public was allowed inside when prisoners staged the Reg-
inald Rose play *Twelve Angry Men*. The play, better known from its
film adaptation starring Henry Fonda, is about a jury deliberating
over a crime. But what it's really about is guilt and innocence.

However, today, some months later, it's April 29 and Lebanese
eyes are on Roumieh for another reason. The four generals arrested
in 2005 as suspects in the assassination of Rafiq al-Hariri are about
to be released, because Daniel Bellemare, the former U.N. commissioner of the Hariri investigation, now the prosecutor of the
Special Tribunal for Lebanon that began operating in March in a
suburb of The Hague, has informed the pretrial judge that he does
not have enough evidence to indict them. It is four angry men
who emerge from Roumieh, notably Jamil al-Sayyed, the man who
had hounded Samir Kassir, once Syria's preeminent enforcer in
Lebanon, who would soon declare that after Lebanon's parliamentary elections in June, if the opposition won, he would accept the

post of justice minister. However, Sayyed's glory days are behind him. The Syrians are no longer in Lebanon, and it is noticeable after his release that he and his colleagues have been taken in hand by Hezbollah. The party has decided to use the generals' case as a battering ram to discredit the Lebanese judiciary, but, more important, to discredit the Hariri tribunal, whose establishment it tried several times to block.

Bellemare had yet to put together a formal accusation, so the generals were not necessarily off the hook. Yet for me their release was the first palpable sign that the trial was in danger. I had published an interview with Detlev Mehlis more than a year earlier in which he had cast doubt on the investigation of his successor, Serge Brammertz. Mehlis had told me that one of the reasons it was necessary to accelerate the investigation and the transfer to a trial process was that you could not forever imprison suspects. But his main point was that he had discerned little progress in Brammertz's work. The release of the generals lent credence to this view, since the U.N. commission was conducting the bulk of the investigation and had recommended detaining the generals in the first place, therefore, presumably, had as one mission the gathering of further information to make that case solid. Mehlis had told me, just as he told the daily *Al-Mustaqbal*, owned by the Hariri family, after the four were released, that there was sufficient reason to detain them, and that his commission and the Lebanese judiciary had agreed. In his *Al-Mustaqbal* interview, Mehlis disclosed that Sayyed had $50,000 at his home and several passports, while another general, Mustapha Hamdan, was planning on the day of his arrest to travel to the United States, which has no extradition treaty with Lebanon. Had he failed to act, Mehlis said in so many words, his behavior would have been legitimately criticized.

And what if the generals were innocent? While the successive reports of Mehlis, Brammertz, and Bellemare never clarified the specific role they played in Hariri's murder, the political environment the documents described made it virtually impossible that the four were, at a minimum, unaware of the dangerous atmosphere surrounding the former prime minister, then did nothing to warn or protect him. Hariri's security detail had been cut back, prompting the first U.N. investigator, Peter Fitzgerald, to write in his report that the "Lebanese security services have demonstrated serious and systematic negligence in carrying out the duties usually performed by a professional national security apparatus." More damningly, he had pointed to the way the crime scene was interfered with, observing that "the manner in which this element of the investigation was carried out displays, at least gross negligence, possibly accompanied by criminal actions for which those responsible should be made accountable." This was accompanied by very reliable reports in Beirut that one of the generals had tried to distribute the videocassette in which one Ahmad Abu al-Adas claimed responsibility for Hariri's assassination to a local television station, which refused to air it on the grounds that it could not absorb the political backlash. The video was later shown on Al-Jazeera. Why was a Lebanese official peddling such a recording, particularly of an individual U.N. investigators doubted had committed the crime?

More generally, while guilt was ultimately a matter to be decided by the special tribunal, the release of the generals unintentionally cast doubt on a relationship that many Lebanese could nevertheless speak to with authority, and that both Fitzgerald and Mehlis had described extensively in their reports: namely that the Lebanese security and intelligence services in 2005 were acting with and under the auspices and authority of the Syrian intelligence services. Hariri's assassination was an extensive conspiracy; therefore it would have been absurd to imagine that the Lebanese security services were not in some way involved. None of the subsequent UNIIIC reports denied this fact, quite the contrary, so obvious was the relationship of dependency linking the Lebanese to the Syrians. That's why anything casting doubt on this, such as the generals' release, spoke more to the failings of the U.N. commission than to errors in Fitzgerald's and Mehlis's findings.

Then there was the revealing behavior of Brammertz and Bellemare with regard to the generals' detention. When Mehlis had recommended their arrest, he had put it in writing. And when he was replaced by Brammertz in 2006, the Lebanese asked whether the Belgian withdrew the earlier recommendation. Brammertz replied that he did not, and when Bellemare took over, he replied the same way, even if he did apparently later tell the Lebanese public prosecutor privately that he no longer believed the generals should be detained. There was an element of political dodgeball here, with the last two U.N. commissioners preferring to keep the burden of the arrests on Mehlis and the Lebanese. Had Bellemare wanted the four released, the proper method of doing so would have been to request this in a signed document, not in a private conversation. So, when he explained in April 2009 that he would not oppose the generals' release—principally because the bylaws of the Hariri tribunal did not give much margin to maneuver in this regard—he found himself in the awkward position of having failed to release them sooner, since the Lebanese judiciary would not have ignored a recommendation from him to that effect. The only convincing explanation for this incongruous conduct was that Brammertz and Bellemare wanted to have their cake and eat it, too. They suspected the generals were involved in the crime, and they had Fitzgerald's and Mehlis's reports to back that up; but then Brammertz, then Bellemare, did not add anything to their files that would substantiate their suspicions. So both men kept the generals in jail on the basis of what Mehlis and the Lebanese had said, until that position was no longer tenable, when the pretrial judge requested that Bellemare inform him whether he could indict.

The release of the generals was a severe blow to Bellemare's case. However, supporters of the trial process put up a front of optimism. Saad al-Hariri went on television to say that the decision proved the tribunal was not politicized as his adversaries in Hezbollah and Syria had claimed. Even in private he didn't let his guard down. "Bellemare is working on a judicial file to solidify his case. I believe his statement that he is on track and has many leads," he told me in early May. Yet there plainly was a problem. After nearly four years of a high-profile international investigation, not a single suspect was in custody. Bellemare had been in office for just over a year, and it was still possible to imagine that he would get to the bottom of things; but what about Brammertz? He had spent two years at his job and there was not much, publicly, to show for it. In April 2009, I contacted his office at the Interna-

tional Criminal Tribunal for the Former Yugoslavia to give him an
opportunity to rebut what Mehlis had said, and what I myself had
written criticizing his investigation. His spokesperson wrote back
that Brammertz could not comment on an ongoing investigation,
and that U.N. rules allowed him to speak only on his current mandate. Since Brammertz had refused to comment to the media on
the Hariri investigation when he was still UNIIIC commissioner,
I found the sentence almost witty.

The generals' release was an eloquent statement on where Lebanon was headed in the post-Doha period. The agreement reached
in the Qatari capital had brought about an arrangement silencing
the guns, but in no way had it resolved a problem at the heart of
the country's post-2005 rupture: the inability to reconcile the project of a sovereign, independent Lebanese state with Hezbollah's
refusal to surrender its weapons and independence, and its capacity to impose this reality through force. That fed more than ever
into regional politics in late 2008 and into 2009, when Barack
Obama replaced George W. Bush at the White House. As always,
Lebanon accumulated the contradictions of the Middle East. With
Obama having campaigned to remove American forces from Iraq
within a relatively accelerated time frame, and seeking to ease tensions with both Iran and Syria, it was only natural for Hezbollah,
Tehran, and Damascus—each for reasons of its own, some overlap-
ping, some not—to sense that the momentum had turned their
way, at least when it came to American willingness to do battle
with them in Lebanon. The May 2008 events had shown that the
U.S. counted for little in Lebanon's alleyways; and while Jeffrey
Feltman, the U.S. ambassador who had played an important role
in helping push Syria out of Lebanon in 2005, was promoted to assistant secretary of state for Near Eastern affairs, his replacement in
Beirut, Michele Sison, was less imposing a figure, marking a retreat
in the activism of the years before.

In light of this, Hezbollah began an understated yet determined effort to undermine the scaffolding of United Nations resolutions that had, since 2004, placed Lebanon under an indirect
form of international trusteeship. Resolution 1559 had led to the
Syrian withdrawal, even if its clauses on the disarmament of mili-

tias had yet to be implemented; a series of resolutions after Hariri's assassination, particularly Resolution 1595 establishing UNIIIC, had created a parallel mechanism of justice to that of the Lebanese judiciary investigating not only the murder of the former prime minister but also other political killings during and after 2005; and Resolution 1701 had reaffirmed Resolution 1559 and laid the groundwork for the Lebanese army's deployment in southern Lebanon, as well as reinforcement of the U.N. force there, making it more difficult for Hezbollah to use its weapons against Israel. The May 2008 takeover of western Beirut by Hezbollah and its allies was the first sign that Resolution 1559 would pass over the party's dead body—or rather the dead bodies of its adversaries (although the two government decisions bringing on the onslaught could not, in any realistic way, have led to the resolution's implementation). The release of the generals provided Hezbollah with an opportunity to discredit the Hariri tribunal and the U.N.-mandated investigation process. That left Resolution 1701, the most substantial of the U.N. decisions and the most delicate to bring down, since this might provoke a violent Israeli riposte that would alienate a Shiite community still reeling from the 2006 war. Hezbollah was careful here, but the post-Doha national dialogue sessions devoted to the party's weapons, not surprisingly, went nowhere. Party officials repeated on numerous occasions that Hezbollah would not disarm, while its leadership awaited political openings to impose a consensus over a so-called "defense strategy" for Lebanon, meaning an officially-sanctioned framework justifying the party's retaining its weapons, in that way transcending Resolutions 1559 and 1701.

Nasrallah did not hide his intentions in a speech on May 15, 2009, when he said: "We look forward to a state able to defend itself, its own decisions, its land, its people, and its security, without needing [U.N.] forces—which, with all due respect as they are our guests in the south, neither make things better or worse—and without needing foreign security apparatuses; we Lebanese have the capabilities allowing Lebanon to have a creditable force on that basis."

In the aftermath of the Doha Agreement, I tried to get a better sense of what the May events meant on the ground, particularly in the northern Lebanese city of Tripoli and in mixed Sunni-Shiite districts in the Beqaa Valley. Even after the Nahr al-Bared battle ended, Tripoli remained a sore spot in Lebanese-Syrian relations. The north was a reservoir of Sunni youth, a place the Alawite-led Syrian regime felt uneasy about not controlling because it felt uneasy about not controlling any Sunni area within its proximity, especially one acutely antagonistic toward Syria for having starkly endured the consequences of Syrian uneasiness in the past. Even after Doha, sporadic fighting continued in Tripoli between the predominantly Sunni neighborhoods of Bab al-Tebbaneh and Al-Qobbeh on the one side and the Alawite neighborhood of Jabal Mohsen on the other. Here was a microcosm of a microcosm, a marginal fight between two groups of poor and marginal people—a minor tributary to the larger confrontation between March 14 and the Hezbollah-led opposition and Syria.

This confrontation took on a dynamism that mocked traditional alignments. The Alawites were led by one Ali Eid and his son Rifaat. The Eids were with the Assads in Syria and with the Lebanese opposition, but like any minority, they were really just with themselves, out to survive and protect their presence. The Sunnis of Bab al-Tebbaneh and Al-Qobbeh were not any better, as poor and as predisposed to manipulation. They were little helped by the vacuum on the ground left by Saad al-Hariri's Future Movement, the most powerful political organization in the north but still only partly effective then in filling the spaces left by Syria. It was no surprise that a consequence of this was instability, as everyone sought to exploit the void for their own political ends. That's why, for example, Sunni politicians belonging to or friendly with the opposition had combatants in Bab al-Tebbaneh firing on their allies in Jabal Mohsen. This was their opportunity to buy a ticket back into communal legitimacy after the Sunnis were routed by Hezbollah in May. Manning the front line against the Alawites, however, were mainly the young men of Bab al-Tebbaneh, with their complicated allegiances potentially profitable in so destitute a place, yet united by local solidarity. There were also Salafist fighters, though a leading Lebanese Salafist, Da'i al-Islam Shahhal, had

some thirty men in arms, more a sign of his limitations than anything else, since Lebanese Salafism is by and large nonviolent. This
situation was without discernible political logic, showing only how
easily local conflicts and calculations could metastasize and take
on inflated importance.

Confusion was no less evident in what a friend and I heard
from Rifaat Eid when we visited him near the top of Jabal Mohsen
in August 2008. As we drove up the hill a few days after a durable
cease-fire was imposed by the Lebanese army, we asked for "the
villa," and soon afterward were ushered into Eid's office. We found
ourselves in the presence of a stocky young man with a shaved
head and a baby face. Here was an offering from the streets.
Friendly, sitting in for his ailing father, Rifaat didn't have the ur-
banity to tell a good lie, so he frequently told an interesting half-
truth. "The last round of fighting started when the men of an
opposition politician fired a rocket-propelled grenade at us." It was
easy enough to guess that he was referring to the former prime
minister, Omar Karami, though he didn't elaborate. As the conversation went on, my eye wandered around the office. There was a
picture of Hafez al-Assad and another of Bashar al-Assad with Ali
Eid; there were also bound books propped up to be displayed
rather than read: a Quran, a boxed collection of several volumes
which, when the spines were placed next to one another, revealed
the face of Hassan Nasrallah; a book on Suleiman Franjieh, a pro-
Syrian Maronite politician from the nearby town of Zghorta. There
was also a plaque showing the Sydney Opera House, probably a
gift from the Alawite community in Australia; and there were photographs of President Michel Suleiman and Sayyed Musa al-Sadr.
I remembered where I had seen a similar office, with its bric-a-brac
of contrasting political statements: It was when I had first visited
Walid Jumblatt. Here was another minority leader who felt that the
best protection was to cover all the bases. The Alawites were no
choirboys; the Eids' Arab Democratic Party militia had served the
Syrians well in the past; the enmity with Bab al-Tebbaneh dated
back to when the Syrian army had entered the quarter in 1986, and
massacred or arrested several hundred men—some say the figure
was in the thousands. Yet there was something persuasive in Eid's

insistence that he and his followers had no interest in provoking a conflict now, surrounded as they were by a crushing majority of Sunnis. "Why would we want war when we don't even have a hospital?" he asked, even as the inhabitants of Bab al-Tebbaneh, Sunni majority or not, similarly saw no advantages in a quarrel that was destroying their already dismal livelihoods.

As we walked out, I pointed to an apartment across the street that had been burned out, asking Eid what had happened. "I ordered my men to set fire to the place. The person living there was a Salafist!" he answered. You could sympathize with Eid for being master of this disconsolate hill, with its little wars and his villa not very much of an improvement over the decaying buildings around it. But you could also see that he exemplified a conflict without clear lines, in a city that needed to be taken in hand quickly because, otherwise, the Syrians might do so themselves; and if they did, the Eids would be a part of it.

Indeed, a few days after our meeting, a bomb went off near a bus in Tripoli, killing several soldiers and civilians. The attack, which came only a few weeks after another against a military intelligence office in the border town of Abdeh, was made to look like revenge against the army by Fatah al-Islam. However, my view at the time, and that of others, was that the Syrians were trying to force a showdown between the Lebanese army and Islamists in Tripoli, which would have split the Sunnis, with some defending the Islamists and others the state, forcing Saad al-Hariri to make an impossible choice between his different constituencies. Fortunately, the army avoided this, although the situation on the ground remained unstable as Syria continued issuing implicit threats, most revealingly a statement Bashar al-Assad made to a Russian newspaper in August in which he said that what Russia had faced in Georgia, Syria was facing in Lebanon. Russia had recently invaded Georgia's border region, making the statement alarming enough for Saudi Arabia and Egypt to take a more direct interest in events in Tripoli. In September, Saad al-Hariri headed to the city to oversee a broad reconciliation effort. This included a meeting with such rivals as Omar Karami and the Eids. The visit substantially calmed tensions in the city and helped Hariri reaffirm his paramountcy in the north, but it also came in reaction to the fact that two major Arab states were deeply worried about the continuing vacuum in the region—a vacuum that should have been filled sooner—since it affected their dispute with Syria and Iran.

Doha had also failed to end sporadic fighting in the Beqaa Valley, specifically in the mixed Sunni-Shiite towns of Saadnayel and Taalbaya, located, strategically, near the crossroads between the Beirut-Damascus highway and the main road connecting the northern and southern Beqaa. In August, I visited the towns with a friend, who introduced me to Radwan Shehimi, a local Sunni activist who had tried to mediate in the recent hostilities. Saadnayel and Taalbaya were a different type of microcosm than the one in Bab al-Tebbaneh and Jabal Mohsen, but the two were similar in showing how thin the Doha reconciliation was. Here, Sunnis and Shiites lived among one another, so that fights frequently broke out between youths in the street. The Shiites tended to control the high ground, however, and, similar to the Alawite militia in Tripoli, were better trained than the Sunnis because their young men were in or had belonged to armed groups. I asked Shehimi what weapons the Sunnis had. He answered that there were some small arms left over from the civil war, and that people were purchasing weapons on the market. After the May assault, the Future Movement had bought and distributed weapons, but there was no easy way of confirming this. As we drove out of Taalbaya into the hills heading toward other Shiite villages, Shehimi told us that we were probably being watched and advised that we head back. He had helped organize the election campaign of Saad al-Hariri in Saadnayel, but he was not much liked by the Future Movement's representatives in the area, who saw him as too friendly with Hezbollah. Here was another case where manifold local loyalties, rivalries, and relationships, in communities by and large socially disfavored, made any reading of the situation difficult, particularly for anyone trying to cool down the situation.

There was also a more critical backdrop to the tensions in the two towns, which showed that while conflict could be kept alive by parochial rancor, this also fed into national realities. Saadnayel and Taalbaya's location made them an essential passage point between areas of Shiite concentration. Lebanon's Shiites, unlike most of the country's other rural communities, are clustered in three distinct areas having no geographical contiguity: Beirut's southern suburbs; southern Lebanon extending into the southern Beqaa Valley; and the northern Beqaa. Hezbollah had long realized that the community was vulnerable, since connecting these areas in times of conflict required occupying territory controlled by non-Shiites. The May fighting in the Druze Mountains seemed a warning from Hezbollah to Walid Jumblatt that he had better not threaten the party's communication lines between Beirut and the south, and between the south and the Beqaa; the incidents in Saadnayel and Taalbaya, a majority Sunni district, came with a similar threat, namely that Hezbollah would not hesitate to open the road between the southern and northern Beqaa using violence if that became necessary. This thinking again derived from the geography of war. When Hezbollah had planned its social protests against the government in the period leading up to the May fighting, it had also done so with urban warfare in mind. And yet these brush fires were eventually brought under control, as much in Tripoli as in Saadnayel and Taalbaya, nothing really resolved, everything attesting to the fragility of Doha, but also to the potency of that invisible hand of equilibrium that stopped so much before the edge.

MICHEL AOUN, who had devastated half his country to fight a war of liberation against Syria in 1989, visited Syria in December 2008. He justified his visit by saying that the Syrians had withdrawn from Lebanon, so it was time to let bygones be bygones: "This is an old story that is now over. We must have better relations with Syria," Aoun declared. The Syrian army may have been gone, but Syria certainly was not, otherwise Aoun would not have troubled himself with the visit. The bombings and assassinations, Bashar al-Assad's threats issued in the presence of Ban Ki-moon in April 2007, Syrian backing for the Lebanese opposition against the parliamentary and government majority, and Assad's recent comparison between Lebanon and Georgia, all indicated how inattentive Syria remained to Lebanese sovereignty.

Aoun got little out of a visit that was a political risk. He did meet with the Assads twice, once in a family context, with his son-in-law and daughter being flown in for the occasion on the Syrian president's jet for a meal. But the Syrians did not give him what he sought most: signs that he would be the preeminent Christian interlocutor with Damascus, displacing President Michel Suleiman. Rather, the Syrians welcomed this opportunity to use Aoun to keep Suleiman in line, and to use Suleiman to keep Aoun in check. However, Aoun did not lose much from the trip either, just as he did not lose much politically from an earlier trip he had made to Tehran. His followers, it seemed, would follow him to hell; in fact, many had during his two-year spell in power from 1988 to 1990, because they saw in him a sort of a savior, even if he was now taking his community in directions it had always resisted.

There was also something more meaningful in Aoun's turnabout on Syria and Iran. It had to do with an original idea circulating in his entourage, particularly through his son-in-law, Gebran Bassil, who appeared to have picked it up from Suleiman Franjieh, the Maronite leader from northern Lebanon who was a friend of the Assad family. The idea was that it was in the interest of the Maronite Christians to ally themselves with other minorities in the Middle East, particularly the Alawites and the Shiites, against the Sunni majority. It was a crackpot notion, one that must have made Bashar al-Assad smile, for while his security edifice was heavily reliant on Alawites, his regime had always protected itself by sticking to Arab nationalist tenets finding favor among Sunnis. The Syrians knew, as did the Shiites, that you could not get very far in a Sunni-majority region against the Sunnis. You could create spaces for yourself, but the game had to be played carefully to avoid provoking sectarian conflagrations.

Aoun had no such touch. He needed Saad al-Hariri and the Sunnis to be elected president when Émile Lahoud finished his term, and what did he do? He attacked Hariri as corrupt and denounced what he called the Sunni hold over Lebanon. Aoun doubtless went to Syria to garner some support for the parliamentary elections scheduled for June 2009; he was too self-centered a man to be completely taken over by an abstraction like the alliance of minorities, except in the way it might advance his political well-being. However, as he visited Christian religious sites in Syria, as he tried to show that Syrian Christians had it good under the Assads and that he, Michel Aoun, could be a new secular patriarch to both the Syrian and Lebanese communities, neither message came through very well. Aoun had already done everything to earn Assad's approval, including implying that Syria was not responsible for Rafiq al-Hariri's assassination; going further would bring only marginal gains. And who could *really* take Aoun seriously as a contemporary Christian Moses leading the community into the Promised Land of new minority relationships in the Middle East? Many Maronites liked Aoun, but as many, if not more, had doubts. And just as Aoun arrived in Syria, he left it, his relationship little deeper than it had been before, though Assad could enjoy watching the Lebanese do anything to gain a leg up on their adversaries at home. And what had it cost him? A table of food and some jet fuel.

If Aoun was a defiant emanation of Maronite deterioration—defiant for wanting to reverse that trend through his own political accomplishments and his innovative alliances—it was clear to him, and to everyone else, that the Maronites in particular, and Christians in general, would play a decisive role in the 2009 elections. The election law agreed to in Doha favored the opposition, by breaking up large constituencies in which March 14 held an advantage. Lebanon votes according to a list system, where powerful politicians or parties lead or sponsor slates of candidates. In predominantly Shiite districts, Hezbollah and Amal had a decisive advantage; in predominantly Sunni and Druze ones, Saad al-Hariri and Walid Jumblatt did; that left the divided Christians to decide the final balance in the 128-member parliament. An overall opposition victory required that Aoun win almost all the seats in Christian districts. If that happened, he would not only be the strongest Christian leader; he would again be in a position to say that he was the community's true representative.

This hunger for communal supremacy raised an interesting

question about Maronite leaders, and how they were faring at so critical a time in their history. Why were they devoid of vision? Why were the Maronites, otherwise so instrumental in building modern Lebanon, now so pathetically focused on petty struggles for power? Part of an answer came when I interviewed the Lebanese Forces leader Samir Geagea in February 2009 with my friend the journalist Hazem al-Amin. Amin, a Shiite who had fought during the war in the ranks of the Lebanese Communist Party, now leaned toward March 14 and was highly critical of Hezbollah. Geagea was intrigued, but then he was thrown off by an observation that Amin made, namely that there no longer seemed to be a Maronite leadership in the city. Geagea lived in an isolated mountain home in Maarab; the Gemayel family spent most of its time in Bikfayya, another mountain town. Michel Aoun was the closest to Beirut, but he still resided in the suburb of Rabieh. What had happened? Previously, Maronite leaders were an essential part of the capital; they lived in it, reveled in it, and spent most of their time in it. That was much less the case today. Why?

Geagea gave some sort of answer that showed he hadn't quite understood. Yet Amin had hit at the essence of where the Maronites were today in their political psychology. The community's rise, in fact Lebanon's, had coincided with the Maronite embrace of the city—both as a physical place and the abstract expression of a Lebanese polity—with the integration of a mainly rural community, and its rural ideology, with an ideology of the city, to again borrow from the historian Albert Hourani. But now most Maronite leaders seemed to have reverted to a form of rural insularism, self-absorbed in the gloom of their waning power, which came at the expense of a multisectarian Lebanese project that the city embodied, and this was manifested, almost banally, in where they lived and functioned as politicians. It was not surprising that Geagea had misunderstood, because he was a son of the poor and secluded mountain village of Bsharri in northern Lebanon, even if, like Aoun, he had since forged strong political ties with Muslims, in his case with Saad al-Hariri, now the leading exemplar of the urban Sunni, regardless of his family's modest roots.

Of the leaders of March 14, Samir Geagea was the one who radiated the strongest sense that he sat atop a strict hierarchy and had not quite overcome his military mind-set. A tall man with an angular bald head and a thin mustache, a natural leader and organizer, Geagea often seemed surrounded by people who, though admiring, weren't altogether relaxed in his presence. His mountain house was described as "fascistic" in its design; in fact, it was nicer than that, though its low linearity and uncompromising lines, so alien to Lebanon's mountain architecture, suggested only that it, too, had succumbed to Geagea's discipline—the discipline of a security-minded former militia leader for whom the outside world is a palimpsest of meticulous considerations, where the whimsical is threatening; a discipline that will drive him to politely inform you, fifty-five minutes into an interview, in the middle of a light-hearted exchange, that you have five minutes left. The first thing Geagea told me when we met was "I used to read you while in prison." He had obviously prepared for the meeting, that line in particular. Geagea had been sentenced to life by the Syrian-dominated Lebanese judiciary in a politicized series of trials—though the accusation that he was involved in the assassination of a former prime minister, Rashid Karami, seemed more credible. While he was denied newspapers, Geagea's jailers did give him apolitical publications, including a business magazine I wrote for. Discipline was doubtless what carried Geagea through his eleven-year stretch in a tiny cell in a basement of the Defense Ministry, where every moment had to be carved up into a meaningful crutch to avoid breakdown. Geagea's toughness had facilitated a view that he had been among the vilest of warlords. Yet he was no worse than the others; perhaps he was better than some who seemed more respectable. Where Geagea had sinned was that his big battles were against his own, against Christians, so that the detractors among his coreligionists could never forgive him. This was one reason why many had rallied to Michel Aoun, and it was why Geagea, between his scrupulous time management, unbending will, dislike of familiarity, and relentless, even finicky, logic when decorticating an idea, could sometimes seem so strange to the Lebanese, who tended toward precisely the opposite.

Geagea's mountain bluntness meant he beat relatively little

about the bush on his election prospects. He was realistic about
the obstacles ahead, but also observed that Aoun could not expect
the wave of support he had gained in 2005. Then there was the
matter of the Maronite Church, its patriarch no great enthusiast
of Aoun, which might play a role against the general that was
"*insidieux*"—Geagea said the word "insidious" in French. Unlike the
Aounists, who sought to capitalize now, he was thinking ahead,
placing candidates around Lebanon, some to win, some to mark
their presence in preparation for the 2013 elections. By then Aoun
would be seventy-nine or so, and Christians, freed of that pied
piper, might see Samir Geagea in a better light.

While Geagea had no innate attraction to the city, in his electoral calculations he was preparing to compete in Beirut, as well as
in Zahleh, the largest town in the Beqaa Valley. Victories for the
March 14 coalition in these constituencies would be vital to preventing Aoun and the opposition from gaining a majority. They
would also represent a way for Geagea to reenter in force the main-
stream of Christian political life. His battle with Aoun, an echo of
battles past between the militia leader and the army commander,
was a subtext to an election with wider regional repercussions. But
it was also the heart of the matter as far as Christians were concerned: Who would dominate the community in the end? And as
Aoun and Geagea tried to answer that question, would it necessarily be one of them?

However, as elections neared, the overriding question became
whether Hezbollah would leverage an opposition victory into
behind-the-scenes control over Lebanon. There was the possibility
of another Hamas moment here, some thought, whereby a militant Islamist group might win control of a country through a democratic process, as Hamas had done in the Palestinian elections of
January 2006. As this impression began circulating, it took on a life
of its own, so that very soon foreign media, even foreign embassies
in Beirut, were openly preparing to watch Lebanon fall into the lap
of Hassan Nasrallah, via Michel Aoun. As journalists spoke to
journalists, one might tell the other, with some satisfaction, that
March 14 was about to "get their asses handed to them." This came
against a backdrop of shifting dynamics in the Middle East, which

only reinforced the sense that the foundations of regional support for March 14 were eroding.

The most significant change came from Saudi Arabia. In the aftermath of the January 2009 war in the Gaza Strip between Israel and Hamas, the Saudi leadership changed direction on Syria when King Abdullah decided to reconcile with Bashar al-Assad. The Gaza War had put the Saudis, like the Egyptians, in the uncomfortable position of appearing before the Arab world as objective allies of Israel because they opposed Hamas, which both countries perceived as serving Iran and Syria. This only compounded a sense in the kingdom that the strategy adopted since 2006 in Lebanon and the region, one focused on isolating Syria, in part to counter Iran, had backfired. After all, it was not the Saudis, but their principal Gulf rival, Qatar, that had brokered the Doha deal. Nowhere were the limitations of Riyadh's diplomacy more manifest than at the Arab League summit in Damascus in March 2008, which the Saudis and Egyptians effectively boycotted by sending low-level representatives. The summit achieved little of value, but most Arab heads of state attended, giving Bashar al-Assad the diplomatic success he sought and showing that it was the Saudis and Egyptians who were the ones on their own.

With Iran deemed the foremost regional threat, the Saudi monarch reversed course on Syria, hoping to gradually break it away from the Islamic Republic. There was not much conviction in this effort, but the Saudis played on Syrian uneasiness. Damascus was not readily prepared to abandon its alliance with Tehran, which made it a desirable regional interlocutor, since Assad could up his price amid all the petitions that he distance himself from Iran. However, since 2005, Syria had lost ground to Iran in Lebanon. The Syrians had never properly institutionalized their hegemony, so that their political proxies were now dependent on the goodwill of a pro-Iranian party. That did not mean Syria opposed Hezbollah—on the contrary; but Assad was also calculating beyond Lebanon, so that in the run-up to the elections there were signs of a tactical change in Syrian behavior, building on the fact that Syria, after Doha, for the first time recognized Lebanon diplomatically. Now the Syrians and the Saudis agreed to permitting a smooth Lebanese vote. For Assad, Syria lost nothing by placing its relations with the Arab states, the United States, and the Europeans on a more solid footing, particularly when the Hariri tribunal seemed less of a priority to everyone, and little more could be gained at this stage by destabilizing Lebanon. But that only disguised Assad's intention of dominating the country through other means, as he now saw that the Saudis would grant him greater leeway in Lebanon, believing this would contain, at least in relative terms, Iranian influence.

The Saudi opening to Syria had also been driven by the decision of Barack Obama to engage Tehran and Damascus. Gone was the Bush-era fervor against the Assad regime that had sustained Lebanon's beleaguered majority. Everyone, it seemed, wanted to do the opposite of what George W. Bush had done, which is perhaps why Western media were so ready to assume that March 14 was about to face defeat. On the ground, however, many Lebanese could sense a different mood. Aoun had benefited from a tsunami of approval in 2005, which anyone who bothered to talk to the Christians could see was changing. The general still had a hard core of supporters, but he had also become a divisive figure, the number of his detractors rising. The election law had been different four years earlier, but under the new law Aoun and his partners still needed to gain thirty seats in Christian districts for the opposition to gain a slight majority of sixty-five seats in parliament. Even under the most realistically optimistic assessments of Aoun's chances, this was difficult.

The opposition, particularly Aoun, had put massive amounts of money into their advertising campaign; however, it was in the homes and minds that outcomes would be decided. There were numerous factors making an Aoun triumph elusive, the most essential one being the increasing number of Christians unhappy with the general's relationship with Hezbollah, which they saw, and feared, was turning Lebanon into a strategic outpost of Iran. Aoun had managed to carry his Christians against the tide of their history, but that couldn't last, not when his coreligionists had financial, educational, familial, and other stakes in the West and in a Sunni-majority Arab world fearful of Iran. Lebanon was not the kind of place that could welcome becoming a frontline garrison state working on behalf of an Islamic regime in Tehran. This seemed obvious to me and to most of my friends, but apparently not to many reporters who shaped opinions overseas about the elections. It was a mistake to underestimate the opposition's chances, but in article after article, the sexy narrative, almost the desirable one from a journalistic perspective, was that Hezbollah would win, even if it was the Christians who had the final word.

In late May, the Hariri assassination returned to the front pages thanks to an article published in the German weekly *Der Spiegel* by one Erich Follath. The journalist argued that "it was not the Syrians, but instead special forces of [Hezbollah] that planned and executed the diabolical attack" against Rafiq al-Hariri. Follath also wrote that while Syria "is not being declared free of the suspicion of involvement, at least President Bashar Assad is no longer in the line of fire."

The article hit like a bombshell, though many Lebanese had long felt that Hezbollah was involved in Hariri's killing, by action or by omission. The next evening I was invited to a dinner organized by the Progressive Socialist Party. There, Walid Jumblatt took me aside and said, "What trap have we fallen into? This will open a Pandora's box between Sunnis and Shiites." It was vintage Jumblatt. He was spinning, saying the same thing to every journalist. By that time the Druze leader had largely given up on the Hariri tribunal, interpreting the release of the four generals as a critical blow to the institution. He was seeking a rapprochement with the Shiites, fearing that if there were more battles like those of May 2008, the Druze would be caught in the middle. Jumblatt was also looking for an opening to Syria, conscious that he would have to patch things up sooner or later with the Assad regime, which was regaining the initiative regionally and internationally. That's why the Druze leader implied that the truth about who had killed Rafiq al-Hariri was not worth a Sunni-Shiite war. Perhaps he was right, but for three years he had insinuated, without flinching, that Hezbollah was involved in Lebanon's series of assassinations. Jumblatt's newfound fear seemed to me much more a pretext to justify his impending reconciliation with Damascus. "Are you particularly surprised about what the *Der Spiegel* story reported?" I asked him. "That doesn't mean we have to publicly say it," he replied.

Yet Follath's story was flawed, and I wrote then how I thought the journalist had been manipulated. The essence of his article was that analyses of cellular telephone intercepts of participants in the crime by Lebanon's Internal Security Forces (ISF) had led them to a senior Hezbollah security official. Follath explained that he had been shown documents confirming the information. That may have been true, but his larger argument was problematical because Follath's conclusions did not necessarily follow from his evidence. Hezbollah may have participated in the crime, but the plot was complex, so that even if Hezbollah played a part, this did not imply that it planned and executed the operation. There were likely separate circles of participation, and U.N. investigators offered a hypothesis in a 2006 report that "there is a layer of perpetrators between those who initially commissioned the crime and the actual perpetrators on the day of the crime, namely those who enabled the crime to occur." Had Hezbollah supplied the "actual perpetrators," or had the party contributed those enabling the crime, let's say by tracking Hariri to the crime scene? In fact, was the party involved at all? No one could tell, but if there were concentric rings of involvement, then there was no way to prove Syria's innocence, and Follath did not. Had Hezbollah participated in the assassination, it was almost impossible to envisage it doing so without a Syrian request, a request that Bashar al-Assad, given the centralized nature of Syria's regime, alone could have conveyed, explicitly or more likely implicitly.

There were three messages in the article, the first two plainly by design: the one Jumblatt had seized upon, namely that if the truth meant accusing Hezbollah, Lebanon could face a Sunni-Shiite conflict as a consequence; that Assad was innocent, and perhaps Syria, too, an assumption Follath never demonstrated; and that the ISF had made progress on analyzing telephone intercepts. It was this last point I saw as the most relevant. Two of the men overseeing analyses of the intercepts—Lieutenant Colonel Samir Shehadeh and his deputy, Captain Wissam Eid—had been the targets of assassination, in Eid's case one that had been successful. Their investigation had been penetrated in the same way that the documents Follath was given apparently came from the inside. The leaked information appeared to substantially damage any conclusions the Hariri tribunal might reach in the future on the basis of the intercepts. Exposure politicized the information, so that even March 14 politicians, keen to avoid domestic acrimony, were now pooh-poohing the *Der Spiegel* article, in the process handing their rivals in Hezbollah valuable denials the party might later use.

Who were Follath's sources? Some accused the Future Movement of being behind the leaks, but that didn't make any sense. It would have meant the Hariri family wanted to embarrass the Special Tribunal for Lebanon, show how undesirable was the search for truth in the killing of their patriarch, and declare Syria blameless. To my mind it was more likely someone close to the Syrians, or perhaps someone wanting to do them a favor, hoping to build on the momentum of the generals' release to decisively cripple the tribunal. I still remembered how Bashar al-Assad had told Ban Ki-moon in Damascus, during their meeting of April 2007, that the Hariri tribunal might cause a civil war, splitting Sunnis and Shiites "from the Mediterranean to the Caspian." Wasn't that what was most frightening in Follath's article? You had to pity Wissam Eid, who had paid with his life for what seemed the only overt sign of progress the Hariri investigation had made since 2006.

ON THE morning of election day, June 7, I picked up a friend, the *New York Times* columnist Thomas Friedman, who had last been in Beirut a decade earlier. We drove up to the mountain town of Broummana, where my wife and I voted. One thing immediately obvious was the high participation level, a phenomenon visible all over, suggesting great polarization. Aoun and his followers were coming out in large numbers, but so, too, were the general's adversaries. We would soon learn that Aoun was responsible for both movements, as results showed that most Christians had really voted either for or against Michel Aoun. The previous day the influential Maronite patriarch, Nasrallah Sfeir, who presided over a divided church when it came to Aoun, had made his preferences known when declaring, "Today we are facing a threat to the Lebanese entity and its Arab identity, requiring alertness." It was obvious that Sfeir, by mentioning Lebanon's Arab identity, was really warning against what Iran might gain through a Hezbollah win. This hardened the doubts many Christians already had, and reminded me of what Geagea had foreseen, namely that the church might affect the final result.

By the middle of that night, returns showed a defeat for the opposition, as Hezbollah and Aoun garnered only 57 seats, against 71 for March 14 and two independents who had collaborated electorally with the majority. The predictions of a March 14 defeat had been wide of the mark. Even in mainly Christian areas where Aoun managed to pull off a victory, his margins were much smaller than in 2005, and in two key mixed-sect constituencies he was carried over the top by a Shiite electorate told by Hezbollah to vote in his favor. That didn't make the victories less legitimate, but it did show that a sizable number of Christians had abandoned him. Aoun was not out—indeed, along with allies he had a larger bloc than previously—but he was down, as the virus of Christian doubt was growing when it came to the Aounist movement.

Beyond the numbers, the election brought Lebanon full circle back to the events of 2005. Friedman later wrote that Barack Obama had defeated Iranian President Mahmoud Ahmadinejad: "Neither man was on the ballot, but there's no question whose vision won here," he observed. "First, a solid majority of Lebanese Christians voted against the list of Michel Aoun, who wanted to align their community with the Shiite Hezbollah party, and tacitly Iran . . . [and] for those who wanted to preserve Lebanon's sovereignty and independence from any regional power."

That was a fair assessment, even if few voters, frankly, had thought about Obama. The Christians and their like-minded partners in the other communities had really voted against the situation imposed upon them between 2006 and 2008, when Lebanon had descended into mayhem, and very nearly into civil war, because there was an armed party in their midst, Hezbollah, that

Lebanon could not absorb and that served Iranian and Syrian interests. Most everyone in Lebanon served the interests of outsiders,
some would reply, but those behind March 14 were not out to un-
dercut the state's sovereignty nor were they massively arming their
local sympathizers, especially with ballistic missiles. In fact, none
of the countries supporting March 14 would have dared say, as did
Mahmoud Ahmadinejad in the run-up to the elections, that an
opposition victory "would change the situation in the region and
would create new fronts for strengthening the resistance," which
did Aoun great damage among voters. Aoun could argue that
there were Christians who had stuck by him, but he had failed
in his ability to unite the community. The Christians in general,
and the Maronites in particular, had always been turbulent and
pluralistic, and now the general was the latest victim of their uncertainty, intensified by the fact that many had earlier put their
highest hopes in him.

This was a sanction vote, a vote against Michel Aoun (who had
yet always thrived among those against something) and Hezbollah. However, while voters had a sense of the general contours of
the Lebanon they wanted, those in March 14 were going in different directions. As in 2005, the triumph was the consequence of
parallel interests. Saad al-Hariri seemed to come out of the experience the strongest and was asked to form a government. In the pre-
election period he had maneuvered astutely between his political
partners. Hariri had also managed to co-opt potential Sunni rivals,
thereby consolidating his hold over his community after a period
when this was in doubt. He emerged as the true leader of March
14, over Jumblatt, who had gravitated toward the middle of the political spectrum, in an effort, with other so-called "centrist" politicians, to create the nucleus of a political grouping friendlier to
Syria. Here Jumblatt once again showed the vulnerability of his
minority status. Everyone was going or preparing to go to Damascus, the Druze leader believed, and he correctly anticipated that if
Saad al-Hariri became prime minister he would do the same, at
the Saudis' urging. After all, Jumblatt had done that himself in
1977 when the Syrians had killed his father, and he was not about
to follow in Kamal Jumblatt's footsteps by being the only Leba-

nese holdout against the Assad regime. He had gambled that the centrists would hold the balance in a new parliament, and he with them. Yet centrist candidates were obliterated as voters gave either to Aoun and Hezbollah or to March 14.

As for Samir Geagea, his was the stratagem of the ant. While the Lebanese Forces parliamentary bloc remained the same size, he had sponsored three nonparty candidates in Zahleh, all of whom were elected, and he contributed significantly to the March 14 win in Beirut, expanding his influence nationally. Geagea could play in the city, even if he was not of it and did not want to be, and he had done so largely through his relationship with Hariri. This was as good an illustration as any of how Lebanon invited advantageous compromise. There was a time during the war when Geagea had been an unbending Christian nationalist, with no real understanding of the Muslims. Much had changed. He was still imbibed with the reflexes of his community, but the alliance with Hariri, for as long as it lasted, showed his appreciation of Lebanon's inclination to spurn absolutes. Geagea would still defend his aims to the hilt, but the election allowed him to break out of his northern power base, a reality, he knew, that could only reap him political rewards if he internalized Lebanon's pluralism.

That left Hezbollah. Could it play Lebanon's pluralist game in the same way? In some ways yes, but beneath this was an unrelenting will to power. For Hezbollah, Lebanese politics were never about perpetuating the pluralistic system; they were about pursuing the party's priorities, even if the ultimate irony was that Hezbollah had no finality in its objectives except the defense of its weapons and continuation of the armed struggle—open-ended objectives reliant on Iran's. The party had hoped to use the election as leverage to impose a political order that it could control more tightly and bend into recognizing its right to bear weapons independently of the state. Aoun would have been the front man for that design, a useful idiot of sorts, for Hezbollah knew that the general was more dependent on the party than the party on him. That's why the Lebanese, not for the first time, showed a gut genius in saying no, in rejecting the real possibility that Hezbollah would mount another coup against the pluralist order as it had tried in May 2008.

Those who voted against them sensed that, once in power with Aoun, Hezbollah would have put a headlock on the institutions of the state—the security bodies, the ministries, the army. By then the international community, particularly the United States and the Sunni Arab states, unhappy with Hezbollah's success, would have reduced their cooperation with Lebanon, leaving the country isolated from a world the Lebanese would never have wanted to be isolated from. If the rhetoric of Hezbollah and Aoun was to be believed, neither much cared for Lebanon as it was, and while many Lebanese shared their skepticism, they had no faith that Hezbollah's Lebanon, or for that matter Hezbollah's Lebanon with Aoun in tow, would be any better. The party could do many things, but under no circumstances could it offer a viable model for a state, nor could Aoun change that. And while Hezbollah retained its weapons, it now received a warning that an expanding portion of society had had enough of weapons: the Lebanese did not want war as their daily lot; they did not want to be cut off from their international bearings, in favor of Iran and Syria; and they did not want their political diversity to be subject to the whims of a totalistic, militarized party. This may have been a simplistic way of seeing things, but underlining it was a realization that a Hezbollah-led victory would have also provoked a backlash in many parts of the country, particularly from Sunnis, in a future holding not only the prospect of pariah status for Lebanon but also of domestic strife. This went against the liberal aspirations of many Lebanese, which is why voters felt that their refusal to accept this state of affairs could make a difference, and for a time it seemed to.

Until something happened that shuffled the deck. On August 2, as the government formation process dragged on, with the opposition determined to drain Saad al-Hariri's and the majority's victory of all significance, Walid Jumblatt called for a special general assembly of his Progressive Socialist Party to announce that he was leaving March 14. The place where he organized the gathering was chosen with great cheekiness: the Beau Rivage Hotel, once the headquarters of Syria's intelligence branch in Beirut. Some weeks earlier, Jumblatt had announced that he was thinning out the security detail near his mountain residence, and he began circulating with minimal protection. Either he had received guarantees that the Syrians would not kill him, or he was sending a message to Bashar al-Assad that his safety was now in the president's hands, a telltale sign that he was preparing a turnaround. In his Beau Rivage speech Jumblatt stated that he regretted his flirtation with "the neocons" in Washington and announced that he was returning to his political roots in Arabism, Palestine, and the left. "Our alliance with March 14 cannot continue," Jumblatt declared, he who had been among those most responsible for allowing March 14 to continue. His strategy was not to join the opposition, though it was doubtful he could calibrate such a thing, but to maneuver between the opposition and March 14 in the government and parliament, using this to improve his relationship with Syria without alienating Saudi Arabia. It was the role he had tried to secure through the elections, but which the results had thwarted.

Jumblatt's thinking also went deeper than that. If the Druze leader was not out in front, he feared, ahead of the curve on the transformations in Lebanon, he would fall to the back, and with him the Druze, political insignificance forever knocking at their door. Jumblatt sought an axial role in a political system that he believed Syria, bolstered by its rapprochement with Saudi Arabia and perhaps the United States, would again dominate—albeit without its army in Lebanon to make his balancing act impossible. The Syrians welcomed Jumblatt's reversal, which was accompanied by the humiliation of having to atone for his years of antagonism by dealing, first, with their most sordid Lebanese partisans—yes-men to their intelligence agencies. The Druze leader accepted this mortification, knowing that in the new alignment of things his life counted for little. Yet, perniciously, Jumblatt needed the Syrians to succeed for his gamble to pay off; for where would the inveterate trapeze artist be if they failed—and therefore *he* failed to become a prize Lebanese interlocutor of Bashar al-Assad? He would be cut off from his former comrades, at the mercy of Syria and of Hezbollah, whose armed men were deployed below his mountain.

Not for the first time the Lebanese had to watch their political choices overturned by the realities of their fractured political system. In a single speech Walid Jumblatt had cast doubt on whether

March 14 remained a majority, overturned four years of defiance against Syria, and largely discarded the memory of the martyrs, all because his political and personal survival, like the defense of his Druze community, dictated a self-centered, bleak reading of what was likely to come next. He would patch things up, sort of, with Saad al-Hariri because he could not afford to incur Saudi wrath, and the Saudis still held the purse strings, but something was fundamentally broken in the post-2004 consensus that had sustained the emancipation movement. It was difficult to blame Jumblatt, since that was the nature of the system: mercurial, often unforgiving, a sheet of ice on an expanse of wet clay. Soon, others too would begin preparing for their Syrian reconciliations, planning their appointments in Damascus. In December 2009, Saad al-Hariri would visit the Syrian capital and embrace Bashar al-Assad. It may not quite have been a reconciliation, but it showed that Jumblatt had been correct. After four years of trying to reimpose its will in Lebanon, principally through violence, Syria seemed closer to its objectives. But could it succeed? Had the parliamentary elections sounded the rebirth or the death of Lebanon's emancipation movement? The Lebanese had no definitive means of answering that question, as their seemingly endless game of pursuits resumed, the answer seldom less than a fingertip away.

8

The Road from Martyrs Square

Wᴇɴ I ᴡᴀs a boy, I recall hearing a fantastic little story, probably taken from a book, of someone walking up a stairway in a tower, counting each step to the top; then doing the same thing on the way down, only to discover, to his horror, that the number of steps had increased, trapping him in an eternal spiral labyrinth. This seems an apt metaphor for Lebanon. Its elections over, we were entitled to go down the stairway and see how far the country had come since 2005, only to discover that, though much had been achieved, there was still the absence of a neat finality to it all as we were no closer to the exit.

This book is about a slice of time, one with particular relevance in Lebanon's recent history, but also with considerable meaning for the Middle East, given that so much that has gone on in Lebanon in recent years has reflected the region and has had a significant impact on it. The 2006 Lebanon war and the growing tension between Sunnis and Shiites are but two examples. This particular Lebanese moment did not end with the 2009 elections or Saad al-Hariri's visit to Damascus. The coming years will continue to be influenced by what happened in 2005 and its aftermath, not least the dilemma of how a Lebanese state with aspirations to be sovereign can coexist with a neighbor like Syria or an armed party like Hezbollah that enjoys Shiite support while its regional loyalties and obligations undermine that sovereignty. However, Hezbollah, its foreign allegiances notwithstanding, could only really gain the power it did in a society like ours, which allowed it to take advantage of the open spaces left for communal autonomy at a particular historical moment in the development of the Shiite community, under the sympathetic eye of Syria, whose long protectorate over Lebanon, at least imposed through the direct presence of its army, was brought to an end after Rafiq al-Hariri's murder.

We will return to that. But what these peregrinations around post-2005 Lebanon are, with the casual dip into a more distant past, is a story about Lebanon in general through miscellaneous particulars—particulars that I've observed with both pleasure and repulsion from up close. Even during the war years, for instance, I don't recall ever having been surrounded by such an intensity of death, of attending so many funerals. Samir Kassir was killed a few hundred meters from my apartment building, and I watched with indignation as he was left there as an exhibit while onlookers came and went. I had written at the time, in an élan of confidence and anger, that he would be avenged, but I'm not sure anymore. For months many of us journalists would, with some embarrassment, look under our cars before getting in, for who could be sure what message the next bomb would bring, no matter how irrelevant we knew we were. That sense of personal danger dissipated, but only because Lebanon entered into a period of indiscriminate danger. In his autobiography, the historian Eric Hobsbawm described the mood in Weimar Berlin this way: "We were on the *Titanic*, and everyone knew it was hitting the iceberg." Such foreboding, the certainty in the foreboding, has permeated Lebanese society in recent decades, and after 2005 we felt it all the more tenaciously because it came after a brief moment that had proven to us the tremendous power, the tremendous liberal power, Lebanon could generate when the dials were in the right alignment. Alas, they usually are not, therefore the volatile, inconclusive years that followed.

This book is an effort to derive a few general interpretations about Lebanon's political culture and society. I make no pretense of being objective, and perhaps know Lebanon well enough to be amused by claims to objectivity whenever the topic is brought up. These observations are all in many ways incomplete, surely in some respects contestable, but all are a result of intimate contact with this disconcerting country of ours, so that the best I can admit to is striving for a form of subjective detachment.

In no particular order, what have I tried to describe? For starters, that Lebanon is a paradoxically liberal country in an autocratic region because its illiberal institutions tend to cancel each other out in the shadow of a sectarian system that makes the religious communities and sects more powerful than the state—to me, the main barrier to personal freedom in the Middle East. This reality, in turn, creates spaces in society for individuals to pursue these freedoms with relative ease. Sectarianism, in imposing communal balance and a weak state, has forced society, in particular the political leadership, to accept compromise and balance as a way of moving things forward. This has deadlocked the system on many occasions, particularly after 2005, so that today it is in desperate need of reform. However, at every juncture the message has been the same: When the fundamentally pluralistic spirit of the sectarian order is in jeopardy, Lebanon risks internal conflict, which acts as a restraining mechanism on all sides.

This dry reading cannot hide that in 2005 there were real people, with real aspirations, who believed that the demonstrations against Syria, particularly the rally of March 14, were the kernel of a Lebanon that could transcend sectarianism. When that didn't happen, the believers cried "foul," saying the sectarian leaders had betrayed the aspirations of the Lebanese. This was simplistic. The leaders had little yearning to move beyond sectarianism, true, but that was never probable in the first place. As the leaders knew, from seeing it day in and day out, they retained their legitimacy because sectarianism retained its own, whatever its many faults, so that the idealists, no less than Amin Maalouf's character Tanios, became invisible in a system they could not comprehend. As far as I was concerned, 2005 was actually the consequence of sectarianism and Lebanon's retribution against those who mistreat its dictates. The Syrians, when they killed Rafiq al-Hariri to stifle the possibility of a Sunni-led rebellion against their leadership, crossed a red line, for at that moment Hariri, by virtue of his foreign relationships and the international consensus in favor of a Syrian withdrawal, was too significant to just kick into a hole. The result was that the Sunnis and the Druze joined forces with the recalcitrant Christians, so that each community, for reasons of its own—reasons based principally on their sectarian reading of Lebanese politics and society—shared a desire to end Syrian hegemony.

In light of this, any realistic effort to reform the sectarian system must come from within the system itself; in other words, using sectarianism to move beyond sectarianism, working within the framework of Lebanon's dysfunctionalities. Justifying such an approach are three things: the desirability of preserving the pluralism, therefore the liberal spaces, that Lebanon's sectarian balancing act has generated; the unlikelihood that the Lebanese can suddenly and unnaturally move from a sectarian system to a nonsectarian one without an evolutionary process of adaptation governing this; and the fact that reforms capable of improving on Lebanon's current constitution, contained in the so-called Taif Accord of 1989, actually outline such an evolutionary process that awaits implementation.

The post-2005 period in Lebanon, while it exposed the paradoxical liberalism at the heart of the country's political and social system, also highlighted the system's profound defects, particularly its remarkable ability to breed division. After all, pluralism can be the unnatural child of dissension. This tendency has had a direct impact on a second thread in the book: the ease with which outsiders have been able to exploit Lebanon's divisions to assert their power over the country. Much of this book is taken up with Syria, its methods of ruling over the Lebanese and its systematic efforts after 2005 to regain the foothold it had lost. The sudden collapse of Syrian hegemony attested to Bashar al-Assad's ignorance of the structure of control his father had set up in Lebanon, so that he unwisely came to feel that terrorization alone would suffice to keep the country in his hands. His failure temporarily allowed Iran to gain the initiative, through Hezbollah, which accepted the varnish of the pluralist system while imposing strict limits when it came to whatever might harm its interests. However, even divided, Lebanon in the post-2005 period was again and again a story of frustration for Syria and Iran, regardless of what happens in the future. Both managed to make Lebanon pay a heavy price for the Syrian pullout, but they were never able to bend the system to their advantage in a conclusive way. Theirs remained only a negative form of influence, which is why they and their local allies waged often indecisive battles against Lebanon's realities. Almost nothing Hezbollah did after 2006 truly consolidated its power within Lebanese society, so that in May 2008 its resort to weapons became an implicit admission that force was its only option, the last rampart, not persuasion. There is Lebanon and there is Hezbollah's Lebanon; one or the other will prevail, but together they cannot long coexist in a stable way.

Deriving from this, a third thread is how Lebanon has suffered from the hubris of individuals who have regarded themselves as better than the system, which hardly ever seems to satisfy their aspiration to be great men. Well before the events of 2005 blindsided him, Hassan Nasrallah expressed his dislike of Lebanese politics, saying it was characterized by "leaders of alleyways, of confessional groups, of districts." Instead, what the country needed was "great men and great leaders." I've always found such statements difficult to stomach, because they are self-reinforcing: When a leader says his country needs great men, he usually means it needs him.

My preference has always been for historical modesty. In rereading Tolstoy's *War and Peace*, for example, I am always struck by the author's views of Kutuzov, the Russian general who defeated Napoleon Bonaparte in 1812. A central theme of the later stages of the novel is that while history tends to be attracted to "great men," men like Napoleon, it is the modest men, like Kutuzov, "those rare and always solitary individuals who, divining the will of Providence, subordinate their personal will to it," who merit our admiration.

Why should they? Because they are less inclined to justify violence in the name of narcissistic change. They are more likely to understand the worth of individuals rather than consider them merely as extensions of themselves. If Lebanon can find a more durable social contract in the years to come, it will do so thanks to the efforts of modest men and women, those who have a realistic understanding of the recompenses and constraints of their system, not the visionaries who will burden the system with their egoism. Yet, it's true that the Lebanese system doesn't impose modesty, so haphazard and unreliable a patchwork of understandings and compromises has it become, so effective its promotion of mediocrity. In its preference for equilibrium over domination, the system has also favored stalemate over progress, one reason why so many young Lebanese are inclined to pick up and leave the country to cultivate their talents.

Still, I can't help but conclude that one of the main domestic problems Lebanon faced once the Syrian army left the country in 2005, the main barrier to the emergence of a stable, sovereign order, was that Hassan Nasrallah and Michel Aoun—both so similar in their readiness to ride roughshod over dissent, both armed with paternalistic disregard for their followers—refused to move beyond withering contempt for the Lebanese system. Of course, there was opportunism here. Hezbollah intended to retain its weapons at all costs and remain relevant as a political-military organization working independently of the Lebanese state on Iran's behalf, in alliance with Syria; Aoun hoped to use his ties with Hezbollah to become Lebanon's president and change the post-Taif order in a way more to his liking. Nasrallah and Aoun each used the other against March 14. Their adversaries could be sublime egoists as well, men and women out to pursue personal welfare at the expense of the general good. Who could deny that corruption prevailed, even if Hezbollah and Aoun presided over as much of it as anyone else? That's what makes the post-2005 struggle in Lebanon so difficult to idealize. Few on either side were particularly virtuous. However, Nasrallah and Aoun alone infused their interests with a higher justification, rarely showing a willingness to subordinate their own will to Providence; least of all to the improvident Lebanese political system that they felt it was their right to overhaul.

What is Lebanon to do about Hezbollah? This question is a

fourth thread I've addressed, without providing any definite answers. For the foreseeable future, the matter of the party's weapons can only be resolved regionally, through agreement with Iran; and since Iran shows no signs of wanting to disarm Hezbollah, the party will continue to oppose any effort, peaceful or violent, to go down that road. And for as long as Hezbollah holds its weapons in the face, primarily, of a hostile Sunni community, Lebanon will be unable to advance on a path toward negotiated political reform.

At one level, Hezbollah is both a consequence of and a reinforcing factor in Lebanon's inability to forge a strong state. But there may be an irony here for the future: the party, by so brazenly reflecting the limits of the state, may compel those Lebanese uncomfortable with Hezbollah to think more carefully about the state they really want, and to find ways of drawing a majority of Shiites over to a project that fulfills the latter's aspirations and encourages them to look beyond Hezbollah. We might ask, in this context, whether we are not in the midst of a much longer undertaking of state-building in Lebanon, one that began with the civil war in 1975, continued on through the decade and a half of postwar Syrian rule, and lasting to this day. That may be too optimistic a reading, and the consequences are by no means predetermined; Lebanon may yet succumb to its contradictions and collapse once more into war, whether a civil war or one imposed by regional animosities. However, the 2007 parliamentary elections, while they did not offer solutions for Lebanon's future, did show that many Lebanese were uneasy about Hezbollah. The party, despite its immodesty, must have known to read the election results as a warning that it has no blank check to conduct new wars, on anyone's behalf. Hassan Nasrallah dreams of a militarized Lebanon under the guidance of a Hezbollah vanguard. Yet this is so at odds with what most Lebanese aspire to, that were the secretary-general to briefly succumb to self-doubt, he might find that his party's reason for existing had, in most respects, evaporated.

Modesty, political modesty, is also a crucial aspect of a fifth thread, namely justice and the rule of law. It is not easy to describe the sense of resentment that overtook many Lebanese when Rafiq al-Hariri and his companions were assassinated on February 14,

2005, and on every occasion afterward when an assassination occurred. It was not just about the victims; it was about the arrogance
of the killers who sensed beforehand that they would get away
with murder. The United Nations–mandated investigation initially showed signs of promise. Peter Fitzgerald, the Irish police-
man who conducted the preliminary international inquiry into the
Hariri bombing, as well as Detlev Mehlis, the first commissioner
of the U.N.'s independent investigative commission, advanced
substantially in their understanding of what had taken place, and
who was behind it. In Mehlis's case, he arrested people and was on
the verge of arresting more, this time Syrian officers. I believe that
Mehlis's successor, Serge Brammertz, intentionally or unintentionally slowed down the investigation, so that four years after Hariri's
murder the Lebanese were still waiting for a legal accusation in the
case. Instead, the imprisoned generals were released and the prosecutor of the Special Tribunal for Lebanon, Daniel Bellemare,
found himself with no suspects in custody. The tribunal is a work
in progress, and the Canadian, or maybe just circumstances, may
yet identify the guilty; however, as the investigation and trial process dragged on, the Lebanese became unconvinced that this represented the beginning of the end for political murder. To them
the deterrence power of the Hariri investigation dissipated as time,
politics, and the interests of states took over. What ultimately happens with the Hariri tribunal will tell us a great deal about how seriously we should take the United Nations when it comes to
dispensing justice. The international organization went to great
trouble to show that the assassination of Rafiq al-Hariri would not
be accepted as business as usual. We will one day be able to judge
whether the U.N. was not guilty of hubris of its own, and if the
confidence of the assassins was justified.

The nature of the Lebanese system has never been favorable to
justice or retribution. Postwar Lebanon is a country built on a
foundation of officially sanctioned amnesia toward what happened between 1975 and 1990. And while the Lebanese themselves
didn't forget, and could not forget, their pluralism, like their
country's fragmented social structure, has frequently meant that if
imparting guilt is not something that can be applied in all cases,

then it is best for stability to avoid imparting it even in specific cases. This has been another aspect, a less luminous one, of Lebanon's system of compromise, and Rafiq al-Hariri himself was one of its prime advocates. His death could have made a difference; it may yet make a difference, but maybe we should ask another question: If it does not, if the tribunal process flounders, then what part of this can we attribute to the Lebanese and their social and political arrangement, which so naturally shies away from unambiguous outcomes?

A sixth and central thread that has preoccupied me here is the city, both as a place of political action and an idea. Martyrs Square, the metaphorical heart of this book, played an essential role in several phases of the narrative: during the intifada against Syrian rule, when its open spaces served not only as a vortex for the actions giving life to the event, but also as their symbolic incarnation. The square was at the crossroads between Beirut's different sectarian neighborhoods and bisected the divided capital of the war years, now united around the tomb of Rafiq al-Hariri. Yet it also accommodated the setbacks of the Independence Intifada, as the place from where the funeral of Samir Kassir began, through which the funeral processions of Gebran Tueni and Pierre Gemayel passed. It was the place, as well, that Hezbollah and its opposition allies sought to empty of its meaning when they began their long protest in the downtown area, tents pitched only a dozen meters away from Hariri's tomb.

This fight over an open space and what it was supposed to represent only mirrored a larger struggle over the meaning of Beirut. The embrace of the city, of the *polis*, is what defines the citizen, in the sense that when one is of the city, he or she takes part in defining the state and the citizen's role in it. What the Lebanese went through after 2005 offered a panoptical view of Beirut as Lebanon in a concentrated form. For many of those who organized the Independence Intifada, the city was a cosmopolitan and liberal place, since only those characteristics could elicit the outrage they felt against Syria after the killing of Hariri. Others agreed with them but pursued more parochial objectives, somehow understanding that the city invited such variety. For Hezbollah, Amal, and their

Shiite followers, the city was no less a setting for political action, where Shiites had as legitimate a right to frolic as anybody else. However, the nature of Hezbollah's actions ultimately turned many in the city against the Shiites (just as Hezbollah had turned many Shiites against the city), so that the violence done to Beirut by the party led to a disturbing counterreaction maintaining that Shiites had no claims to the city's favors. This displayed ignorance of what cities are about. For what possible value can there be in demanding that Shiites take their distance from Hezbollah and reintegrate into the state if those issuing the demand are not prepared to integrate them into Beirut itself?

If Lebanon is ever to know stability, the way to achieve this is through a common understanding of what it means to be of the city, beyond the narrow confines of sectarianism. I've repeatedly tried to defend aspects of sectarianism in this book, an ungrateful task when the politically correct position is to argue how odious sectarianism is. But my position has been a sociological, not a normative, one. I have preferred to deal with what we have rather than with what we would like to have, but cannot. However, that does not alter my conviction that Lebanon can only ever emerge from its seemingly incurable instability once its paradoxical liberal impulses can unite and rejuvenate the society. Sectarianism will not do that. It is no ideal, offers no conclusiveness. At best, thanks to the pluralism it elicits, it can be a way station on the path toward a Lebanon that is a common concern for all its citizens, a Lebanon in which we no longer have to pay such a heavy tribute to the martyrs, whose ghosts speak to, cry out against, our tragic disagreements.

Acknowledgments

M UCH THANKS GOES to the dozens of people whom I interviewed for this book, most of them cited, some not, who always made room for me in their often busy schedules. There isn't enough space to list them all here, and it would be unfair to name some and not others. However, their banishment to the notes in no way diminishes my deep appreciation for their assistance, without which this book could not have been written.

I must also mention close Lebanese friends who provided valuable input or advice, including Hazem al-Amin, Jabbour Doueihy, Samir Khalaf, Najib Khazzaka, Ziad Majed, Chibli Mallat, Farés Sassine, and Waddah Sharara. Ziad and Jabbour took it upon themselves to read several chapters, providing very helpful comments and corrections. Eli Khoury and Jamil Mroueh deserve particular mention, both as friends and employers, for never having tried in any way, shape, or form to influence what I've written for them over the years, despite the headaches this entailed and despite their own views.

In the United States a special dollop of gratitude goes to my old friend Charles Paul Freund, as well as to Nick Gillespie and

Jack Shafer, who all in their own way gave impetus to this project. Chuck, who is responsible for the book's title, read an earlier proposal of mine, and because of his modesty, talent, and editorial flair, has always been a model to me. Nor can I fail to mention David Ignatius, the first person to tell me in 2005 that what he really wanted to read was the story of Lebanon's emancipation movement. I had initially planned something more extensive about the country, before finding myself adopting David's more sensible approach. Alex Star was also instrumental in pushing this project forward in my mind by commissioning an article on the 2006 Lebanon war for the *New York Times Magazine*, in the midst of the conflict. The way Alex framed the argument transformed itself into a central theme of this book.

I've never met Barry Rubin, but that didn't prevent him, when I begged off contributing to a book he was editing because I wanted to focus on my own, from putting me in touch with his agent, Andrew Stuart. This was generous and fortuitous. When I spoke to Andrew, to my delight I saw that we wanted to do the same book. Andrew's savvy made the initial phases of this project effortless. Much the same can be said of those with whom I worked at Simon & Schuster. Dedi Felman merits heartfelt thanks for accepting my proposal and making early editorial suggestions that were simple but essential to improving the book's style. Alice Mayhew then took over, and nothing I write could possibly add to Alice's reputation as an editor. Her subtlety and encouragement throughout the later writing and editing stages make me, a novice, feel highly privileged to have been given the chance to work with her. I'm also grateful to her two collaborators, Karen Thompson and Roger Labrie, for their patience and time, as well as to Gypsy da Silva and Fred Wiemer for their excellent copyediting.

My great regret is that my uncle, Marcel Bakhos, will never read this book. He arrived in Beirut from Montreal in early January 2009, and one of his first questions to me was how it was coming along. Four days later he was dead. It was to be near him and his family that my mother and I moved to Lebanon in 1970. Many of my most powerful memories I still view through the prism of a world that he and my late aunt, Myriam, helped create and define, perhaps because, despite the long Lebanese nightmare, their humanity and openness tended to generate much happiness.

My wife, Mireille, has always showed me that while familiarity need not necessarily breed contempt, it allows for candor far more valuable in making a text readable. She has never been attracted to politics, which is why she was my final filter for a book not directed at a specialist audience, enhanced by her unsparing eye for the boring and superfluous. She also happened to believe in this book—as is her way quietly, without any fuss. Lebanon's civil war revolted her about many things Lebanese, but it never made her indifferent, and as I wrote, I tried repeatedly to borrow from her skepticism and compassion in reaching my conclusions.

Finally, a word on my parents. For most of my life that concept has been in the singular. My mother made many sacrifices to bring up an obstinate boy on her own, through hard times. For parents from her generation, Lebanon's collapse into war during the mid-1970s broke the momentum of lives at their cruising speed. That they strived to lend normality to abnormal surroundings, mainly on behalf of their children, was a valiant struggle that we could only truly appreciate later on. Finally, there is my father, largely absent from this narrative, yet essential to it in so many ways. He died a young man, having barely turned forty-four. When those who knew him mention him fondly, his gentleness and elegance, I believe they mean it. Absence is also a form of discretion, these days an underrated quality I will try to emulate by stopping here. This book is dedicated to his memory.

Notes

Introduction

1   *the many instead of the one:* The clever phrase is borrowed from Paul Berman, although I've reversed the order. The correct quote can be read in Chapter 3.

3   *or face Saudi enmity:* "Al-riyadh nasahat bi-insihab souri min lubnan fi asra' waqt li-muwajahat al-dughut wa ha'l al-azma" (Riyadh Recommended a Syrian Withdrawal from Lebanon as Soon as Possible, to Confront the Pressure and Resolve the Crisis), *Al-Hayat*, March 4, 2005. This article in particular did not mention that Bashar al-Assad had sought a delay or that Syria would face Saudi enmity, but several other Arabic sources did, and both were implied in the Saudi position.

3   *The Saudis had few doubts about who had killed Hariri:* Email exchange with Jamil Mroueh, the publisher of the *Daily Star* newspaper. In a meeting in Riyadh with then Crown Prince Abdullah on March 6, soon after Abdullah's meeting with Bashar al-Assad on March 3 in the Saudi capital, Mroueh heard Abdullah say, "[I]t is our assessment that the Syrians arranged the operation" ("tarjeehuna anna al-souriyoun dabbaru al-'amaliyah"). The email exchange occurred on March 6, 2009, although Mroueh and I discussed the conversation more generally in the spring of 2005. In an interview in May 2009 with the Lebanese Broadcasting Corporation, the former Saudi ambassador to Lebanon, Abdul Aziz Khoja, recalled that "the Saudi leadership was afraid for the life of President Rafiq al-Hariri. I told him of the necessity to take precautions and leave Lebanon for a specific period of time." The obvious question was, who would Hariri have left Lebanon to escape from? Crown Prince Abdullah

provided the obvious answer. For a summary of Khoja's statements, see, online in Arabic, http://nowlebanon.com/Arabic/NewsArticle Details.aspx?ID=95385, or in English this imperfectly translated version: http://nowlebanon.com/NewsArticleDetails.aspx?ID=95382.

10   *"uniting them in one day":* Michel Chiha, "Introduction à une Politique Libanaise," *Politique Intérieure* (Beirut: Éditions du Trident, 1980), p. 17.

10   *down the hierarchical ladder:* For an English-language description of the development of the National Pact, see Eyal Zisser, *Lebanon: The Challenge of Independence* (London: I. B. Tauris, 2000), pp. 57–67.

11   *a cosmopolitan Mediterranean city:* Samir Kassir, *Histoire de Beyrouth* (Paris: Fayard, 2003), p. 274.

11   *a " 'state that cannot be found' ":* Georges Corm, *Le Liban Contemporain, Histoire et Société* (Paris: La Découverte, 2003; edition updated in 2005), pp. 31–33.

1. A Voluptuous Vibration

PAGE

20   *an X drawn through their faces:* Interview with Giselle Khoury, Beirut, June 13, 2008.

21   *Lebanon's French-language daily:* Sandra Iché, *L'Orient-Express: Chronique d'un Magazine Libanais des Années 1990* (Beirut: Presses de l'Ifpo, Cahiers de l'Ifpo 03, 2009), 184 pp.

22   *Arabism and the Arab nationalist idea:* Samir Kassir, *Considérations sur le Malheur Arabe* (Paris: Actes Sud-Sinbad, 2004), p. 26.

26   *the term of President Émile Lahoud, Hariri's enemy:* In this context, it's worth recalling what Machiavelli wrote: "[T]here is nothing more difficult to handle, more doubtful of success, and more dangerous to carry through than initiating changes in a state's constitution." *The Prince* (London: Penguin Books, 2004), p. 24.

26   *"I will break Lebanon":* Neil MacFarquhar, "Behind Lebanon Upheaval, 2 Men's Fateful Clash," *New York Times*, March 20, 2005. This version is the same one Jumblatt repeated to me in a conversation.

26   *some Security Council members voting in favor:* Conversation with a diplomat in Beirut who was aware of one such message from Hariri to his own government.

28   *there were thousands with us:* Email interview with Ziad Majed, June 10, 2008.

28   *"that this alone could move the Muslims":* Interview with Nabil Aboucharaf, Beirut, June 5, 2008.

30 *"free and indeterminate and therefore negotiable":* Samir Khalaf, *Heart of Beirut: Reclaiming the Bourj* (London: Saqi Books, 2006), p. 180.

31 *hanged by the Turkish governor, Jamal Pasha:* For a remarkable history of Martyrs Square, see *El-Bourj: Place de la Liberté et Porte du Levant,* a collection of texts, presented under the supervision of Ghassan Tueni and Farés Sassine, in French and Arabic on the history of the square and its surrounding area. (Beirut: Dar al-Nahar, 2000). On the history of the martyrs themselves, see (in Arabic) the chapter "Shuhada al-saha, 1915–1916" (The Martyrs of the Square, 1915–1916), a collection of three texts on who they were and the specifics of their executions, pp. 217ff.

31 *(bombed Beirut's medieval walls from there):* Ibid., p. 181.

32 *"to allow more sensation, more liberty . . .":* Farés Sassine, "Modernisme et Folklore: Les Cinémas du Bourj," ibid.

33 *"the neighborhood's access to* Al-Nahar*":* Interview with Ziad Majed, June 10, 2008.

34 *Everything seemed to fall into place:* As Khodr Ghadban, then the student representative in the Progressive Socialist Party of Walid Jumblatt, put it: "The youths seemed to have worked together all their life." Interview with Khodr Ghadban, Beirut, June 13, 2008.

34 *meaning the resignation of the government:* Interview with Asma Andraos, Beirut, June 11, 2008.

34 *a jeweler hanging out with Andraos:* Conversation with Selim Mouzannar, Beirut, June 20, 2008.

38 *" 'This one is for real' ":* Interview with Eli Khoury, Beirut, May 21, 2008.

39 *who above all wanted Syria out:* Interview with Shireen Abdullah, an employee of *Al-Nahar* and assistant to Gebran Tueni, Beirut, May 28, 2008.

40 *not surprisingly by the Syrians:* The portrait of Walid Jumblatt was published in the March 20, 2005, issue of the *New York Times Magazine* under the title "The Survivor."

44 *"it was the start of a new Arab world":* David Ignatius, "Beirut's Berlin Wall," *Washington Post,* February 23, 2005, p. A19.

44 *running the security services in Lebanon:* Report of the Fact-Finding Mission to Lebanon Inquiring into the Causes, Circumstances, and Consequences of the Assassination of Former Prime Minister Rafik Hariri, S/2005/203, United Nations Security Council, March 24, 2005.

45 *unnecessarily alienating Syria:* See, for example, Flynt Leverett, "Don't Rush on the Road to Damascus," *New York Times,* March 2, 2005.

45 *the behavior of American neoconservatives:* Francis Fukuyama, *America*

at the Crossroads: Democracy, Power, and the Neoconservative Legacy (New Haven and London: Yale University Press, 2006).

45   *"the eradication of terrorism and its sponsors":* The full passage of the PNAC letter is even more damning to Fukuyama. It reads: "We agree with Secretary of State Powell's recent statement that Saddam Hussein 'is one of the leading terrorists on the face of the Earth. . . . ' It may be that the Iraqi government provided assistance in some form to the recent attack on the United States. But even if evidence does not link Iraq directly to the attack, any strategy aiming at the eradication of terrorism and its sponsors must include a determined effort to remove Saddam Hussein from power in Iraq. Failure to undertake such an effort will constitute an early and perhaps decisive surrender in the war on international terrorism. The United States must therefore provide full military and financial support to the Iraqi opposition. American military force should be used to provide a 'safe zone' in Iraq from which the opposition can operate. And American forces must be prepared to back up our commitment to the Iraqi opposition by all necessary means." The full letter can be found, online, at the following address: http://globalresearch.ca/articles/NAC304A .html.

48   *were not sure how to read Hariri:* Email interview with Ambassador Jeffrey D. Feltman, June 25, 2008.

51   *parliamentary consultations to name a prime minister:* For an English translation of the speech, see Nicholas Noe, ed., *Voice of Hezbollah: The Statements of Sayyed Hassan Nasrallah* (London & New York: Verso Books, 2007), pp. 319–327.

54   *and a third person to be agreed upon:* Interview with Samir Abdelmalek, Beirut, June 2, 2008.

56   *he hated how politics in Lebanon were played:* Interview with Ghassan Atallah, Beirut, June 2, 2008.

2. A Forest of Fathers

PAGE

59   *A Forest of Fathers:* The title of this chapter is taken from a book review of *The Rock of Tanios* by Farés Sassine in the *Beirut Review*, no. 8 (Fall 1994), published by the Lebanese Center for Policy Studies.

59   *skill in evading himself:* Amin Maalouf, *The Rock of Tanios* (London: Abacus Books, 1995). The passage translation is mine, from the original French version of the book, *Le Rocher de Tanios* (Paris: Grasset, 1993).

62 *Lahoud was the choice, like it or not:* Interview with Elie al-Firzli, a former deputy speaker of parliament and information minister, Beirut, July 7, 2008.

63 *Lebanon's sectarian relations:* Albert Hourani, "Ideologies of the Mountain and the City," in Roger Owen, ed., *Essays on the Crisis in Lebanon* (London: Ithaca Press, 1976), pp. 33–41.

65 *if they ever got out of line:* See Amnesty International, "Samir Gea'gea' and Jirjis al-Khouri: Torture and Unfair Trial," published on November 23, 2004. The document can be accessed online at http://www.amnesty.org/en/library/asset/MDE18/003/2004/en/dom=MDE 180032004en.html.

66 *over the Druze:* That was how Jumblatt described himself in an interview with me. See "The Survivor" in the March 20, 2005, issue of the *New York Times Magazine.*

66 *now lorded over Lebanon:* The Document of National Accord, known as the Taif Accord, was negotiated in the Saudi resort of Taif between September 30 and October 22, 1989. Many of its clauses were integrated into the Lebanese constitution, establishing what would become known as the Second Republic. One of the primary results of Taif was to take most executive power out of the hands of the Maronite president and place it in the Council of Ministers. Despite the accord, the conflict in Lebanon would continue until October 13, 1990, when Syrian forces overran the areas controlled by units loyal to Michel Aoun, forcing the general to take refuge at the French embassy, before his exile in France.

67 *aid networks in Lebanon:* Muhammad Abi Samra, "Al-Ihya al-sha'biyya wa-ahluha fi zaman al-munathamaat al-'askariyya wa 'amalaha al-sha'bi" (The Popular Neighborhoods and Their Inhabitants in the Period of Military Organizations and their Popular Activities), in *Al-Nahar* (Beirut), August 3, 2008, on how Hariri began distributing Saudi aid to predominantly Sunni popular areas of Beirut in 1982, after Israel's invasion of Lebanon.

68 *(Hassan Nasrallah, would grow up):* Interviews with Lebanese sociologist Waddah Sharara, July 10 and August 8, 2008. Sharara followed Musa al-Sadr's rise from up close in the early 1970s, when he was a social activist in the northeastern suburb of Burj Hammoud. For an English-language account of Musa al-Sadr and the transformations in the Shiite community during the period leading up to and after the beginning of the civil war, see Fouad Ajami, *The Vanished Imam: Musa al Sadr and the Shia of Lebanon* (Ithaca: Cornell University Press, 1986).

69 *Syrian military intelligence:* For the discussion of Ghazi Kanaan, I have greatly benefited from interviewing General Adnan Shaaban, a for-

mer senior Lebanese intelligence officer close to Kanaan during his years in Lebanon, although the two later had a falling out. The interview was conducted in Beirut on July 9, 2008. For a discussion of the Alawite tribes, see Patrick Seale, *Asad: The Struggle for the Middle East* (Berkeley: University of California Press, 1988), p. 9. For a discussion of Syria's political and security leadership and its origins, see Hanna Batatu, *Syria's Peasantry, the Descendants of Its lesser Rural Notables, and Their Politics* (Princeton: Princeton University Press, 1999).

70   *"ours, politics and security":* Cited and translated by Fawwaz Traboulsi in *A History of Modern Lebanon* (London: Pluto Press, 2007), p. 246.

70   *"keep out of politics":* William Dalrymple, "Syria Shouldn't be Demonised," *The Spectator*, October 24, 2007.

71   *he was dead:* Conversation with Wardeh Zamel, the host of two very popular political talk shows on the Voice of Lebanon radio station, Beirut, August 1, 2008.

72   *his Lebanese chessboard:* Kanaan's actions and his way of exercising power have been gleaned from my own observations, numerous conversations with Lebanese politicians, army officers, observers, and newspaper stories over the years. Watching Kanaan at work was a favorite pastime in Lebanon.

73   *and humiliate Salim al-Hoss:* Interview with Adnan Shaaban, July 9, 2008. This was confirmed to me by another former Lebanese intelligence officer.

73   *not a Sayyed trait:* Sayyed was then head of military intelligence (the so-called Deuxième Bureau) in the Beqaa Valley, until his promotion as number two in military intelligence, where he was the real head of the service, since as a Shiite he could not take the top post. In 1998, he was appointed head of the General Security directorate, whose role was expanded to match his expanding power.

73   *"the* muqaddams *still ruled Lebanon":* Conversation with Farés Sassine, August 6, 2008.

74   *"at the hands of heartless people":* See Michael Young, "Assad's Forgotten Man: A *Reason* Interview with Syrian Intellectual Yassin al-Haj Saleh," at Reason Online, accessible at http://www.reason.com/news/show/34033.html. For a barely fictitious novel on the Palmyra prison, see Moustafa Khalifé, *La Coquille: Prisonnier Politique en Syria* (Paris: Sinbad, Actes Sud, 2007), 262 pp. The book is a French translation of a little-distributed Arabic book titled *Al-Qawqa'a.*

75   *"we believe in trusting" the United States:* The attack was officially blamed on a Sunni Salafist group named 'Asbat al-Ansar, which issued a statement warning against the intention of "anyone, even if they are powerful and influential, to fire poison arrows at the heart of the resistance." However, very few observers in Beirut, including

numerous politicians, believed anyone but the Syrians had the leeway and means to mount such an attack, whether directly or through
a proxy. One could read the statement released as a direct response
to Hariri's comments in Brazil, warning him against any effort to
disarm Hezbollah, which for all intents and purposes was the "resistance." Indeed, Hariri had sinned in two ways: He had spoken about
talks with Israel, and he had spoken of his "trust" in the United
States. Both were unacceptable transgressions for a Syrian regime
that systematically sought to undermine any Lebanese foreign policy
independent of Syria.

76 *doubly vulnerable to Syrian retribution:* Conversation with then Tripoli
parliamentarian Mosbah al-Ahdab, Beirut, July 29, 2008.

76 *not be a good idea to attend:* For a breakdown of Syrian intelligence officials in Lebanon in March 2004, see the document "A Recent Report Detailing the Structure of the Syrian Intelligence Service's
Network in Lebanon," available online at http://www.milnet.com/
archives/Syrian-Intel-Service.pdf.

77 *when Israel occupied the Lebanese capital:* Ze'ev Schiff and Ehud Yaari,
Israel's Lebanon War (New York: Simon & Schuster, 1984), 320 pp. See
also the more recent book by French journalist Alain Ménargues, *Les
Secrets de la Guerre du Liban* (Paris: Albin Michel, 2004), 553 pp.

77 *Cobra's book was an illiterate masterpiece:* Robert Maroun Hatem, *From
Israel to Damascus: The Painful Road of Blood, Betrayal, and Deception*
(La Mesa, CA: Vanderblumen Publications, 1999), 172 pp. For a review of the book, see Walid Harb, "Snake Eat Snake," *The Nation*,
July 19, 1999, which is also accessible at http://www.thenation
.com/doc/19990719/harb/single. Walid Harb is a pseudonym that I
used to author the article, because at the time Elie Hobeiqa was still
alive. To my enduring regret, and for the only time in my career, I
opted to hide behind a borrowed name.

80 *"would increase or decrease his power":* Adam Cohen and Elizabeth
Taylor, *American Pharaoh* (Boston, New York, and London: Little,
Brown, 2001), p. 8.

82 *enhanced his popularity:* See Muhammad Abi Samra, "Irth al-
munazamaat al-filastiniyyeh bayn al-mukhabaraat al-suriyyeh wal-
'amal al-ijtima'i li mu'assassat al-hariri (The Heritage of the
Palestinian Organizations Between the Syrian Intelligence Services
and the Social Work of the Hariri Institutions), in *Al-Nahar* (Beirut),
August 10, 2008, on how Rafiq al-Hariri managed to build on the
social networks in the popular Sunni neighborhood of Tariq al-
Jadideh in Beirut. The article is Part Two of a four-part series, of
which the first is cited in the note for p. 67.

82 *with no compelling leaders:* Traboulsi, *A History of Modern Lebanon,*

p. 229. See also "Al-mujtama' al-ahli bayn al-'amal al-ijtima'i lil-hariri wal mukhabaraat al-suriyyeh" (Civil Society Between the Social Work of Hariri and the Syrian Intelligence Services), in *Al-Nahar* (Beirut), August 17, 2008. The article is third in a four-part series, of which the first two are cited in notes for pp. 67 and 82 (above).

83   *he admitted in an interview:* Interview with Saad al-Hariri, Beirut, May 5, 2009.

85   *set up electricity networks:* For a brief rundown of some of the kinds of networks Hezbollah can call upon, see Waddah Sharara, *Dawlat hizbullah, lubnan mujtama'n islamiyyan* (The Hezbollah State: Lebanon an Islamic Society) (Beirut: Dar al-Nahar, 1996), pp. 1–8.

86   *handed down to him:* Of Hafez al-Assad's patience, the British journalist Patrick Seale has written: "Throughout his life the most consistent characteristic of Asad's moves was the cautious, patient planning which preceded them. He learned to examine the ground carefully before venturing out on it." *Asad: The Struggle for the Middle East.* For those Lebanese who were happy to see the Syrians leave their country, it was a relief that the son was less accomplished than the father.

3. Total War

PAGE

91   *what was going on:* Michael Young, "Hezbollah's Other War," *New York Times Magazine,* August 13, 2006, pp. 34–39.

93   Story of a Secret State: Jan Karski, *Story of a Secret State* (Boston: Houghton Mifflin, 1944), 391 pp.

95   *when the civil war started:* According to the former head of Lebanon's military intelligence service, Johnny Abdo, one of those who had played a key role in engineering Bashir Gemayel's ascent, "Bashir wanted a strong state that defended minorities, including Christians. He did not consider the Sunnis a minority." Interview with Johnny Abdo, Paris, October 30, 2008.

96   *within a two-year period:* Ménargues, *Les Secrets de La Guerre du Liban,* pp. 11–19, for the details of this effort. Ménargues reportedly had access for his book to the papers of Fadi Frem, who was appointed head of the Lebanese Forces after Bashir Gemayel's assassination.

97   *"will have been in vain":* As quoted in Karim Pakradouni, *Stillborn Peace* (Beirut: Éditions Fiches du Monde Arabe, 1985), p. 262.

98   *"abandoned to visionaries":* René Grousset, *Figures de Proue* (Paris: Balland, 1992), p. 229.

98   *a terse official biography:* There are several biographical articles or interviews with Nasrallah, including Noe, ed., *The Voice of Hezbollah,*

pp. 116–143, an English translation of an interview conducted with Nasrallah in August 1993 by the now-defunct Lebanese daily *Nida' al-Watan*. See also, "Al-sayyid nasrallah yarwi siratahoo" (Sayyid Nasrallah Tells his Biography), an Arabic translation of an interview that appeared in French in Lebanon's weekly *Magazine*, November 28, 1997. The Arabic translation of the article can be accessed online at darkulaib.com/vb/showthread.php?p=536547. See also Ali al-Ruz, "Min madrasat 'al-najah' fil karantina ila al-najah fi-madrsat al-nasr" (From the "Al-Najah" School in Karantina to Success in the School of Victory), *Al-Ra'i al-'Aam* (Kuwait), which can be accessed at http:// www.bintjbeil.com/A/nasrallah.html. A biographical interview, translated from the Persian, was published, oddly enough, on the site of the Federation of American Scientists, and was taken from the weekly Iranian magazine *Ya Lesarat Ol-Hoseyn*, the organ of the Ansar-e Hezbollah. The document can be accessed at www.fas.org/ irp/news/2006/08/nasrallah.html.

99   *a militia known as the Amal Movement:* Augustus Richard Norton, *Amal and the Shi'a: Struggle for the Soul of Lebanon* (Austin: University of Texas Press, 1987), p. 48.

100   *urged them to combat Israel's occupation:* Ahmad Nizar Hamzeh, *In the Path of Hizbullah* (Syracuse: Syracuse University Press, 2004), p. 24.

100   *the reborn Islamists among its members:* Ibid., p. 24.

101   *outlining its political program:* A slightly abridged English-language translation of the Open Letter can be found in the *Jerusalem Quarterly*, no. 48 (Fall 1988). It is accessible online at http://www.stand withus.com/pdfs/flyers/hezbollah_program.pdf.

102   *the communal umbrella he was setting up:* Interview with the sociologist Waddah Sharara, who writes extensively on Shiite affairs, Beirut, July 10, 2008.

103   *Majed Nasser al-Zubaydi:* Majed Nasser al-Zubaydi, *Karamaat al-wa'd al-sadeq* (The Miracles of the Sincere Promise) (Al-Ruwayss, Lebanon: Dar al-Mahja al-Bayda', 2007), 231 pp.

103   *a key stage in his rise to power:* For one version of the battle, see Maxime Rodinson, *Muhammad* (New York: Pantheon, 1980), pp. 164–168.

103   *Hezbollah's resistance against Israel:* The poll, which posed a number of other questions as well, can be found online at the Beirut Center for Research and Information's Web site: http://www.beirutcenter.info/ Default.asp?contentid=690&MenuID=46; and an English-language summary of the poll can be found at http://www.beirutcenter.info/ default.asp?contentid=692&MenuID=46.

104   *between the different factions:* Conversation with a March 14 parliamen-

tarian present at a meeting with Prime Minister Siniora to address such concerns.

106   *particularly of electricity and water stations:* This was the conclusion many reached during the war, but which was confirmed in my private conversations afterward with U.S. officials who wish to remain anonymous.

107   *"the birth pangs of a new Middle East":* The statement was made in a briefing in Washington on July 21, 2006. It can be accessed online at http://www.state.gov/secretary/rm/2006/69331.htm.

109   *"a thousand rockets fired on Israel":* Michael Young, "The Accidental Prime Minister," The Weekend Interview with Fuad al-Siniora, *Wall Street Journal,* October 7, 2006. The interview can be accessed online at http://www.opinionjournal.com/extra/?id=110009061.

111   *"moved its oppression to the minds":* Interview with Luqman Slim, Beirut, August 5, 2008.

112   *"not a political party that conducts jihad":* Hamzeh, *In the Path of Hizbullah,* p. 44.

112   *"destruction and human sacrifice":* Ian Buruma and Avishai Margalit, *Occidentalism: The West in the Eyes of its Enemies* (New York: Penguin, 2004), p. 58.

113   *"We need to find a middle ground":* Interview with Ali Fayyad, Beirut, August 18, 2008.

113   *Mahdi Army in Iraq:* See, for example, the article in the Abu Dhabi daily *The National,* titled "Hizbollah Training Us: Mahdi Army," August 23, 2008, in which combatants of the Mahdi Army in Iraq described their training in Lebanon in camps belonging to Hezbollah. This can be accessed online at http://www.thenational.ae/article/20080823/FOREIGN/514250997/1133.

114   *"the total movement":* Paul Berman, *Terror and Liberalism* (New York: W. W. Norton, 2004), p. 46.

115   *close ties to Syria's Alawite regime:* For an overview of the foundations of Musa al-Sadr's political and intellectual thinking, see Saoud Mawla, " 'An al-shi'a wa lubnan" (On the Shiites and Lebanon) in *Tariq zhat al-shawqah, al-shi'a al-lubnaniyoun fi-tabalwur wa'ihim al-watani* (A Road with Thorns: Lebanon's Shiites and the Crystallization of Their National Consciousness), a series of essays published by the Haya Bina association in its Dafater series, March–June 2008, pp. 3–34. On the Musa al-Sadr–Alawite connection, the sociologist Waddah Sharara traces the relationship back to the late 1950s and '60s, when Sadr established contact with Syrian Alawite officials who would become more prominent subsequently. Interview with Waddah Sharara, Beirut, July 10, 2008.

116 *absolute leader of Iran:* For a text of the speech, see *Al-Nahar* (Beirut), May 29, 2008, p. 9. In its Open Letter, Hezbollah stated, "Our behavior is dictated to us by legal principles laid down by the light of an overall political conception defined by the leading jurist." See *Jerusalem Quarterly*, no. 48 (Fall 1988).

116 *"what was lost during the war":* Interview with Ali Fayyad, Beirut, August 18, 2008.

116 *firms, vehicles, and agriculture:* The report, released in November 2006 in Arabic, was released in English in February 2007 as "The Comprehensive Survey of Economic Sector Losses Resulting from the July 2006 Aggression on Lebanon," Consultative Center for Studies and Documentation, Beirut.

117 *many of them Lebanese:* The statement can be read at the Web site of Engage, and can be accessed at http://www.engageonline.org.uk/blog/article.php?id=601.

119 *"many people here have chosen that":* The interview can be seen online at http://www.memritv.org/clip/en/1676.htm, and a transcript can be read at http://www.memritv.org/clip_transcript/en/1676.htm. The interviewer was Najat Sharafeddine, herself a Shiite, who at one point engaged in this remarkable exchange with Finkelstein:

Interviewer: The war could have been avoided.

Norman Finkelstein: It could not have been avoided. There is no way that the United States and Israel are going to tolerate any resistance in the Arab world. If you want to pretend it can be avoided, you can play that game. But serious people, clear-headed people, knew there was going to be a war sooner or later. . . . Now, how can I not respect those who say no to that? You know, during the Spanish Civil War there was a famous woman—they called her "La Pasionaria"—Dolores Ibarruri, from the Spanish Republic. She famously said: "It's better to die on your feet than to walk crawling on your knees."

Interviewer: But that is up to the Lebanese people in its entirety.

Norman Finkelstein: I totally agree. I am not telling you what to do with your lives, and if you'd rather live crawling on your feet, I could respect that. I could respect that. People want to live. How can I deny you that right? But then, how can I not respect those who say they would rather die on their feet? How can I not respect that?

121 *"not just a military reaction":* Qassem made the statement at a book-signing ceremony in June 2008. The statement can be found online, in Arabic, at http://www.nowlebanon.com/Arabic/NewsArticleDetails.aspx?ID=48252.

4. Invisible City

123 *among the battle dead for years:* For a firsthand account of that experience, see Paolo Caccia Dominioni, *Alamein, 1933–1962* (Milan: Longanesi & C., 1962), 606 pp.

126 *control over the governmental agenda:* Article 65 of the Lebanese constitution specifies that the legal quorum for the Council of Ministers is two-thirds of ministers present, and requires that "basic national issues" be decided by a vote, with approval requiring a two-thirds majority. Basic national issues are clearly defined in the text as "[t]he amendment of the Constitution, the declaration of a state of emergency and its termination, war and peace, general mobilization, international agreements and treaties, the annual government budget, comprehensive and long-term development projects, the appointment of Grade One government employees and their equivalents, the review of the administrative map, the dissolution of the Chamber of Deputies, electoral laws, nationality laws, personal status laws, and the dismissal of Ministers." For an English-language text of the constitution, see the *Beirut Review*, vol. 1, no. 1 (Spring 1991), pp. 122–160.

128 *allowing it to remain constitutionally in place:* The cabinet had twenty-four ministers, so that the resignation of six ministers still left two-thirds of the ministers in place.

128 *proved the contrary:* Conversation with Walid Jumblatt, Beirut, November 2006.

131 *between rich and poor was nonsense:* See, for example, Mohamad Bazzi's article, "People's Revolt in Lebanon," in *The Nation*, January 8, 2007, in which he wrote: "The protests are being portrayed in much of the Western media as a sectarian battle, or a coup attempt—engineered by Hezbollah's two main allies, Syria and Iran—against a US-backed Lebanese government. Those are indeed factors underlying the complex and dangerous political dance happening in Beirut. But the biggest motivator driving many of those camped out in downtown isn't Iran or Syria, or Sunni versus Shiite. It's the economic inequality that has haunted Lebanese Shiites for decades. It's a poor and working-class people's revolt." Bazzi's interpretation was not wrong when it came to motivations, but in playing up the matter of economic inequality and implying that the Shiites alone were the victims of that inequality, he greatly overstated things. He also, unintentionally, seemed to confirm the views of those who argued the protest was primarily provoked by social envy.

133   *to love life:* Indeed, at the end of the 2006 war, the head of Quantum Communications in Beirut, Eli Khoury, began an advertisement campaign centered around the theme "I Love Life," which was directed against the cult of martyrdom that Hezbollah had highlighted during the summer war of 2006. The campaign hit a sensitive spot among Hezbollah and its allies, including the Aounist movement, who responded with a campaign of their own that insisted "We Also Love Life."

136   *furnished for nothing but use:* The useful sentence is taken from Graham Greene, *The Confidential Agent* (London: Penguin, 1971), pp. 70–71.

137   *"We are very happy," Mehlis said:* Interview with Detlev Mehlis, Monteverde, December 5, 2005.

138   *backbone report for future reports:* This point was made to me by Mehlis himself, but also more extensively by his spokeswoman, Nasra Hassan, in conversations we had in Beirut in late 2005.

138   *"without their knowledge":* Report of the International Independent Investigation Commission Established Pursuant to Security Council Resolution 1595, October 20, 2005, p. 5. The report is accessible online at www.un.org/News/dh/docs/mehlisreport.

139   *"considerable resources and capabilities":* Ibid.

139   *I conducted with him in January 2008:* Interview with Detlev Mehlis, Berlin, January 19, 2008. The interview was conducted for the *Wall Street Journal*, but an extended version was published on the Web site of *Reason* magazine, titled "Under Suspicion: A *Reason* Interview with German Prosecutor Detlev Mehlis." It can be accessed at http://reason.com/news/show/124674.html. In that interview this is what Mehlis had to say about the 2005 track changes episode: "When I prepared the original report, it was my impression that it would be confidential; that we would release to the public a version containing fewer details. However, in New York I learned that [U.N. Secretary-General Kofi] Annan wanted to make the report public. I intervened to say that, therefore, we needed to remove the names in question, because the persons mentioned were not suspects, but had merely been mentioned by a witness. Only the names of suspects and certain prominent witnesses were in the report. The U.N. press office made an unfortunate mistake in releasing the document with the track changes. It was definitely not intentional."

141   *"the very existence of such places is a profanity":* Christopher Hitchens, "Our Friends in Bombay," Slate, December 1, 2008. The article can be accessed at http://www.slate.com/id/2205710/.

143   *criticized by urban planners and others:* For a critical assessment of the 1991 master plan, as well as a look back at previous master plans for

the reconstruction of Beirut, see Nabil Beyhum, "The Crisis of Urban Culture: The Three Reconstruction Plans for Beirut," *Beirut Review*, vol. 2, no. 4 (Fall 1992), pp. 43–62.

144   *Hariri held a controlling interest:* Ayman Trawi, *Beirut's Memory* (Beirut: Published by the author, 2004).

150   *were still keen to meet Majed:* Conversation with Ziad Majed, December 4, 2008. It is significant that the altercation took place in Shiyah, an area of the southern suburbs settled earliest, therefore with more established solidarity networks, creating a situation in which Hezbollah tended to be less dominant than in other parts of the suburbs. It is also a place where the Amal Movement is influential.

5. The Crack-Up

PAGE

153   *the French daily* Le Monde: Cécile Hennion, "Dialogue de Sourds Entre Bachar Al-Assad et Ban Ki-moon," *Le Monde*, June 28, 2007.

154   *(through Resolution 1757):* Some prominent Lebanese jurists point out that while the tribunal was *passed* under Chapter VII authority, that did not mean it would *operate* under such authority; instead, on the matter of state cooperation with the tribunal, a new U.N. resolution would be required. Interview with Judge Shukri Sader, who as president of the Department of Legislation and Consultation at the Lebanese Justice Ministry, helped negotiate the tribunal's statutes on Lebanon's behalf, Beirut, February 13, 2009. Sader articulated his thinking in a paper read at the Yale Law School, titled "The Very Special Tribunal for Lebanon," on October 26, 2008.

154   *as Syrian officials later frequently explained:* This longstanding position was reversed in 2008, and in 2009 Syria named an ambassador to Lebanon for the first time since the two countries' independence.

159   *he was being besieged in Beirut:* This was reported in newspapers the following day, and was later confirmed to me by Jumblatt in a conversation.

162   *to Aoun's irritation:* As recounted to me by people who heard this from Aoun's close entourage.

163   *the conditions of his homecoming:* In a television interview with a program produced by the Lebanese Broadcasting Corporation (LBC) aired in spring 2005, one mediator, Fayez Qazzi, described going back and forth between Aoun and the Syrians, adding that he was aware of other parallel lines of communication. He didn't specify who was involved in these, but one was a mission undertaken by Émile Émile Lahoud, the son of President Émile Lahoud, along with

Karim Pakradouni, who had opposed Syria before being co-opted and placed by the Syrians at the head of the Kataeb Party. Pakradouni described his mission and the conditions imposed on Aoun in a book on the Lahoud presidency. See Karim Pakradouni, *Sadmeh wa Sumud* (Shock and Resistance), 2nd ed. (Beirut: All Prints Distributors and Publishers, 2009), pp. 371–381. It remains unclear whether there were direct contacts between Syrian officials and Aoun, though there were persistent reports in Beirut that there had been, involving a senior Syrian official close to the late Hafez al-Assad.

165 *Aoun's exile personified their regression:* In reality, Taif took executive power away from the Maronite president and gave it not to the Sunni prime minister, but to the Council of Ministers as a collective body. A prime minister, if he was a powerful figure like Rafiq al-Hariri, could appear dominant. However, in 1998 the prime minister happened to be Salim al-Hoss, who was a much weaker figure than the Maronite president at the time, Émile Lahoud. The Taif reforms were vague enough that the president's, prime minister's, and speaker's powers could be defined by individuals and circumstances, so that the perception among Maronite Christians that the Sunnis had inherited their presidential power was not really accurate.

172 *robbed a bank in a nearby town:* For an excellent analysis of the Nahr al-Bared fighting, which will be discussed later in this chapter, see Bernard Rougier, "Fatah al-Islam: un Réseau Jihadiste au Cœur des Contradictions Libanaises," in Bernard Rougier, ed., *Qu'est-ce que le Salafisme?* (Paris: Proche-Orient, Presses Universitaires de France, 2008), pp. 179–210. In his article, Rougier notes that it was never established if the Internal Security Forces sought to arrest the militants for the bank robbery, or whether they were after a Fatah al-Islam militant who went by the name of Abou Yazin, suspected of involvement in the bombing of two buses in the Christian village of 'Ain 'Alaq three months earlier.

174 *use him in some capacity:* Shaker Absi, a Jordanian-Palestinian, was also condemned to death *in absentia* by a Jordanian court for the assassination in October 2002 of an American diplomat, Lawrence Foley, in Amman.

175 New Yorker *of March 5, 2005:* Seymour Hersh, "The Redirection: Is the Administration's New Policy Benefiting Our Enemies in the War on Terrorism?" *New Yorker*, March 5, 2007.

175 *Hassan Nasrallah in 2003:* The word "friend" was used by Hersh himself in describing his relationship with Michel Samaha in a conversation Hersh and I had over lunch in Washington in March 2004. In

an email exchange with me, Hersh mentioned that Samaha had introduced him to Nasrallah in 2003. Email exchange with Seymour Hersh, June 12, 2009.

176   *familiar with what had happened:* See Rougier, "Fatah al-Islam." For another interesting account of Nahr al-Bared and the events surrounding it, see Nir Rosen, "Al Qaeda in Lebanon: The Iraq War Spreads," *Boston Review*, January–February 2008. On a number of key issues relating to Fatah al-Islam's rise and relationship with northern Lebanese Salafists, or the hidden intentions prevailing on all sides, Rosen and Rougier tend to agree. Rosen writes: "The Future Movement still insisted that Fatah al Islam was a Syrian tool, and the movement's leader, Saad al Hariri, described the organization as 'the gang of Asef Shawkat,' head of Syrian military intelligence and the brother-in-law of the Syrian president. Others in the opposition claimed it was a creation and tool of the Future Movement. Both were wrong." Where Rosen's account comes up short is in his failure to go more into depth when investigating Syria's role in the rise of Fatah al-Islam. He is fair in describing the group's movements in and through Syria, and in citing sources who believe Syrian responsibility was more pronounced, but he doesn't draw conclusions of his own on how Syria might have exploited Fatah al-Islam against its foes in Lebanon.

177   *Salafist networks in the north:* Hazem al-Amin, "Irhab bayn bibnin wa trablos wa mukhayyamay al-baddawi wa 'ayn al-hilweh" (Terrorism between Bibnin and Tripoli, and the Two Camps of Baddawi and Ayn al-Hilweh), Parts 1 and 2, *Al-Hayat* (London and Beirut), November 7 and 8, 2008. Amin's article is an investigation of a Fatah al-Islam cell formed in Bibnin after the Nahr al-Bared fighting that was linked to Salafist networks in both Baddawi and Tripoli. The networks he described brought together Salafists who worked in institutions belonging to Islamists close to Syria as well as Salafists who, on certain occasions, were allied with the Future Movement. Amin's implicit point is that within the context of these highly intricate relationships, the matter of political loyalty could be easily lost, as could the notion of strict command and control by leading political actors, whichever side of the Lebanese political divide they were on.

178   *than was really the case:* For example, according to news reports and to Suheil Natour, an official of the Democratic Front for the Liberation of Palestine, with whom I spoke in early 2007, Bahiyya al-Hariri, the aunt of Saad al-Hariri and the sister of Rafiq al-Hariri, paid money to Islamists based in the Taamir district of Sidon, abutting the Palestinian refugee camp of Ain al-Hilweh, so they could clear out of the

district. She did so in order to solve a long-standing problem between the Islamists and inhabitants of Sidon, which she represents in
parliament. Natour noted that some of these combatants took the
money and disbanded, while others moved to Nahr al-Bared to join
Fatah al-Islam. The Taamir incident was used by some to claim that
Bahiyya al-Hariri had financed Fatah al-Islam, when the likelihood
is that she was trying to resolve a local dispute, and in doing so only
displaced the Taamir problem, or part of it, northward. That does
not mean, however, that Bahiyya al-Hariri does not have relationships with Salafist groups in the Palestinian camp of Ain al-Hilweh
in Sidon, even militant Salafists. However, there is no evidence
that the Hariris have used these groups against the Lebanese state or
Hezbollah; rather, these relationships can be explained as necessary
for the Hariris to insert themselves into the various power centers of
the Sunni community in Lebanon in order to protect their influence
and ward away possible dangers and threats.

178 *keeping tabs on their activities:* For example, one northern Salafist who
mediated with Fatah al-Islam during the Nahr al-Bared fighting was
widely viewed in Tripoli as being an informer working on behalf of
the Information Department, even though he doubtless had several
simultaneous loyalties.

179 *more closely affiliated with Syria:* Interview with Johnny Abdo, Paris,
October 30, 2008. Abdo made the same claim in interview shows on
Lebanese television.

182 *several exchanges between us:* Mehlis and I exchanged several emails
when I was in Paris, but the email quoted here, sent on November
26, 2007, included his conclusions of what we had discussed earlier.

183 *so much slack, including me:* I had written a number of pieces defending Serge Brammertz's reports. However, as it became painfully apparent that the reports were offering nothing new, and as I heard
gradually more open criticism from Mehlis, but also others, particularly Lebanese politicians, lawyers, and judges, I began to get a sense
that something was indeed not right. In this context, credit goes to
my friend Chibli Mallat, a distinguished lawyer and specialist on Islamic law, who also stood as a candidate for the Lebanese presidential election in 2007 and 2008. Mallat was one of the first to publicly
express doubts about Brammertz and to criticize his reports. I disagreed strenuously with him at the time, until my subsequent reporting convinced me he was closer to the truth than I was.

6. The Crack-Up Continues

188 *(it was never voted upon):* It was never voted upon because the amend-ment process required a preliminary request by the government, and the parliament speaker, Nabih Berri, a leading opposition member, refused to permit any steps that might legitimize the government he was trying to overthrow.

190 *"the possibility of an evolution" with Damascus:* Background interview with a source intimately familiar with French thinking at the time, who insisted on remaining anonymous. Paris, November 12, 2008.

190 *his most senior advisor:* For an account of the disagreement within the French government over the opening to Syria, see James Traub, "A Statesman Without Borders," *New York Times Magazine,* February 3, 2008.

192 *the same district as he:* He would later change his attitude toward Su-leiman.

193 *could be a stalled career:* Conversation with retired General Tannous Mouawad, a former head of the Lebanese army's eavesdropping de-partment, who described such an episode to me.

193 *men whom the Syrians mistrusted:* Interview with General Adnan Shaa-ban, Beirut, July 9, 2008. Some details in this account were con-firmed in private conversations with other army officers.

195 *that would be that:* In fact, that wouldn't be that. Mehlis granted an interview to May Chidiac of the Lebanese Broadcasting Corporation in March 2008. He also granted an interview to Raghida Dargham of the Arabic daily *Al-Hayat* on the occasion of the formal start of the Special Tribunal for Lebanon in February 2009, and he spoke to Farés Khashan of the pro-Hariri *Al-Mustaqbal* daily in May 2009. The interviews were eloquent reminders that Lebanon very much remained a preoccupation of the former commissioner.

196 *"handled things differently," he answered:* "Justice for Lebanon," *Wall Street Journal,* January 26, 2008. It can be accessed at http://online .wsj.com/article/SB120130736626218217.html. However, for the text of the full interview, see "Under Suspicion: A *Reason* Interview with German Prosecutor Detlev Mehlis," at *Reason* Online, January 31, 2008. It can be accessed at http://www.reason.com/news/ printer/124674.html.

198 *in his investigation than he was:* Interview with a Lebanese judicial source who asked to remain anonymous, but who had firsthand in-formation on Bellemare's contacts with the Lebanese. Beirut, Febru-

ary 13, 2009. As a general rule, Lebanese officials ask to remain anonymous, particularly judicial sources.

198 *to conclude the work:* Ibid. My source's pessimistic assessment was shared by a senior Lebanese government official who also asked to remain anonymous but who did not go into the details of what Brammertz had said. Beirut, April 16, 2008. In conversations with this person, however, criticism of Brammertz was recurring.

199 *Brammertz had progressed:* In April 2009, I contacted Brammertz's office at the International Criminal Tribunal for the Former Yugoslavia (ICTY) to allow him to address what Mehlis had said. I wrote his information assistant the following: "As Mr. Brammertz perhaps knows, Mr. Mehlis (as well as myself in articles written here), and other sources in Lebanon, have been critical of his tenure as commissioner of UNIIIC, the commission investigating the Hariri killing. I believe it only fair, therefore, that in writing my book, Mr. Brammertz should be offered an opportunity to give his side of the story. Would he be willing to respond to some questions from me by email, or over the telephone?" On April 24, I received an email from his spokesperson, Olga Kavran, asking me what I hoped to address in an exchange with Brammertz, but also informing me: "For your information, the Prosecutor is generally not in a position to discuss the Hariri investigation both because it is an ongoing investigation and also because of his current position as Prosecutor of the ICTY (and the general rule within the United Nations that officials can only discuss matters which are part of their current mandate)." I sent what I expected to cover, and on May 11, when I sent Ms. Kavran a follow-up email asking what Brammertz had decided, she confirmed what she had stated in her earlier email, writing: "Unfortunately, the Prosecutor is not in a position to discuss these matters for the reasons I outlined in my previous message."

199 *"within the Commission's mandate":* "Tenth report of the International Independent Investigation Commission established pursuant to Security Council resolutions 1595 (2005), 1636 (2005), 1644 (2005), 1686 (2006) and 1748 (2007)," March 2008. The statement is found in the summary of the document, and again in paragraph 25.

200 *Eid had made a breakthrough:* Interview with the well-informed Lebanese judicial source mentioned four notes earlier, Beirut, February 13, 2009. Eid's role in analyzing communications was widely known, and was repeated by numerous politicians or officials whom I interviewed.

202 *"a repeat of the February 1984 intifada":* Qassim Qassir, "Tas'id al-mu'arada amam mun'atif hasim ba'd al-idrab al-'am: fawda siyas-

siya wa dusturiyya wa khawf min tawaturaat sha'biyya wa amniyya"
(The Opposition's Escalation Faces a Decisive Junction after the
General Strike: Political and Constitutional Chaos, and Fear of Popular and Security-Related Tension), *Al-Mustaqbal* (Beirut), January
22, 2007.

204   *challenge the better-armed Shiite groups:* Muhammad Barakat, "Sirat
shabb min tariq al-jadideh" (The Biography of a Young Man from
Tariq al-Jadideh), Parts 1 and 2, posted on the NOW Lebanon Web
site, January 7 and 23, 2009. The articles can be accessed online.
For Part 1, see http://nowlebanon.com/arabic/NewsArticleDetails
.aspx?ID=73926&MID=100&PID=46, and for Part 2, http://now
lebanon.com/Arabic/NewsArticleDetails.aspx?ID=76843#.

205   *as tensions in the streets rose:* Interview with Farouq Itani, Beirut, February 27, 2008.

207   *convince Siniora to go along with them:* Conversation with Walid Jumblatt, Beirut, March 10, 2009.

207   *replace him as army commander:* This is the view of Johnny Abdo, the
former head of Lebanon's military intelligence service, who is close
to March 14. I interviewed him in Paris on October 30, 2008.

207   *Jumblatt had made a mistake:* This was, for example, the view of Samir
Geagea, the head of the Lebanese Forces. I interviewed him in his
home in Maarab on June 27, 2008.

208   *he had indeed fallen into:* Jumblatt had deep doubts not about the role
of Georges Khoury, but about that of the defense minister, Elias
al-Murr, who, while he was nominally allied to the March 14 movement, could have been pursuing a separate agenda. The reason for
Jumblatt's doubts was that the information on the cameras was apparently leaked to a daily newspaper by Murr, suggesting that he
sought to provoke a confrontation. Conversation with Walid Jumblatt, Beirut, March 10, 2009.

209   *described what happened:* Interview with Khodr Ghadban, who was
the student representative of Jumblatt's Progressive Socialist Party,
Beirut, June 13, 2008.

213   *"what would have happened?":* Interview with Saad al-Hariri, Beirut,
May 5, 2009.

214   *with no place for Shiites:* This statement, from a Future Movement
parliamentarian from Beirut, Ghinwa Jalloul, provoked a disapproving response from Walid Jumblatt, a political ally. See "Jumblatt:
Al-Hariri asil wa Nasrallah yulaqihi" (Jumblatt: Hariri Is Noble, and
Nasrallah Joins Him in That), *Al-Hayat*, September 10, 2008.

7. The End of the Beginning

217   *enough evidence to indict them:* "Submission of the Prosecutor to
the Pre-Trial Judge Under Rule 17 of the Rules of Procedure and
Evidence," Doc. CH/PTJ/2009/004, released by the Special Tribunal for Lebanon, April 27, 2009, Leidschendam, The Netherlands,
p. 8.

218   *would have been legitimately criticized:* Farés Khashan interview with
Detlev Mehlis, "Al-generalat al-arba' fi 'marhalat lubnan': li maza
tam tawqifihim, wa li maza lam youfraj 'anhum?" (The Four Generals in "the Lebanon Period": Why Were They Arrested and Why
Were They Not Released?), *Al-Mustaqbal,* May 8, 2009, p. 5.

219   *"should be made accountable":* Report of the Fact-Finding Mission to
Lebanon Inquiring into the Causes, Circumstances, and Conse-
quences of the Assassination of Former Prime Minister Rafik Hariri,
S/2005/203, United Nations Security Council, March 24, 2005.

219   *absorb the political backlash:* I heard this from a source in a position of
responsibility at the television station, who knew what had happened. He was speaking privately, however, and asked that he not be
quoted by name.

219   *he had put it in writing:* As Mehlis wrote me in an email, the process
went this way: "[A] formal UNIIIC-letter [was sent] to [public prosecutor Said] Mirza to suggest the arrests, accompanied by the judicial evidence this suggestion was based upon. Mirza checked and
supported it and passed it on to [Elias] Eid, who was the [examining
judge]. Email exchange with Detlev Mehlis, June 3, 2009.

220   *the generals should be detained:* Two very senior judicial officials confirmed this to me in private, although, because of their positions,
they would not do so on the record. In an interview with the MTV
television station on May 16, 2009, the former head of Lebanon's
military intelligence service, Johnny Abdo, who is close to the Hariri
family, repeated this version publicly. In an interview with the Lebanese newspaper *Al-Akhbar* on February 11, 2009, Bellemare did try
to get across that he had had his disagreements with the Lebanese
over the generals' continued detention. When asked about their detention (in what is an English translation from the Arabic text),
Bellemare replied that "[t]he Lebanese judiciary is sovereign and I
cannot, as commissioner, intervene with the Lebanese judiciary. . . .
However that does not mean that I don't express my opinion to the
Lebanese public prosecutor." The clear implication from this passage was that Bellemare disapproved of prolonging the detention of

the four. This is also the distinct sense I got in a conversation with a non-Lebanese person working with the tribunal, who was speaking off the record.

220 *not in a private conversation:* Detlev Mehlis, the first commissioner of UNIIIC, described the procedure in an email he sent me: "[I]f at any point, and for whatever reason (time, evidence . . .), one of the [two U.N. commissioners that followed me] had come to the judicial conclusion [that the] provisional arrest [of the generals] was no longer justified, *it was their judicial duty to express this officially, immediately, and in writing under a UNIIIC letterhead.* The arrest of suspects is not a personal affair of the individual working on the case, which can simply be ignored by his successor" (Italics mine). In other words, since it was incumbent on the U.N. commissioner to recommend the arrests in writing to the Lebanese, it was necessary for him to reverse this in the same way. Email exchange with Detlev Mehlis, July 20, 2009.

220 *in early May:* Interview with Saad al-Hariri, Beirut, May 5, 2009.

222 *"creditable force on that basis":* An English text of the speech, though the translation is wanting, can be accessed at www.nowlebanon .com/NewsArchiveDetails.aspx?ID=94029. For an Arabic summary of the speech, see "Nasrallah: iza fazna fil intikhabaat lan natawassal musharakatahum al-hukm" (Nasrallah: If We Win the Elections, We Will Not Beg Them to Participate in Governance," *Al-Hayat*, May 16, 2009, p. 6.

223 *allies in Jabal Mohsen:* According to one Abu Rashed, a coffee seller in Bab al-Tebbaneh, weapons were being sold by an arms dealer said to be close to the former prime minister, Omar Karami. However, one weapon the inhabitants bought didn't even have a firing pin. The arms market was bustling, he said, so that a Kalashnikov was worth $1,000. He expressed confusion about what was going on and admitted that the Sunnis were less organized than the Alawites. Conversation with Abu Rashed, Bab al-Tebbaneh, August 11, 2008.

224 *by and large nonviolent:* The weakness of the Salafists was described by Samir al-Hassan, an individual long active politically in Bab al-Tebbaneh, who stressed that there were at most about forty Salafists fighting in the neighborhood. As he put it, "When the Salafists fought, their real size was shown. It showed how few they were." Conversation with Samir al-Hassan, Tripoli, August 11, 2008. As for the generally nonviolent nature of Lebanese Salafists, I spent, along with the journalist Hazem al-Amin, an hour hearing the Salafist cleric Omar Bakri dismiss Lebanese Salafism, adding, "Don't be afraid of the Salafist situation in Lebanon." Bakri is hardly the most credible of individuals, and his feuds with other Salafists were well

known, but there was an essential truth in what he said, namely that the jihadist element was not widespread among Lebanese Salafist groups, even if we cannot dismiss its potential given the right, or some may say wrong, circumstances. Interview with Omar Bakri, Tripoli, November 19, 2008.

224 *interesting half-truth:* Interview with Rifaat Eid, Tripoli, August 11, 2008.

226 *weapons on the market:* Conversation with Radwan Shehimi, Saad-nayel, August 22, 2008.

227 *between the south and the Beqaa:* I raised this question with Jumblatt a few days after his reconciliatory meeting with Hassan Nasrallah in June 2009. He disagreed that this was Hezbollah's motive, arguing that Nasrallah had been evasive on his question of why Hezbollah had attacked the Druze in the mountains. From his comments I understood that he suspected that the party had been asked to attack Druze areas. He didn't say by whom, but from the context I inferred he meant Syria. I still believe, however, that a significant objective of Hezbollah in May 2008 was to warn Jumblatt not to threaten its communication lines, even if there were other reasons. Conversation with Walid Jumblatt, Beirut, June 21, 2009.

228 *it had always resisted:* See, for example, Muhammad Abi Samra and Waddah Sharara, *Aqni'at al-mukhalles* (The Mask of the Savior) (Beirut: Al-Nahar, 2009). The book is an interesting series of personal testimonies of individuals who were once followers of Michel Aoun, before breaking with him.

232 *"get their asses handed to them":* Michael Crowley, "Lebanon Spares Obama a Headache," the Plank blog at the *New Republic,* June 8, 2009. The post can be accessed at http://www.tnr.com/blog/the-plank/lebanon-spares-obama-headache.

234 *was about to face defeat:* On the errors of Western media predictions before the Lebanese elections, see Tony Badran, "Why Western Media Got Lebanon's Elections So Wrong," NOW Lebanon, June 16, 2009. The online commentary can be accessed at http://nowlebanon.com/NewsArticleDetails.aspx?ID=98885.

235 *by one Erich Follath:* Erich Follath, "New Evidence Points to Hezbollah in Hariri Murder," SpiegelOnline, May 23, 2009. This is an English version of an article written in German, and it can be accessed online at http://www.spiegel.de/international/world/0,1518,626412,00.html.

236 *the journalist had been manipulated:* Michael Young, "Understanding the *Der Spiegel* Upheaval," *Daily Star,* May 27, 2009. The commentary can be accessed online at http://michaelyoungscolumns.blogspot.com/2009/05/understanding-der-spiegel-upheaval.html.

236 *"enabled the crime to occur":* "Third report of the International Independent Investigation Commission established pursuant to Security Council resolutions 1595 (2005), 1636 (2005), and 1644 (2005)," March 15, 2006, paragraph 36. The full report can be accessed online at http://www.al-bab.com/arab/docs/lebanon/brammertzl.htm.

238 *"independence from any regional power":* Thomas L. Friedman, "Ballots over Bullets," *New York Times*, June 10, 2009, p. A29.

8. The Road from Martyrs Square

PAGE

246 *"hitting the iceberg":* Eric Hobsbawm, *Interesting Times: A Twentieth-Century Life* (New York: New Press, 2005), p. 57.

Index

About the Author

MICHAEL YOUNG IS opinion editor of the *Daily Star* newspaper in Lebanon and a contributing editor at *Reason* magazine in the United States. Young has written for *The Wall Street Journal*, *The New York Times*, *The New York Times Magazine*, the *Los Angeles Times*, *Newsweek*, *Slate*, the *San Francisco Chronicle*, *The Spectator* (London), the *Times* (London), and many others.